Islands and Oceans

GEOGRAPHIES OF JUSTICE AND SOCIAL TRANSFORMATION

SERIES EDITORS

Mathew Coleman, *Ohio State University*
Sapana Doshi, *University of Arizona*

FOUNDING EDITOR

Nik Heynen, *University of Georgia*

ADVISORY BOARD

Deborah Cowen, *University of Toronto*
Zeynep Gambetti, *Boğaziçi University*
Geoff Mann, *Simon Fraser University*
James McCarthy, *Clark University*
Beverley Mullings, *Queen's University*
Harvey Neo, *National University of Singapore*
Geraldine Pratt, *University of British Columbia*
Ananya Roy, *University of California, Los Angeles*
Michael Watts, *University of California, Berkeley*
Ruth Wilson Gilmore, *CUNY Graduate Center*
Jamie Winders, *Syracuse University*
Melissa W. Wright, *Pennsylvania State University*
Brenda S. A. Yeoh, *National University of Singapore*

Islands and Oceans

REIMAGINING SOVEREIGNTY AND SOCIAL CHANGE

SASHA DAVIS

THE UNIVERSITY OF GEORGIA PRESS
Athens

© 2020 by the University of Georgia Press
Athens, Georgia 30602
www.ugapress.org
All rights reserved
Set in 10.25/13.5 Minion 3 by Kaelin Chappell Broaddus

Most University of Georgia Press titles are
available from popular e-book vendors.

Printed digitally

Library of Congress Cataloging-in-Publication Data in process

ISBN: 9780820357331 (hardcover: alk. paper)
ISBN: 9780820357355 (pbk.: alk. paper)
ISBN: 9780820357348 (ebook)

CONTENTS

ACKNOWLEDGMENTS

This book was made possible through the kindness, hard work, and generosity of many people. I first want to thank those who gave me their time during my stays on Jeju, Okinawa, Yap, Hawai'i, O'ahu, Guåhan, Vieques, Saipan, Tinian, Majuro, Ebeye, Kili, Luzon, Honshu, and Koror. I talk a lot about assemblages in this book, and this book itself definitely is one. It has been created through a combination of ideas, emotions, tactics, ethics, insights, and stories shared through countless interactions with people generous enough to give me their time. Not only must I thank my (anonymous) interviewees, but I am thankful for all the conversations, formal and informal, that have shaped the perspective I put forward in this book. In particular, I want to thank Jessica Hayes-Conroy, Allison Hayes-Conroy, Francis Hezel, Kyle Kajihiro, Robert Rabin, Hideki Yoshikawa, Shinako Oyakawa, Daniel Broudy, Koari Sunagawa, Weston Watts, Masaki Tomochi, Koohan Paik, Yukari Akamine, Yoko Fujita, Sung-Hee Choi, Emily Wang, Sunwoo Kim, Lina Koleilat, Vid Raatior, Jennifer Everett, Mark Hartman, Lorraine Dowler, Tiara Na'puti, Sylvia Frain, and Michael Bevacqua.

I also want to thank everyone at the University of Georgia Press. I especially want to thank Mick Gunsinde-Duffy, Jon Davies, Beth Snead, and Sapana Doshi for giving me another chance to publish in this exciting book series dedicated to fundamental social change. I also want to thank the anonymous reviewers and Mat Coleman for their valuable comments on earlier versions of the book. Their critiques were incredibly helpful and enabled me to develop my argument in ways I never could have without their insights. I am also thankful for Kerrie Maynes's and Thomas Roche's excellent comments throughout the copyediting and production process.

I also want to thank my colleagues and administrators at Keene State College and at the University of Hawai'i at Hilo. Not only did I receive financial help from both institutions for the travel associated with the research for this book, they also gave me encouragement and support while I worked on this project. I am also incredibly thankful for the grants I received from the Marion and Jasper Whiting Foundation and the Human Geography Institute, which also helped me conduct this research.

Lastly, I want to thank my family for supporting me throughout the writing of this book. My mother, Susan Justice, passed away as I began this research project, but I am indebted to her for always reminding me of the power of the persistent ocean to wear down any obstacle. I also want to thank my dad, Frank Davis, and my stepmother, Alicia Davis, for their support over the years. I also want to thank my sister, Mya Dee. I never gave her enough credit for all the help, protection, and love she has given me. As the younger sibling, I had the benefit of being able to grow up somewhat oblivious to many of the things going on in our crazy childhood because she was there for me. I am sure that without her I would be in a much worse place. Thank you! I also want to acknowledge my kids—Huxley Davis, Luca Davis, Mariposa Davis, and Sabine Maloney—whom I have missed terribly while I travel and hide myself away while writing. The person deserving the most thanks for this book, however, is my partner, Hillary Washburn. For every hour I have put into research and writing for this book, she has put in just as much effort or more holding our family together. I cannot thank her enough for her love, support, hard work, and patience through this long project.

Some of the material in this book was adapted from the previous publications listed below. The writing has been updated, revised, and reshaped, and I appreciate the work of the reviewers and editors that helped develop some of the ideas in this book that were in these earlier publications. This book is derived in part from the article "Sharing the Struggle: Constructing Transnational Solidarity in Global Social Movements" published in *Space and Polity* (2017) 21 (2): 158–72 (copyright Taylor & Francis; available online at https://doi.org/10.1080/13562576.2017.1324255). This book is also derived in part from the article "Apparatuses of Occupation: Translocal Social Movements, States and the Archipelagic Spatialities of Power" published in the *Transactions of the Institute of British Geographers* (2017) 42 (1): 110–22 (available online at https://rgs-ibg.onlinelibrary.wiley.com/doi/abs/10.1111/tran.12152).

LIST OF ABBREVIATIONS

A2/AD	anti-access / area denial
COFA	Compact of Free Association
EEZ	exclusive economic zones
ETG	Exhibition and Travel Group
FSM	Federated States of Micronesia
GAO	Government Accounting Office (United States)
IMF	International Monetary Fund
PLA	People's Liberation Army (military of the People's Republic of China)
RMI	Republic of the Marshall Islands
SLOC	sea lines of communication
TTPI	Trust Territory of the Pacific Islands
UNCLOS	United Nations Convention for the Law of the Sea

Islands and Oceans

INTRODUCTION

Visions of Sovereignty

Dreams of Control versus the Limits of State Power

In the first summer of Donald Trump's presidency, two major news stories simultaneously saturated media reports in the United States. One of these was the rally of white supremacist groups in Charlottesville, Virginia, that caused the death of one counterprotester and two police officers. During the rally, right-wing participants called for a strengthening of U.S. sovereignty while criticizing globalists and chanting infamous Nazi slogans such as "blood and soil!" that claim a link between racial purity and the control of territory.

The other major news story of the summer was the exchange of fiery rhetoric between Trump and the government of North Korea. This war of words provoked North Korea into threatening to launch missiles toward the island of Guam in the western Pacific (known locally as Guåhan). In the media frenzy that followed, residents of Guåhan strongly—and repeatedly—emphasized that one of the main reasons they were being targeted was because of their nonsovereign political status as a military colony of the United States. With no effective political representation in either U.S. or global institutions, the 160,000 people living on Guåhan were essentially caught between two nuclear-armed powers. In response, residents of Guåhan held rallies emphasizing their desires for the establishment of local sovereignty and self-determination (Aguon 2017; Leon Guerrero 2017; Raymundo 2017).

These two examples demonstrate both how prominent, but also how malleable and different, calls for sovereignty have become in contemporary politics. While to many people sovereignty may appear to be a relatively straightforward concept that specifies how a nation-state controls its formally recognized territory, in practice the concept is rather ambiguous and flexible. For instance, in these two cases the calls for sovereignty are similar in that people in both places are aspiring for more control over a specific territory. In particular, they appear to be calling for the kind of power usually associated with a state. There is an appeal for the creation, or strengthening, of an apparatus of power capable of managing other social processes, such as immigration flows, economic circulations, cultural mores, and external political powers (variously defined as imperialist, globalist, etc.).

Despite those similarities, however, these calls for sovereignty obviously have substantially different political bents. In the case of Guåhan, a group of people that has endured close to five hundred years of imperial and discriminatory formal political relationships has deployed the term to advocate for political representation (Guåhan has been occupied by the Spanish and Japanese as well as the United States). In Charlottesville, long-dominant groups have used the concept as a tool of exclusion to maintain superiority over perceived threats from both foreign influences and an increasingly diverse domestic population.

Sovereignty, then, is a term deployed by both stateless people seeking decolonization and by members of traditionally dominant social groups in the centers of global power struggling to reassert their socially privileged positions in the face of global processes and shifting ethnic mosaics. On the left side of the political spectrum, Indigenous groups, anti-imperialist social movements, and progressive anticapitalists have looked to enhancing sovereignty as a way to resist the exploitation of transnational capitalism or to break free from occupying imperial powers (Goodyear-Ka'ōpua 2011; Goodyear-Ka'ōpua, Hussey, and Wright 2014; Lutz 2009; Na'puti and Bevacqua 2015; Shigematsu and Camacho 2010; White 2016). Meanwhile, for political conservatives—from supporters of the United Kingdom's exit from the European Union (Brexit) to Donald Trump devotees in the United States calling for immigration restrictions and border walls—protecting national sovereignty has become an increasing source of political anxiety (Patrick 2017). Donald Trump himself used the word *sovereignty* ten times in a speech to the United Nations General Assembly in 2017 to assert that nation-states should have greater power than global institutions such as the one he was speaking to. In September 2019, Trump unequivocally doubled down on his position when he said at the United Nations, "Wise leaders always put the good of their own people and their own country first. The future does not belong to globalists. The future belongs to patriots. The future belongs to sovereign and independent nations who protect their citizens, respect their neighbors, and honor the differences that make each country special and unique" (Trump 2019).

Many political actors, it seems, are interested in sovereignty. What is less clear, however, is just what the term means and whether calls for sovereignty promote a politically progressive or conservative agenda. In short, increasing sovereignty is a widely advocated political aim, but one that needs to be interrogated more closely. In this book, my aim is to pick apart how sovereignty functions in order to better understand the dangers, promise, and limitations of relying on it as a political strategy. Since sovereignty is, at its core, not just about political control but also about political control *over a space*, I examine the concept through an explicitly geographical perspective that looks at how power functions both in places and across space. To do this, I embed my theoretical discussions in grounded examples of contemporary political contests occurring today, especially in East Asia and the island Pacific region. As I describe in more detail throughout the book, when we pick apart just how sovereignty is constructed and how it functions in real-world environments and political contests, then traditional conceptualizations that define political sovereignty and state power as autonomous processes that stand above—and manage and order—other social practices begin to unravel. I will also question whether calls to strengthen sovereignty are the most ethical or effective political strategies in a fundamentally interconnected world.

As an alternative to focusing on sovereignty to solve social problems, I emphasize how states and other political actors are embedded in wider contexts that both construct and constrain their ability to act and govern. Using the metaphorical device of "islands and oceans," I emphasize how sovereignty is produced at both the local scale of everyday life (islands) and in the larger milieus of globally circulating ethics and material practices (oceans). By shifting the focus to these sites that are usually considered to be outside, below, or above the apparatus of the state—or even outside what we might usually categorize as the realm of the political—I aim to highlight alternative approaches to addressing social and environmental issues that can move us beyond merely advocating for more sovereignty. To tell this story, I will largely challenge traditional conceptualizations of sovereignty. However, since these traditional views still inform a great deal of political action and scholarly debate, I will first consider them in order to better understand critiques of them.

Conceptualizing Sovereignty

One reason invoking the term *sovereignty* can serve so many purposes across the political spectrum is it is as ambiguous in the academic realm as it is in popular politics. As Jens Bartelson has noted, the term is so central to discussions and debates in political science, international relations, international law, and political geography—and it is invoked so frequently in different contexts—that just what is meant by the term is a "a perennial source of theoretical confusion" (1995, 12). He adds, "In political discourse, centrality and ambiguity usually condition each other over time. A concept becomes central to the extent that other concepts are defined by it, or depend on it for their coherent meaning and use within a discourse. These linkages—whether inferential or rhetorical—saturate the concept in question with multiple meanings that derive from these linkages, which make it ambiguous; an ambiguity that is open to further logical and rhetorical exploitation" (Bartelson 1995, 13). The ambiguity of *sovereignty*, therefore, does not so much deter its use in political discourse as much as it enables it. In essence, sovereignty is what Leigh Star refers to as a "boundary object" (2010)—something over which there is much discussion, collaboration, and debate but little actual precise consensus.

That said, there is still widespread agreement about what characteristics can be used to define a traditional view of sovereignty. As Wendy Brown contends,

> A composite figure of sovereignty drawn from classical theorists of modern sovereignty, including Thomas Hobbes, Jean Bodin, and Carl Schmitt, suggests that sovereignty's indispensable features include supremacy (no higher power), perpetuity over time (no term limits), decisionism (no boundedness by or submission to law), absoluteness and completeness (sovereignty cannot be probable or partial), nontransferability (sovereignty cannot be conferred without cancelling itself), and specified jurisdiction (territoriality). If nation-state sovereignty has always been something of a fiction in its aspiration and claim to these qualities, the fiction is a potent one and has suffused the internal and external relations of nation-states since its consecration by the 1648 Peace of Westphalia. (2010, 22).

While traditional approaches to sovereignty may accept many of those assumptions, there are of course still arguments about the finer points of how sovereignty functions. For instance, some theorists who still hold to these traditional notions of sovereignty note that there are different aspects of sovereignty, which must be examined separately. According to Stewart Patrick (2017) for instance, sovereignty can be disassembled into several facets, such as sovereignty-as-authority (the unfettered supremacy of state power vis-à-vis other actors), sovereignty-as-autonomy (the ability of state power to have independent freedom of action without external interference), and sovereignty-as-influence (the ability of a state to shape its own destiny within the international arena). Importantly, these different forms of sovereignty are sometimes in conflict or at least at cross-purposes. For instance, entering into alliances or international agreements decreases autonomy but will likely increase influence.

Additionally, there are prominent debates within traditional approaches to sovereignty regarding the source from which the authority of a sovereign power derives. Does sovereign authority come from a popular mandate of the governed in which a given people enact self-rule? If so, what happens when immigration or colonial population transfer changes who the people in a given area are? Does sovereignty come from the ability of a sovereign to claim an exception and suspend normal law? Or does it arise from a theologically defined divine source? Perhaps it comes from an agreement among other sovereigns to not interfere with another sovereign's territory?

While these debates are important to consider, in this book my goal is not so much to engage in debates that accept the traditional presumptions that sovereignty is characterized by supremacy, decisionism, absoluteness, completeness, and formally bounded jurisdiction. Instead, I aim to tell a story that supports Brown's position that these characteristics of sovereignty "*are indeed fictions*" (2010, 22). Through a geographic exploration of how power and sovereignty function across the Asia-Pacific region, I hope to demonstrate that traditional assumptions about sovereignty are incorrect for the purposes of political analysis, and that holding on to these assumptions is ethically problematic and constrains effective political action. My critique of traditional forms of sovereignty therefore is threefold. I question that sovereignty works the way some scholars and political actors assume it does. I also question the political efficacy of relying on calls for a change or enhancement of formal political sovereignty. Furthermore, I question the morality of relying on conceptualizations of sovereignty that accept that governance over a place is an either/or dichotomy where the only question is *which* state reigns supreme.

A short vignette about an event that took place where I used to work can help further illustrate the traditional view of sovereignty that I am aiming to critique. As on most college campuses, at the front entrance to the University of Hawai'i at Hilo there is a flagpole. On most days the flagpole serves as a rather banal marker of the political order of the site (Anderson 1991). At the top of the pole flies the flag of the United States, while below it—in the subordinate position—sits the flag of the state of Hawai'i (which is also the flag of the previously independent kingdom of Hawai'i). One day in December 2014 a group of residents of Hawai'i Island (a.k.a. the Big Island) came to the flagpole to contest this symbol and the political arrangement that it represents. One activist blew a long note on a pū (conch shell), and the others lowered the flags, removed the U.S. flag, and then raised the Hawaiian flag alone. The group stated that their rationale for this action was that Hawai'i had been illegally annexed to the United States and that the sovereignty of the Hawaiian Kingdom over the islands had never officially been ceded.[1] U.S. control over the island chain was therefore best characterized as an unjust occupation.

Even if the group of activists participating in this particular event was rather small—less than a dozen people—this kind of ceremonial protest is not uncommon in Hawai'i. There are many people in in this state who question U.S. sovereignty over the islands. There are several reasons for this, both historical and contemporary. There are many ways in which U.S. control of the island chain is a contested project, from the manner in which the United States came to claim sovereignty over the islands (through an overthrow of the independent government in 1893 and its annexation by the United States against majority public opinion in 1898) to the ways in which the government in Washington, DC, treats the islands today (Akaka et al. 2018).

On the surface, the taking down and replacing of a flag demonstrates a binary debate: either the United States has complete sovereignty over the islands *or* a Hawaiian entity does. While there appears to be a contest over *who* should have sovereignty, there does not appear to be much of a debate over the *way* that sovereignty operates. However, as I will discuss in more detail, there is much more going on here (and in the actions of sovereignty movements across the region) than just contesting *who* has sovereignty. Some of that nuance is not always immediately apparent. It also may be lacking entirely from political debates in other contexts where sovereignty can commonly be portrayed as a totalizing form of power over a particular territory. Frequently, if a governing apparatus (usually a state) is seen as having sovereignty, it carries the connotation that the state has complete control over what goes on in a given space. In fact, dictionary definitions, such as the one in *Merriam-Webster*, define *sovereignty* as "*supreme* power especially over a body politic" and "freedom from external control: *autonomy*" (emphasis added).

Using the term *sovereignty* therefore frequently assumes that in any given place there is some unitary apparatus of power that has political control to the exclusion of other actors. As noted above, events on Guåhan and in Charlottesville demonstrate that the traditional view of sovereignty still saturates the imagination of political movements across the political spectrum—within imperial states as well as within Indigenous movements. Blocking the sovereignty of a foreign power, bolstering the sovereignty of one's own nation against transnational economic flows and processes, or replacing an occupying sovereignty with a local one—these are all common aims of political movements that share this basic conceptualization that political sovereignty involves the exercise of a supreme and autonomous power that is capable of managing and purifying the complex social field. In other words, some believe that sovereignty *stands above* the messy tangle of economic and cultural relations. Calls for sovereignty that accept this view of power tend to follow two scripts. One calls for more state power because the mess of complex social relations seems out of control and dangerous (this would be, for example, a staple of recent right-wing arguments in North America and Europe). The other views current state power as the problem and calls for resistance via a form of autonomous sovereignty that will carve out a space, stand above current social relations, and order things differently.

What if, however, the traditional assumptions about sovereignty are not accurate? What if the governance of a space by any state is anything but unitary, autonomous, and mutually exclusive? What if control in a place is actually much more fragmented, contested, partial, hybridized, and woven from threads that emanate from different places and actors? What if there are other ways to imagine sovereignty? What might the implications be for the strategies and tactics of political action and social change?

Islands and Sovereignties

As the quote by Wendy Brown explicitly contends, the traditional view of sovereignty may be popular, but it is also a fiction. My goal in this book is to use grounded examples of politics and social activism in the Asia-Pacific region not only to demonstrate how traditional views of sovereignty are fictions but also to explore how different conceptualizations of sovereignty could inform movements for the creation of more just political processes. To do this I use a geographical approach that combines theoretical considerations of social processes with research experiences in specific locations across Asia and the Pacific. My research approach is geographical in two senses. First, I insist on taking academic concepts of how sovereignty supposedly operates and examining whether these theories accurately portray what is going on in particular places. Second, I focus particular attention on the spatial components of sovereignty. Sovereignty, of course, is not just about power: it is also about the way that power flows across space and covers particular territories. Therefore, focusing on the spatiality of sovereignty—and drawing on other spatial concepts, such as territory, enclosure, jurisdiction, property, and imperialism—offers a useful perspective that can show some of the flaws in traditional views of sovereignty, as well as clarify the strengths and limitations of invoking sovereignty as a remedy to processes of colonialism, exploitation, and domination in world affairs.

The particular study sites that I discuss in this book are ones in which I have done research over the past seventeen years. These research sites are on islands in the Pacific and on the rim of Asia, but I completed the book in the United States during the Trump administration's ascension to state power. The resulting analysis comes from established research methods such as semistructured interviews and participant observation,[2] but it is also formed from an urgency to develop an effective political response to the continued colonialism and militarization of the Asia-Pacific region as well as the rise of a xenophobic regime in the United States that frequently invokes the strengthening of state sovereignty as a means for creating a more nationalistic and racially exclusionary corporatocracy.

As for the Asia-Pacific focus, this book will specifically build on my research endeavors between 2002 and 2019. During that time I completed my doctoral studies in the Marshall Islands and then conducted research on militarization, environmental issues, contemporary colonialism, geopolitics, tourism development, and social movements during multiple visits to Guåhan, the Federated States of Micronesia (specifically Wa'ab, or Yap Island), the Commonwealth of the Northern Mariana Islands (Saipan and Tinian), Palau (Koror/Babeldaob), Okinawa, Korea (Jeju Island and Demilitarized Zone), Japan (Fukushima prefecture and Hiroshima), China (Sichuan Provence), Tibet (Lhasa), and the Philippines (Subic Bay / Olongapo; see maps 1 and 2). I also had two stints living, teaching, and doing research in Hawai'i (on O'ahu and Hawai'i Island). For the sake of grounding the theoretical narratives, each chapter focuses on a particular island or group of islands. In this introduction I use Hawai'i Island and Bikini Atoll (in the Marshall Islands) as examples, while I primarily reference events in Okinawa for chapter 1. In chapters 2 and 3, the islands of the Micronesia region are the primary sites of discussion. In chapter 4, islands in South Korea (Jeju Island), Okinawa, Hawai'i, and Puerto Rico are the anchoring locations for discussion. Chapter 5 then aims to integrate the discussions from the previous chapters and serves as more of an exploration—or a how-to perspective—on the way a more nuanced view of sovereignty can inform alternative political practices in the Asia-Pacific region and beyond.

There are many reasons why I focus my discussion of sovereignty on the often-overlooked islands of the Pacific and Asian littoral. First, this is a criti

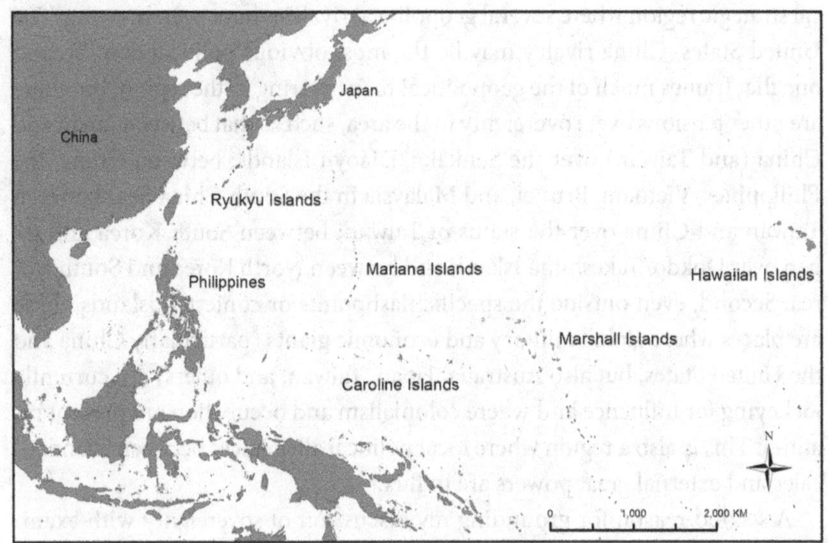

MAP 1. Island groups of the northern Pacific. Map by the author.

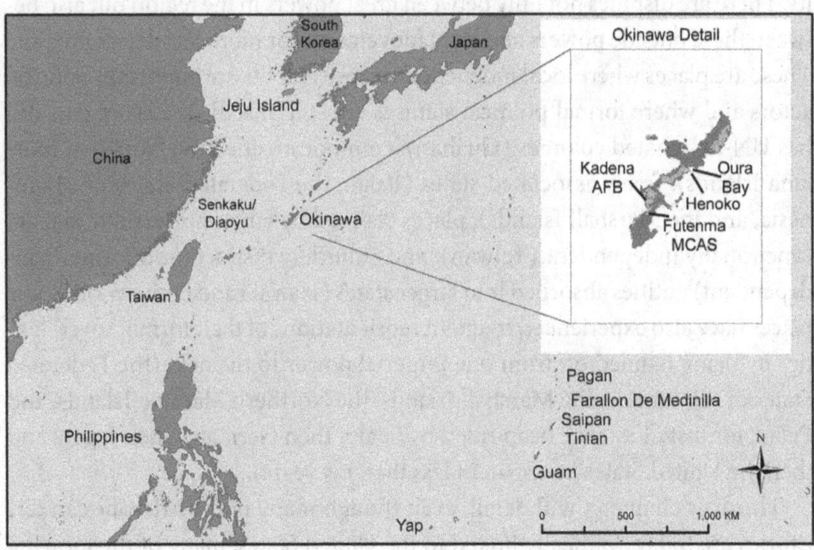

MAP 2. Key locations in the western Pacific discussed in the book. Lighter gray areas of Okinawa inset map are U.S. military installations. Map by the author.

cal strategic region where several geopolitical rivalries have been brewing. The United States–China rivalry may be the most obvious political contest, and one that frames much of the geopolitical maneuvering in the region, but there are other tensions over sovereignty in the area, such as that between Japan and China (and Taiwan) over the Senkaku/Diaoyu Islands; between China, the Philippines, Vietnam, Brunei, and Malaysia in the South China Sea; between Taiwan and China over the status of Taiwan; between South Korea and Japan over Dokdo/Takeshima Island; and between North Korea and South Korea. Second, even outside the specific flashpoints or contested islands, these are places where global military and economic giants (particularly China and the United States, but also Australia, Japan, Taiwan, and others) are currently jockeying for influence and where colonialism and occupation are present realities. This is also a region where local political allegiances between island locales and external great powers are in flux.

A second reason for grounding my discussion of sovereignty with examples from this region is that these are also places where formal sovereignty is anything but straightforward, and where colonialism is a contemporary reality. There are disputes not only between great powers in the region but also between these outside powers and local movements for more self-determination. These are places where local independence movements are important political actors and where formal political statuses are still unsettled. This region still has UN-designated colonies (Guåhan), commonwealths (the Northern Mariana Islands), freely associated states (Palau, the Federated States of Micronesia, and the Marshall Islands), places claimed by larger powers but that are functionally independent (Taiwan), and culturally distinct (and formerly independent) entities absorbed into larger states (Hawai'i and Okinawa).[3] These places have also experienced frequent reorientations of their formal sovereignties by being handed off from one imperial power to the next (the Federated States of Micronesia, the Marshall Islands, the Northern Mariana Islands, and Palau, for instance, have been ruled by Spain, then Germany, then Japan, and then the United States in a span of less than 125 years).

Third, as chapter 3 will detail, even though many of the Micronesian territories are today politically linked to the United States, many of the growing economic influences come from Asia (particularly from China, Japan, Taiwan, and South Korea). The fact that the locus of formal political power in this region has been Washington, DC, but that economic influences come from very different places helps demonstrate just what role economic processes have in weaving webs of influence in place. In other words, an examination of how different kinds of social processes entwine in place shows us how local-scale contests over political sovereignty are entangled with grander-scale political and economic processes. In turn, we will also see how these supposedly local contests reverberate back across the region and affect emerging patterns of global politics and international relations. This analysis will therefore demonstrate the ways in which processes we might perceive as happening at local *or* global scales are actually more fluid multiscale processes in which the local and global are quite entwined.

A fourth reason for the Pacific focus in this book is that for decades social movements and scholars in the Pacific region have been at the forefront of pointing out the flaws in traditional views of sovereignty. While the above vignette about lowering a flag in Hilo may appear to characterize Hawaiian movements as taking a traditional view of sovereignty, that is far from the case. What Indigenous sovereignty movements such as those in Hawai'i have done is demonstrate different and innovative ways of thinking beyond simplified traditional Western versions of sovereignty. By examining how landscapes can be thought of as actors in their own right (rather than merely canvases for human action), how power can operate differently, and how interconnection is woven into place, scholars in the Pacific region have demonstrated how sovereignty is *anything but* an autonomous process that floats above and manages the economy, the land, the water, and culture (Aguon 2005, 2006; Akaka et al. 2018; Alexander 2016; Diaz 2011; Frain 2017; Goodyear-Ka'ōpua, Hussey, and Wright 2014; Kajihiro 2013; Louis 2017; Natividad and Kirk 2010; Oliveira 2014; Perez 2014; Trask 1999). As Hawaiian concepts of sovereignty such as *ea* extol, there is no sovereignty separated out from larger hybridized environmental and cultural processes (Goodyear-Ka'ōpua, Hussey, and Wright 2014). This critique is one that scholars and activists—Indigenous and nonindigenous—can apply to understanding sovereignty in broader contexts.

These Pacific examples, therefore, are apropos for examining sovereignty not because of their unique qualities but because the tensions and acute debates over sovereignty in the region more easily lay bare how sovereignty works as a process on these islands and elsewhere. The flexible, contested, colonized, graduated, hybridized, and debated forms of sovereignty in the region bring to the visible surface what is happening in more subtle ways in other places, too. The point of view I take in this book, therefore, is to stand on these islands, look outward, and examine how threads of power coming from various directions and centers of global power are weaving together in these places. My goal here is not to speak for Indigenous persons or native movements on these islands but rather to listen to them and combine their insights with other critiques of the universality of traditional views of sovereignty. By doing so I hope to examine how sovereignty has functioned in places within and outside the region. While I will detail the way foreign powers—especially the United States and China—view these islands on their contested imperial margins, the majority of the sections in this book flip this perspective around and attempt to explore what the imperial powers mean to the islands. I conclude the book by clarifying what the experiences of these places can tell us about how sovereignty functions in the centers of power. While it may be more common to take mainland (European, Asian, or North American) examples of political processes and then apply them to realms deemed to be peripheral, I take the opposite tack here.

Geographies of Power, Part One: Sovereignty contra Flows?

Although in this study I use geographic methods to untangle the operation of sovereignty, geographical representations of power have in fact strengthened the myth that sovereignty is unitary, autonomous, and mutually exclusive (Flint 2016; Ó Tuathail and Dalby 1998). As most common world maps demonstrate, the world is typically represented as a mosaic of solid-colored countries where one government rules one space, and the government of a neighbor rules another. A viewer of a typical world map may easily assume that inside the monochromatic shapes everything is ordered by a unitary power that controls all that occurs inside the country and whose influence stops at the border. Map after map reconfirms in our perceptions, as well as in the world, the territorial outlines of modern countries. We see where red country A ends and blue country B begins.

More recently, however, geographers have demonstrated that this is far from an accurate picture of how governance over space functions. As John Agnew has convincingly shown, to view countries in this simplistic way is to fall into a "territorial trap" (Agnew 2005). A government's control is hardly total within a country's internal territory and it frequently does not end at its official borders. This is particularly true for countries that have been the perpetrators or targets of colonialism. Take, for example, the United States. Where does its sovereignty end? The continental margins? In the fifty states (including Alaska and Hawai'i)? What about Puerto Rico, Guåhan, and American Samoa? What about the U.S. military bases in Okinawa, Germany, Diego Garcia, Guantanamo, and elsewhere? Furthermore, there are holes in the U.S. government's control even within its official territory. From officially recognized distinct political zones such as Native American reservations to unofficial areas where it is difficult to make pronouncements in Washington, DC, effective—the rangelands of the American West, urban neighborhoods with strong animosity toward the dominant society, and a university in Hawai'i where people lower the U.S. flag and raise the Hawaiian one—a quick look at U.S. sovereignty shows that it does not end at the formal borders, and varies from place to place within it.

This spatial ambiguity and unevenness of power demonstrates a key distinction in discussions of sovereignty. Namely, that it can be characterized as either "formal sovereignty" (the space over which a state has official, internationally recognized rights to rule) or "effective sovereignty," which denotes where a state (or other entity) has an *actual ability* to direct what is happening on the ground (Agnew 2005, 2009; Pasternak 2017). The form and spatiality of this latter conceptualization of sovereignty is quite different from the former. Formal sovereignty may be relatively easy to map, but effective sovereignty is a much more slippery entity. Just where a state has actual control (and to what degree that control is resisted), what things a state has control over and what things it does not in a particular space, and where subnational or transnational actors hold political sway over territory instead: mapping these more nuanced aspects of power is a more complex and ambiguous endeavor.[4] Agnew (2005, 445) does, however, construct a typology of "sovereignty regimes" to categorize the different effective sovereignties of states. He categorizes states as either classic (a strong central state authority and consolidated territorial control), integrative (a weaker state authority but still with a consolidated control over territory), globalist (a strong central authority but with ill-defined boundaries of sovereignty—typified by the United States, with its propensity to project power far outside its formal borders), or imperialist (a weak state with low ability to control its territory, such as islands that are on the *receiving end* of imperialism and transnational processes).

This typology shows that while the formal sovereignties of all countries may be *officially* equal in terms of international relations, their actual abilities to project power over their territories (and beyond them) are quite different. As Stephen Krasner (1999) asserts, sovereignty can be framed as "organized hypocrisy" where stronger states regularly violate the sovereignty of weaker ones while portraying their own sovereignty as sacrosanct. Stronger states *may* respect the sovereignty of other countries, but only so far as it suits their own nationalist desires. Former U.S. secretary of defense James Mattis provided a telling example of this point of view when resigning over a spat with Donald Trump. Mattis protested Trump's denigration of U.S. allies not because the allies deserved respect in general (or to further a universal order of peace, human rights, or even unfettered trade and capital accumulation) but because collecting allies allows the United States to further its own self-centered security agenda. Mattis stated, "While the US remains the indispensable nation in the free world, we cannot protect our interests or serve that role effectively without maintaining strong alliances and showing respect to those allies. . . . We must do everything possible to advance an international order that is most conducive to *our* security, prosperity and values" (2018; emphasis added).

Military strategists and scholars are not the only ones, of course, who have noticed that effective control over space is more complex than formal sovereignty would suggest. Many political actors, commentators, and citizens have noted that states do not always control everything they want in the international realm, or even within their borders. The spatial disjuncture between formal and effective sovereignties can be portrayed as evidence that something is wrong with the functioning of a political apparatus (usually a state). A state unable to control its official territory is frequently viewed as a problem or, at worst, as a failed state in need of intervention. A state unable to manage actors within its borders, or the effects of flows across its borders (whether it be flows of people, information, capital, or trade), is portrayed as a political problem in need of remedy (O'Tuathail 2000; Sparke 2007; Patrick 2017).

Because this is not an unusual circumstance, there is no shortage of scholarship, or political rhetoric, addressing how transnational processes undermine the ability of states to control their borders or the markets within their borders.[5] It has become somewhat cliché in studies of global society to note that there is a battle of sorts between territorial-based state powers supposedly fixed in space and the power of economic (and other) flows that challenge or overwhelm state power (Arrighi 2005; Harvey 2007). In these narratives the sovereignty of a state is undermined as it struggles to capture or block these mobile flows of footloose capital, human migration, and instantaneous communication. Meanwhile discussions of network geopolitics focus on the tensions between sovereign control over a place and the need for a society to participate in transnational circulations for economic (and political) survival (Flint 2016; Foucault 2007). While the problem of maintaining sovereignty in the face of mobilities and circulations is a centuries-old dynamic conundrum, it also comes up as a source of intense political anxiety over globalization today.

This emphasis on the logic of economic flows versus territorial-based political control is an important perspective that helps undermine the idea that sovereignty is unitary, autonomous, and mutually exclusive. Since this perspective shows that there are multiple influences in a given country's space that do not originate from within it, it undermines the idea that social processes are ruled from a unitary domestic source. In other words, states are clearly not the only political actors. Instead, a host of corporations, international institutions, religious organizations, crime syndicates, unions, social movements, paramilitaries, and other actors also take part in deciding what happens. It also shows that transnational economic processes can overwhelm a state's ability to govern its territory. For instance, when in the 1980s and 1990s the International Monetary Fund (IMF) forced Jamaica, Thailand, Indonesia, and many other countries to accept harsh "structural adjustment policies" in order to receive loans to stay financially solvent, these were clear cases of the diminishment of state sovereignty, as governments were forced to cut spending on domestic programs—a political decision many government leaders would rather have not made (Harvey 2007). Thus the authority of nation-states, even within their formal borders, can be limited and circumscribed by transnational processes. This diminishment of power does not represent an entire "hollowing out" of the state or complete *negation* of its power but rather demonstrates that there are other actors who wield effective sovereignty within the territory of a given state. And it seems to have increased as a result of greater transnational connection in the past decades. As Jens Bartelson notes, "So while the sovereign state certainly has not withered away, much of its former authority has been dispersed to other levels of governance, above as well as below the institutions of central government" (2006, 466).

One aspect of these analyses of globalization is that they tend to represent territorially based political power and economic flows as not just oppositional *sources* of power but as entities that have different ways of functioning within and across space: economic processes that flow and circulate, versus state power that barricades, limits, and blocks. This view has definitely affected political views on both the political left and right. Leftist activists have long railed against the negative effects (economic, environmental, and social) of an unbridled neoliberal globalization and have called for the sovereignty of states to be strengthened to block free trade agreements, maintain government spending on social programs, and rein in and tightly regulate the movements of transnational capital (Klein 2007; Sparke 2013). In this way activists have portrayed the exercise of more sovereign power by states (which have—in some places—at least ostensibly democratic institutions that must follow the will of at least part of a populace) as a way to check the rapacious and clearly undemocratic processes of global capital accumulation. In the 2010s, however, it was the political right in the United States and United Kingdom that was able to elect governments committed to increasing their nations' sovereignty in order to manage transnational flows. While the right deployed a similar critique of the negative effects of transnational economic processes (namely that global flows hurt local economies), this was mixed with strong elements of xenophobia, racism, and religious intolerance that fed anxieties that foreign influences and immigrants were threatening a supposed national or racial unity within the countries. It was also not just elections in 2016 in the United Kingdom and United States in which sovereignty became a heightened issue. Many European countries witnessed nationalist resurgences while immigrants were increasingly blocked from coming into Europe across the Mediterranean (Jones 2016). In Asia and the Pacific, Australia continued to block and detain would-be immigrants, while tensions increased between Japan, China, Taiwan, the Philippines, Vietnam, and others over long-standing disagreements on control of maritime spaces in the East and South China Seas, which serve as conduits for global trade (Baldacchino 2016; Mountz 2013; Loyd, Mitchell-Eaton, and Mountz 2016).

In the face of the challenges posed by these flows, political actors tend not to think about sovereignty differently but rather to dig in and *reassert* the primacy of political sovereignty precisely because it is imagined to be a supreme and *autonomous* power that is capable of managing the threats of these mobilities. These appeals to nation-state sovereignty as if it were *the* remedy to the ills of global flows are based on assumptions that state power can be brought to bear to effectively manage flows in a decisionist manner. Many believe that there is a sovereign (as traditionally defined) who has supreme power and that whatever the sovereign decides will become the reality of the land. Donald Trump and his supporters, for instance, may imagine that they can build a wall on the southwest border of the United States and that flows between the United States and Latin America will cease simply because the state said so. This is clearly not the case. Walls are ineffective at stopping many of the flows they claim to be able to stop, and they also tend to be evidence of a diminishing and beleaguered state sovereignty (Brown 2010; Jones 2016, 2019).

This drive for the reassertion of state sovereignty, however, is applied not only to land spaces but increasingly to other kinds of spaces as well. As geographers have been noticing, the logics of enclosure and territorialization are being applied to all sorts of nonland spaces (Peters, Steinberg, and Stratford 2018). In this book I will look at the ocean as frontier and the way that territorializing logics and sovereignty claims are being applied to the seas—such as competing claims in the South China Sea and logics of resource capture in the exclusive economic zones (EEZ) around islands (Steinberg 2018). This drive to assert sovereign power over traditionally open spaces also applies to ice caps, seafloors, and even outer space (as exemplified by Trump's plans, announced in 2018, for an armed U.S. "space force"). These assertions of state sovereignty over traditionally nonstate spaces such as oceans and outer space (even when these claims risk provoking conflict) appear to be attempts to alleviate states' anxieties about their perceived lack of control in global common spaces. Like border walls, these territorial grabs do not indicate political strength but rather make visible a diminishing and anxious state sovereignty.

When these crises of sovereignty are seen across a wide array of circumstances—from the United States to Europe, and from Palestine to the western Pacific—it is not just the sovereign power of a particular government that ought to be brought into question. While that does occur, what also erodes is *the general idea* that sovereign political power operates the way some assume it should. When a supposed total, supreme, exclusive power over territory is shown to be anything but, it demonstrates not just the failings of a particular political machine but the failings of the whole ontological basis of the concept of sovereignty itself.

Geographies of Power, Part Two: Colonized Places and the Limits to Sovereignty

While the examples of threatened sovereignty in strong states in North America, Europe, and the Middle East are important for an analysis of sovereignty, we would miss some critical points if we focused only on states such as the United States, the United Kingdom, Israel, China, and Russia. This is why a discussion of islands in the Pacific can be helpful for getting a broader picture of the limits of sovereignty—both as a supposed attribute of states, and as a blueprint for decolonization. As mentioned above, sovereignties in the Pacific (especially Micronesia) tend to be partial, hybridized, and still deeply entwined with U.S. colonial projects. Also—using Agnew's ideas of "sovereignty regimes"—clearly the islands of the Pacific fall into the "imperial sovereignty" regime in which they have been subordinated to other powers (2005). A view from this other end of the sovereignty spectrum can shed light on how sovereignty functions more generally.

While I will delve into other examples more fully throughout this book, it is useful to briefly examine one case here to demonstrate what I mean about the limits to sovereignty in this Pacific context. In my previous research on Bikini Atoll in the Marshall Islands I examined how this former nuclear weapons test site was turned into a tourism attraction (J. S. Davis 2005a, 2005b, 2007; S. Davis 2015). Tourism activities went on for a number of years in the 1990s and early 2000s and consisted of visitors—largely from the United States, Japan, Europe, and Australia—scuba diving among old warships sunk during the initial two atomic tests that took place on the atoll in 1946. The atoll was (and still is) contaminated with radioactivity from the twenty-three nuclear tests the United States conducted there between 1946 and 1958, and while there is still debate over the safety of the atoll for long-term habitation, most see short tourist visits as safe (J. S. Davis 2005b).

The atoll itself is under the direct political control of the Bikinian government based on Majuro Atoll in the Marshall Islands, and land use (and nearby sea use) decisions are largely up to the Bikinian government council. The council operated the dive tourism enterprise itself and decided to distribute the profits of the operation relatively evenly throughout the community (unlike what most private tourism companies would have done). Between formal political control and the direct ownership of the primary economic activity, it might seem the sovereignty of the local government over life on the atoll was essentially total. On closer examination, however, one sees that this was not the case. There were many external factors and flows that influenced and constrained the council's decisions. For one, there were the radioactive particles and how they migrated through the ecology of the atoll. As "actants" in their own right, these particles—and their complex movements within ocean and terrestrial ecologies—had tremendous effects on whether people could live there, where they could go, and so on (Latour 1993; Steinberg and Peters 2015). Also, even though the government itself ran the tourism operation and had control over land use decisions, it could not simply do whatever it wanted if it hoped to run a *successful* tourism operation. Tourists would come and spend money there only if the experience matched their expectations. This exerted pressure to make sure the island looked like the tropical tourism paradise of Western cultural imaginations. This even extended to discussions about whether a repatriated Bikinian community would harm the tourist aesthetic of the deserted island that many tourists said they craved (J. S. Davis 2007). Eventually, the tourism operation ceased most of its operations—even though the local government wished to continue it—due to a slew of things outside the government's control. As stated on the Bikinians website, "In 2008 the Council had to close their operation due to local airline reliability issues, soaring energy costs and U.S. stock market conditions that impacted the local government budget."[6]

In this brief example we can see just how circumscribed control is for the Bikinian people and its government (even over an uninhabited island supposedly under its complete sovereign control when it comes to land use and economic activities). In this case, many of the important social and environmental factors affecting the atoll would still escape control even if territorial sovereignty were stronger or more forcefully asserted. Too many of the flows that matter escape the government's control. An island government such as the Bikinian's finds itself in a position in which it may have formal sovereignty and managerial oversight of its own (tourism) resources but not have "sovereignty over the financial-technical-logistical *means of producing and selling* those resources within the context of a competitive world market" (Emel, Huber, and Makene 2011, 73; emphasis added). If we add in environmental factors such as the movement and decay of radioactive particles and the dangers presented by anthropogenic climate change and sea level rise, this lack of control becomes even more apparent. All that the government here could do was make decisions that attempted to manage the place and its people *in response to* these flows of international tourist desire, the migrations of radioactive particles, and rising tides. They could do very little directly about the nature of the flows themselves.

The lessons that can be learned from this modern Pacific example are not all that different from those that Michel Foucault (2007) described in the walled cities in medieval Europe. Namely, Foucault posited that an apparatus of sovereignty, if it is to succeed at governance at all, cannot just make whatever decisions its leaders want. Instead, it must make decisions that are attuned to the larger milieu of economic and environmental flows (the "reality," as Foucault puts it) in which it sits. Yes, all entities can affect these larger milieus *to some degree* in that the larger milieu is constructed from a massive aggregation of prior decisions—such as explained in Anthony Gidden's (1984) theories on structuration—but these changes are incremental and occur within the larger existing processes that construct the milieu. The point here is that no state, strong or weak, has the decisionist, autonomous, and supreme power that traditional theorists such as Hobbes and Schmitt may attribute to it.

If this is true, what does this say about pursuing a strategy of strengthening sovereignty as a solution to the perceived perils of globalization, imperialism, or the influence of mobile subjects (whether agents of empire, migrants, or refugees)? What if an incomplete sovereignty challenged by global flows is not a mistake or a malfunction of governance that needs fixing? What if total state sovereignty, as traditionally defined, is just a dream of state power that has been strived for but has never actually been realized by any state actor in any era? If that is the case, should we who want to challenge imperialism, occupation, transnational capitalism, hierarchy, or domination dream the same dream? Perhaps what we need to question is not just whether we should be using existing state apparatuses for change (creating change from within existing governments). Maybe we need to question using the state *form* that insists that power must be exercised as a unitary, supreme, territorially exclusive, hierarchical form of governance. Is there something to the point made by Adam Grydehøj and Zuon Ou that "to fight on the grounds of territory are to accept the state's rules of engagement, to acquiesce to coloniality" (2017, 70)? Or, as Grydehøj and Ou add using Audre Lorde's well-known quote, are those invoking sovereignty forgetting the dictum that "the master's tools will never dismantle the master's house?" (quoted in Grydehøj and Ou 2017, 70).

While sovereignty is an important concept to grapple with in colonial situations, perhaps we should not limit debates on decolonization and self-determination to questions of how to reassert the primacy of some different sovereign power that is still assumed to be autonomous, mutually exclusive, and supreme. To do so may be falling into a "state trap." Instead, perhaps we ought to recognize that this is not how power works. This would require that we strategize more about how to deal with and influence sovereignties (plural) that are fundamentally hybridized. What if we *accept* that control in any given space is profoundly plural, partial, contested, and shot through with influences emanating from across the world? Furthermore, what if we recognize that territorial state power is not just some kind of fixed bulwark that opposes transnational economic, political, or cultural flows within a containerized national space but something that *itself flows*?

In many ways, academic analyses of political sovereignty that portray it as operating in *opposition* to economic flows reinforces an inaccurate view of sovereign power. While these analyses do recognize that political control is contested by nonstate actors and by processes that flow across borders, they also tend to incorrectly reify sovereignty as something spatially fixed and mutually exclusive within the formal borders of a country. Increasingly, however, many geographers, social scientists, political activists, and philosophers have performed more nuanced analyses of how political control functions in space. As Brown emphasizes, "Sovereignty is never simply held and wielded, but from the beginning *circulates*" (2010, 57; emphasis in original). Other theorists take this one step further and note that sovereignty is not an already made thing that fills a determined territory or even a mobile thing that arises in one place and is then projected into other spaces. Instead, it is more accurately viewed as an active and continual process—a *performance*—that not only reaches across space but rearranges space itself (Allen 2011; Anderson et al. 2012; Dewsbury 2011; Featherstone 2011). Following these theorists, I aim to show examples of how sovereignty is not as geographically solid or as fixed as it appears. Instead sovereignty flows just as much as the mobile processes it is said to rein in and contest.

Everything Flows: Objects, Persons, Places, and Power as Assemblages

Unlike traditional views of sovereignty, many of the recent theories regarding how power works across space take as a given that the world—in terms of human and environmental processes—is an intensely interconnected and shifting place (Agnew 2009; Deleuze 1998; Steinberg and Peters 2015). This point, while at one level fairly obvious, cannot be emphasized enough. The following chapters go into great detail about the myriad ways in which entities of all sorts are *assemblages*: things created and reproduced in webs of interactions with other people, ideas, and places (Deleuze 1998). In this section, however, I want to introduce some of the key points of these perspectives in order to discuss their implications for understanding how sovereignty operates in space. The key point of these theoretical perspectives—sometimes labeled under the banner of "assemblage theory" that stems from perspectives of relational ontology—is the insistence that everything is quite literally constructed out of relationships with other things. This viewpoint creates serious problems for views of sovereignty that emphasize that states, or any other political actor, can be autonomous.

This questioning of the autonomy of political power has disquieting implications for those of us (myself included) who have long advocated for decolonization, greater local political autonomy, sustainability, and self-determination. While the perspectives I present in this section critique the political strategies of the political right in the imperial centers that have been clamoring to build walls and maintain cultural stasis in the face of globalizing influences, it will also appear at first glance to pull the ontological rug out from under decolonization struggles and the efforts of those striving to create spaces autonomous from global capitalism. While reimagining how sovereignty functions can destabilize many kinds of political endeavors, my aim is not to condemn those that are trying to get more control over their lives or to criticize those building a more equitable and peaceful world. Instead, my goal is to explore new possible avenues for realizing those goals given that disconnection, air-tight borders, and unfettered political autonomy are impossible dreams born of theories that do not adequately address just how power actually functions in place and across space.

I contend that we ought to think of sovereignty as a relationally constructed assemblage. What, however, does that mean? To answer that question, we have to examine some of the theoretical positions of relational ontology.[7] While some readers will already be familiar with this perspective, I realize that some may not. It seems then that a brief digression can clarify some of the central points I am trying to make.

Simply put, relational ontology posits that all things—places, people, objects, states, ideas, and so on—are literally constructed though their interactions with other things. Without interaction, these things do not exist. Before I move on to examine more abstract concepts such as how state sovereignty is constructed relationally, examples of some everyday objects can be useful here. Take, for example, an ordinary palm tree. What is this tree? More traditional philosophical approaches, sometimes referred to as "object ontology," would posit that the tree has some kind of essence. Its genetic code is perhaps its essence, and the effects of climate, topography, soil nutrients, pests, and so on might affect it and alter the tree's basic essence. Relational ontology, however, would say that the tree has no essence. It would suggest that the palm tree is an amalgamation of other elements *related* to each other in a particular way. From this perspective the tree is the combination of its genetic code, the soil nutrients it incorporated into its structure, the sun's energy it absorbed into its sugars, the insects that have gnawed on it, the winds that have ravaged it, and even the different meanings people attribute to the tree and the way those meanings affect the tree's cultivation. The tree would literally be all these non-tree elements related together in a particular way.

This perspective can also be applied to individual people. Who am I as a person? An object ontology perspective might propose there is some kernel of pure me, or a soul, that is my essence. From a relational ontology perspective, however, I would be a constellation of materials, energies, and more that are related in a particular way. I am a machine of sorts organized by an inherited genetic code, *and* my cells are literally made partially of the sandwiches I ate last week, *and* my psyche is constructed through a collection of experiences over my life course that range from the pleasant to the traumatic, *and* my mind is constructed by my experiences and the things I have read. In other words, from a relational ontology perspective I have no essence. I am constructed—body, mind, and soul—from a certain way of relating all sorts of things that are not me: from sandwiches and loving encounters to childhood conflicts and ice cream cones, from Deleuze's books to research trips. From this perspective it does not make any sense to ask whether I have been created by nature or nurture, or if I am deep-down one kind of person or another (introvert/extravert, good/evil, masculine/feminine, etc.). What if a person is not *either* this *or* that but rather is constructed from multiple elements that are themselves constructed out of arrangements of still other elements? This is the main point of Deleuze and Guattari's contention that when we speak of any entity it is best not to describe its construction as "either/or" but rather as "and, and, and . . ."—an additive amalgam of a vast assortment of disparate elements (1988, 25).

While this may seem a fine point that is far from the discussion of geography and realms of sovereignties, let us now take this idea, change the scale a bit, and see how this relational approach applies to place. After all, any examination of sovereignty—with all the connotations of it being about power being *exercised in place*—deserves as nuanced an analysis of place as it does of power. So, what is a place? Since the idea of place is quite foundational in geographic studies, it should be no surprise that there is quite a lot of geographic research and theorizing on this question. One of the more popular approaches is to represent places as a combination of a location, locale, and sense of place (Agnew 1997). In this schema a particular place—a spot on the earth—can be described from three major perspectives. As a *location* a place is described in terms of its spatial relationship to other places. Hawai'i Island, for example, as a *location*, is at roughly 19 degrees north latitude and 155 degrees west longitude. Its location can also be described as a five-hour flight from Los Angeles or a strategic spot a third of the way across the Pacific from North America toward Asia. *Locale*, on the other hand, is what is actually at a particular site. What buildings are there? What is the physical environment like? What is the stage like on which social activities occur? Hawai'i Island as locale is mountainous, volcanic, relatively rural, and prone to natural hazards of almost every type. It also has fertile agricultural soils (where the geology is old enough), an ethnic mix affected by waves of plantation-oriented immigration, and is formally politically administered by the United States. The third approach—*sense of place*—emphasizes the "subjective and emotional attachment people have to place" (Cresswell 2015, 14). It is the varied meanings people have accumulated based on their history within that landscape. In Hawai'i, sense of place would vary substantially from person to person and also from one part of the island to another. To a visiting tourist the island may link to a sense of adventure and an old Western narrative of experiencing paradise, while to residents it means quite different things that have to do with spiritual attachment, memories, and the routines of daily life. Of course, these different regimes of sense of place have important political ramifications. Different people are going to have disparate opinions on how a locale ought to be managed, governed, or changed. A tourist (or hotel investor) may think a golf course on the side of Hawai'i's Kilauea volcano is a splendid and appropriate idea. Many residents, however, would see it as out of place and a socially inappropriate act of destruction.

Other approaches to understanding place center on the ways in which a person approaches or experiences a given site. One common basic categorization counterposes *place* to the term *space*. Here *place* denotes a more lived-in and experienced site, while *space* is a term reserved for when someone is thinking about a site in a more detached and abstract manner. This distinction is taken a step further in the highly popular tripartite schema of Henri Lefebvre (1991) in which places are categorized according to how people experience and conceptualize a place (Soja 1996). In this view the emphasis is on a person's approach to a site. Is it being abstractly considered in the way a planner, government agent, or other entity might view it from a map or from on high? Or is it being imagined based on prior experiences in places deemed to be like it? Or is the place directly experienced by being lived in and moved through? Lefebvre's views on space and place are quite popular and have been used to analyze relationships to place from Colombia to Papua New Guinea (Oslender 2016; West 2006). It is, however, also slightly misleading. As I have argued elsewhere in more detail, these different ways of experiencing space/place are actually all underpinned by similar *processes* of conceptualizing and representing places (J. S. Davis 2005a; S. Davis 2015).

This brings me to my next point, which signals a return to how the idea of relational ontology is useful for understanding the way places are constructed and governed. While there is analytical value to different categorizations of what a place is and what produces a place, I want to explode these categories a bit by drawing on more contemporary research that characterizes places as assemblages (Cresswell 2015; Featherstone 2011; Massey 1994). The assemblage view is steeped in the tradition of relational ontology and insists that places are created from innumerable physical and social elements brought together and related in a particular way. From a relational perspective, places are hybrids constructed by physical and social processes that emanate from within a local site and from far away. From this perspective Hawai'i Island is a conglomeration of hot spot basaltic lava, the shaping waves of the Pacific, the mo'olelo[8] (stories) of Pele and her siblings, the heiau and fishpond walls of Indigenous

Kanaka Maoli, the immigrant communities who have arrived over generations (from Japan, Okinawa, the Philippines, China, Puerto Rico, Portugal, Micronesia, and the United States), the activities of Christian missionaries, the millions of tourists who have trod upon it, the tsunamis of 1946 and 1960, the telescopes on Mauna Kea, the U.S. flag flying over buildings, and the American flag being taken down and replaced. Here again we see the perspective of "and, and, and . . ." in operation. While some of these influences are stronger than others—and we can, of course, debate which attributes the island *should* have and which ones it should not, and what influences we should promote and what we should discourage—the relational perspective would recognize that these are the disparate elements that have constructed the place as it is. This perspective would also hold that different people (or administering entities) viewing the island from different abstract, imagined, or lived perspectives would emphasize, valorize, or vilify some of these elements more than others. Still, viewing the island as an assemblage constructed out of all these disparate elements acknowledges that all of these threads—for better or for worse—are woven into the tapestry of the place.

This example of Hawai'i Island demonstrates that even geographic islands far from continents are not islands in the Western metaphorical sense of being disconnected, isolated, or unaffected by larger global processes. They are much more connected to global circuits of materials, peoples, process, and ideas than Western romantic notions would suggest (Diaz 2011; Hau'ofa 1994; Nadarajah and Grydehøj 2016; Pugh 2013, 2016; Stratford et al. 2011). As the coming chapters explore further, the fact that I am using islands as examples is not just due to my previous experiences in these places. Instead, I use islands to illustrate these concepts in part because realms of sovereignty have long been portrayed in a way similar to the (mistaken) Western view of islands as disconnected and autonomous spaces.

Reimagining Sovereignty as a Relational Assemblage: The Example of *Ea*

What happens, then, when we apply this relational perspective to considerations of sovereignty? What does it mean to speak of sovereignty as being "assemblage-like" and what does it mean to view power over territory as following the model of "and, and, and . . ." as opposed to either/or? A particularly potent example of this more nuanced view of sovereignty is embedded within the Hawaiian concept of ea. Ea is frequently translated into English as *sover-*

eignty, but, like relational approaches that draw from Deleuzean assemblage theory, it too challenges many of the Western assumptions of how power and territory are constructed. For one, ea emphasizes that the legitimacy of power does not come from a divine source, or the ability to dominate others, or from the ability to call for an exception and suspend normal social rules. It also does not necessarily come from a popular mandate either. Legitimacy does not even derive exclusively from the social realm. Instead, ea is conceptualized as deriving from the land (ʻāina) itself (Osorio 2014). Here we see a flip of how sovereignty functions. Rather than sovereignty being about a human system of governance (aupuni) exercised *over* an expanse land, the land exerts governance over humans and their political systems (Goodyear-Kaʻōpua 2014). In other words, a human authority is legitimate only if it is able to follow the dictates that the land demands. Contrary to Western views in which a human authority controls, establishes, and orders territory (Elden 2009), ea is about organizing the right *relations* (pono) between people (kanaka), land (ʻāina), and other elements so that they work optimally in concert. Ea, then, is not necessarily territorializing and ordering—but rather functions through a recognition of relational actions. Here ʻāina serves a similar function as economy in Foucault's (2007) work on the limits of sovereign power in medieval Europe. ʻĀina is the truth to which governance must bend and adapt, not vice versa. It demands a management that seeks relational righteousness rather than a production of territory in the Westphalian sense.

As Noelani Goodyear-Kaʻōpua explains, "After a rogue British captain claimed the islands for Great Britain in 1843, Hawaiian emissaries secured the restoration of sovereign government. King Kamehameha III famously proclaimed ʻUa mau ke ea o ka ʻāina i ka pono.' Roughly translated: 'The sovereignty of the land continues through justice and proper acts'" (2014, 4). Goodyear-Kaʻōpua emphasizes that it is not the sovereignty of the government that was reaffirmed but rather the sovereignty of the land itself (ʻāina). The preservation of the land's sovereignty was upheld not because an Indigenous government was maintained but because a government was maintained that understood that real human *authority* comes from the ability to successfully bring the land, elements, and people into proper productive relations.

With ea, rather than governance ordering the landscape, the landscape is the agent that orders human systems of sovereignty. Human political decisions that are out of step with the sources of real power (the land, elements, and the needs of the people) sow their own consequences. Governance here cannot be seen as autonomous from other social and environmental processes, and certainly not as something that orders these other elements. Instead, it is a practice relationally embedded within them. Ea is therefore a constant process, never an accomplished fact (Goodyear-Ka'ōpua 2014). It is a process of ordering human life in *relation* to flows, movements, and natural processes, like steering a ship in an ever-moving ocean.

While the concept of ea is tightly connected to both the Hawaiian archipelago and Kanaka Maoli, there are also lessons in this discussion of ea for people in other contexts who are aiming to change systems of government or who are striving for self-determination, equality, and justice. First, it is important to appreciate the lessons inherent in Hawaiian conceptualizations of sovereignty because they show the possibility for creating proactive and *productive* alternative apparatuses of governance. Ea is more than a philosophy of political *resistance*. It is a philosophy of what *should be*. It is based on a recognition that saying no is not enough. Second, an appreciation of ea demonstrates that formal political independence does not, in itself, make one autonomous or able to do whatever one wants. As Goodyear-Ka'ōpua puts it, "Political autonomy may be a baseline minimum for the restoration of functional ea, but it is also only one piece of the puzzle" (2014, 30). Because governance must follow the dictates of the relational socioenvironmental context that one finds oneself in, formal political sovereignty means that one can *begin* to deal productively with the larger enveloping milieu, but it does not divorce anyone from it. To put it in more concrete terms, if Hawai'i achieved political independence we would still have to take into consideration the larger assemblage of environmental, economic, political, and social relations in which it sits in order to understand what connections, threats, and potentialities exist.

While ea is a promising perspective for motivating social movements seeking sovereignty, there are still some questions about the context in which an ea-inspired governance can be constructed. Ea is, I believe, a vastly more useful concept of sovereignty for an interconnected world than traditional Western conceptualizations that assume political sovereignty equals a supreme, autonomous, ordering power. The emphasis in ea on interconnections between the human and natural world, and between materiality and spirituality, are incredibly valuable, but the focus is more on those relationships *within* place than on relationships across vast global spaces. Also, there is the practical question of how ea is made real in the context of unequal global power politics and foreign occupations. How does one promote and produce a more decolonized sovereignty in a world of such intense interconnectivity and unequal power relations?

Toward Better Assemblages of Sovereignty: A Look at the Coming Chapters

This book not only analyzes how sovereignty functions but also seeks to inform and inspire political activism that aims to produce more egalitarian and representative systems of governance in the spaces of our everyday lives. I argue that to do so, one must appreciate the practical limits of sovereignty and state power. Rather than advocating for strengthening state power, making appeals to state power, or constructing new states, I argue that we need to think about how state power is produced and limited by the assemblages in which it is embedded and how those larger more-than-state assemblages can be altered and shifted. In practical terms, this means I want to examine how political action can be deployed at sites outside the state (and even in realms we may not necessarily consider to be political). I argue that there are two foci on which individuals and social movements must work simultaneously. The first focus is the localized metaphorical "islands" of everyday living where struggles over ethics of governance take place and where assemblages of sovereignty are territorialized and produced from the ground up. The second focus is the larger context—or what I metaphorically refer to as the "ocean"—in which state power is shaped and in which local struggles are embedded. These two foci are of course intertwined in many ways, but I think it is tactically valuable to discursively tease them out. I do this in the remainder of this book by first examining in chapter 1 just how effective sovereignty is produced within local places. I then broaden the view in chapters 2 and 3 to examine more regional assemblages of human and environmental activity in which sovereignty is constructed and in which local struggles occur. Then in chapters 4 and 5 I combine these approaches to show how new political possibilities being produced by social movements can inspire broader political struggles for equality, environmental protection, and social inclusion.

More specifically, in chapter 1 I delve deeper into conceptualizations of sovereignty as a performed assemblage in order to elaborate on just why this is a useful approach to sovereignty—both analytically and strategically. By combining discussion of Deleuzean philosophies on assemblages with Foucault's views on apparatuses (*dispositif*) of governance, chapter 1 engages in a more theoretical examination of the translocal way apparatuses of sovereignty are constructed and deployed across space as well as how that power becomes territorialized in place. To ground this discussion, I combine this theoretical conversation with examples of transnational social movements, especially those of antimilitarization groups in Okinawa. I examine how these groups contest power in place—and how they organize across space—before then turning to analyzing what these examples can tell us about the functioning of the regimes of state power that they contest. It may seem somewhat unusual to examine how sovereignty operates by first starting with a discussion of how state sovereignty is resisted and *then* moving on to how it operates, but I think this approach better highlights just how assemblages of sovereignty are produced and deployed.

In chapter 1, I also examine the ethics that order competing assemblages of sovereignty. If, as discussed in the example of ea, structures of governance are about constructing the "right relations" between things, it is important to examine just what contemporary states and social movements imagine these right relations to be. Drawing on the concepts of "regulative principles" (Foucault 2007; Lemke 2001), "molar agency" (Deleuze 1998), and "regimes of living" (Collier and Lakoff 2005), I analyze the values that coordinate assemblages of sovereignty and enable them to hold together across space in archipelago-like constellations.

The second section of the book consists of chapters 2 and 3 and takes a more regional view that examines the context in which local contests over sovereignty take place. In this section I represent the contemporary context of the Asia-Pacific region as one of hegemonic competition between multiple powers, in particular the United States and China, but also including other states such as Australia, Taiwan, Japan, South Korea, North Korea, Russia, New Zealand, and the Philippines. This competition for influence in the region exerts particular pressures on the communities within it, but it produces opportunities as well. The discussions in the second part of the book are centered on the details of contemporary political, economic, and cultural practices in the Pacific realm. While the empirical focus is on the Pacific, this discussion is meant to demonstrate how the threads that come together to produce and sustain assemblages of sovereignty in *any* particular place circulate and flow into places from elsewhere. In other words, it emphasizes that sovereignty over any place—whether on an island or in a continental environment—is not something that sits over a given place but rather is a relational construction of mobile elements.

To show this, chapters 2 and 3 get into more empirical detail and examine the structure of assemblages of sovereignty as they are constructed across the islands of the Pacific, particularly in Micronesia. In these chapters I tease apart the webs that construct sovereignty by analyzing two categories of influence over governance in a place. Chapter 2 focuses on the geopolitical imaginings of this region; both the more traditional views of so-called realist geopolitics and views informed by the alternative outlooks of critical and feminist geopolitics. In chapter 2 I explore the history of how major outside powers (mostly the United States and China) have considered the military and national security value of the islands that sit between them and the ways these outside powers attempt to shape the space for their own ends. While the chapter looks backward in time to World War II, I predominantly focus on more contemporary contests in the region over how the area is influenced by competing projects for building and maintaining global hegemony.

Also in chapter 2, I examine the U.S. military base network in the region as an assemblage. I look at the way in which the United States has viewed the region for purposes of national security and how it has attempted to topologically fold the space of the Pacific in ways that serve its desires (Allen 2011, 2016; Mezzadra and Neilson 2012). The idea of topological space is a revealing one for looking at contemporary political processes in general, and it is particularly relevant for looking at the way in which histories of military colonialism have shaped the western Pacific. The idea of topological space comes from mathematical formulations of how space can be folded and twisted in ways that make geographic distance less important than the way in which places are connected together with infrastructure. In contrast to topo*graphical* representations of space that more or less faithfully represent geographic distances between sites, topo*logical* renderings show how technologies, infrastructures, and geosocial connections make some places functionally more connected than others through processes of "presencing and absencing" (Bickerstaff and Simmons 2009). As John Allen puts it, "The gap between 'here' and 'there' is measured less by miles or kilometres and more by the social relationships, exchanges and interactions involved" (2011, 3).

This topological perspective has great explanatory power across the Pacific region, where places are functionally near and far in many ways that have little to do with actual location. As anyone who has attempted to travel in the region can appreciate, whether a given island is accessible has much more to do with transportation infrastructure (Is there an airstrip or functioning airline that goes there?) and colonial histories than with straight-line distances (for instance, most airline and shipping routes are still aligned from colonial powers to former—or current—possessions rather than to other nearby island groups). What is made present or absent, or closer or further, in this region is more an effect of power than of geographical distance. This is critical to appreciate because, as chapter 2 and the following chapters detail, the proximity of a place to other places is not necessarily an effective predictor of the interaction between them, or a determinant of where allegiances in a place may be directed. Also, it emphasizes that sovereignty and control in a given space may not originate within a place, or even close by. Instead, power can be exerted from afar through the very process of folding space by actively creating (or maintaining) infrastructures of connectivity or separation. As Allen puts it, "The so-called far-reaching powers of transnational corporations or actors like the state and global social movements are often best understood less as something extended across borders and networks and rather more as an arrangement which enables distant actors to make their presence felt, more or less directly, *by dissolving, not traversing* the gap between 'here and there'" (2011, 15; emphasis added).

In chapter 2 I use this topological lens to also look at the common conceptualization that the power of the United States in the region is waning as China's increases. The point is not so much to understand the ramifications for the United States or for China as much as to examine how the process of constructing hegemony on the global scale is affected by how islanders in these supposed out-of-the-way places adopt or resist the influences of competing larger powers. In other words, I look at geopolitics in this strategic region more from the islands looking out than from the Pacific margins looking in. By doing so I argue that we can see better how influence over territory is constructed in a translocal process of assemblage-building rather than just being projected from an imperial center based on military superiority.

In chapter 3 I look at influences in the Pacific that may not necessarily be traditionally thought of as political but that have important political effects. I examine how transnational environmental processes, patterns of human mobility, and economic influences draw the territories of Micronesian states toward different parts of the region, regardless of their close political affiliations with the United States. By doing so, I aim to demonstrate how formal political sovereignty is but one aspect of influence or control in any given space. Of course, the idea that economic processes threaten, or even supersede, political sovereignty is a widely appreciated point by both Marxist and neoliberal theorists (Arrighi 2005; Foucault 2007; Hardt and Negri 2000; Harvey 2007).[9] However, I merge this discussion with the preceding chapter on geopolitics to examine more specifically how—in the Pacific context—economic processes undo some forms of political control, open some avenues for local governance, but also present new dangers of informal imperial control. In particular, I focus in this chapter on the recent surge of Chinese investment, diplomacy, and tourism spending in this region and examine how these new flows and connections alter the topological space of the region. While some may see tourism as a frivolous economic activity for the participants, the economic, cultural, environmental, and political ramifications of tourism development—especially in a realm of tropical islands with few other major income-earning industries—cannot be underestimated (S. Davis 2015; Fregonese and Ramadan 2015; Gonzalez 2013; Teaiwa 2000). As Chinese out-bound tourism becomes far and away the largest potential tourism market for American-affiliated island nations in the Pacific, the lure of Chinese investment and spending is causing countries to reconsider their political allegiances as well as their positions on greater political autonomy, cultural preservation, and environmental protection.

In chapter 3 I also focus on geosocial connections in the Pacific. The term *geosocial* comes from more recent research that theorizes how social processes—including those that have serious implications for geopolitical and geoeconomic circulations—are enacted across space through intimate person-to-person connections (Mitchell and Kallio 2017). In chapter 3 I examine how life in many of these Pacific places is constructed through interactions between people in these places and people outside of them. Through circuits of migration, communication, and family/social networks, the assemblages of sovereignty within these spaces are constructed from various elements that are connected topologically across vast stretches of ocean. These connections are always shifting and changing and can have great effects on political allegiances and desires. For instance, in chapter 3 I examine how Micronesian social connections to the United States through migration, educational opportunities, and enlistment in the U.S. armed forces strengthen the region's geopolitical and geosocial ties to the United States and counterbalance some of the increased economic pull of China. These relationships, however, are shifting, and as they shift, so do other geopolitical and geoeconomic influences. For instance, China is extensively ramping up programs to entice islanders to take advantage of cultural and educational experiences in China rather than in the United States (Jaynes 2017). Meanwhile, new anti-immigration policies being implemented by the Trump administration, along with overall cuts to education and the drying up of U.S. aid to the area, all serve to diminish the influence of the United States in the region.

In chapter 4 I take a closer look at how political assemblages cohere across space. Using examples of antimilitarization social movements from South Korea, Hawai'i, Okinawa, Guåhan, and other island locales, this chapter will explore how the regulative principles discussed in chapter 1 are constructed and travel as they animate geosocial assemblages in the region. Drawing heavily from scholarship in the field of feminist geopolitics—as well as social movement activities and declarations—this chapter highlights the emotional, affective, and physical aspects of assemblages. The chapter also shows the way in which body-centric ethics of care order assemblages of sovereignty that compete over territory against more traditional state-centric sovereignties ordered by ethics of nationalism, capital accumulation, racism, patriarchy, and militarized national security. At the chapter's conclusion these discussions of activism in the Pacific are then tied to their impacts on geoeconomic and geopolitical relationships to show how activist assemblages of sovereignty are not resistances to colonialism as such but rather are *productive* performances that create alternative governances.

The final chapter takes the concepts developed in the rest of the book (assemblages of sovereignty, their topological spatialities, the regulative principles that cohere assemblages, and the analyses of environmental, geopolitical, geoeconomic, and geosocial processes within the Pacific realm) and demonstrates how they can be applied in practical ways by both researchers and political movements in the Asia-Pacific region and elsewhere. In this chapter I discuss four major points that I believe can inform political struggles that aim to destabilize hierarchical and colonial forms of governance. I argue that recognizing the porous and assemblage-like nature of political sovereignties creates potentially novel and effective forms of social action that can advance the principles of justice, equality, and political freedom in an interconnected world. Instead of a fixation on state power, I argue for the need to focus social action on realms outside of state apparatuses: namely the islands of everyday life where effective sovereignty is actually constructed as well as the oceans (contexts) in which state apparatuses are embedded. I contend that struggles for decolonized, healthier, and more inclusive communities can be advanced through the *production of certain kinds of interconnection* rather than depending on traditional Western conceptualizations of sovereignty and autonomy that are not only defined by connotations of domination, disconnection, and exclusion but that are, to a large degree, illusions.

CHAPTER 1

Sovereignty as Assemblage

Competing Global Regimes of Occupation in Okinawa

On a November morning a group of thirteen kayakers pushed off from the shore of Henoko village in Okinawa to confront the combined power of the U.S. and Japanese states (figure 1).[1] Henoko has become the site of a political contest that will not only shape the future of this seaside town—and the adjacent Oura Bay—but may also determine the regional balance of geopolitical power in an increasingly volatile East Asia. As occurs most mornings, the kayakers had set out to test the Japanese Coast Guard's ability to dictate that this sea space—adjacent to the existing U.S. Marine Corps Camp Schwab—is the property of the United States and a suitable site for the building of a new air base (see map 2 in introduction). As the kayakers paddled into the bay, they approached a floating barrier that marks the boundary of the proposed construction area. A circling Coast Guard boat began to crisscross in front of the kayakers to harass and impede them. Once at the barrier, another Coast Guard boat attempted to check the activists' advance while the kayaks parried and probed the perimeter of the construction zone. Eventually, one kayaker paddled across the barrier with a Coast Guard boat in pursuit. Next, other kayakers moved through the unguarded opening, and soon the Coast Guard boats backed off—defeated but still monitoring—while the thirteen kayakers affirmed, for at least another day, that the bay belongs to them.

The actions of these thirteen protesters may appear to be of small significance when measured against the power of the Japanese state and the allied U.S. military. While in 2019 construction on the base was proceeding slowly, these kinds of tactics—occupying space and transgressing boundaries—have enabled activists in Okinawa to impede the complete landfilling of Oura Bay that is required for the construction of the new base that was first proposed in 1996 (Broudy, Simpson, and Arakaki, 2013; Inoue 2007; Lummis 2019; McCormack and Norimatsu 2012). I focus in this chapter on these contests over

FIGURE 1. Protesting kayakers in Henoko, Okinawa, 2012. Photo by the author.

the land and sea at Henoko because they demonstrate the more general processes by which sovereignty over a space is constructed. By looking at how *effective* sovereignty is contested by social movements in a particular small island of space, I make the argument that we can better understand how regimes of formal sovereignty are constructed, undone, and remade through struggles over *jurisdiction* in the spaces of everyday living (Pasternak 2017). Also, by showing how multiple global assemblages of governance intersect in this particular place, I will use this example of Henoko to broaden the view geographically to see how sovereignty over a local space is constructed in quite expansive assemblages that exist at, and across, a range of spatial scales but that are most certainly not geographically containerized or spatially contiguous.

Through this exploration, my aim is to better explain the idea of "sovereignty as assemblage" that denotes how sovereignty can be conceptualized as partial, hybrid, incomplete, constantly resisted, continually performed, and spatially discontinuous. Furthermore, I hope that by showing this in the context of social movements in Henoko, the discussion will also demonstrate some of the political possibilities of this view of sovereignty. Starting from the local and the particular, and then moving toward the general—as well as starting from the perspective of social movements and then moving on to states—

may seem like a backward, or at least unusual, method. I hope, however, that by the conclusion of this chapter the rationale for this approach will be clear.

Social Movements, States, and the Process of Producing Sovereignties

To ground my examination of how social movements can illuminate the larger processes through which effective sovereignty is produced, there are a few important details about these movements that are worth discussing at the outset. First, antimilitarization protests such as the ones occurring in Okinawa are examples of *translocal* activism in which there are strong linkages between groups across the globe (Baird 2015; Davies 2012; Koopman 2011, 2015; McFarlane 2009; Nicholls 2009; Oslender 2016). Many military bases, especially those belonging to the United States, are situated in a far-flung network of (mostly) colonized spaces that form a "repeating island" or archipelago of militarization, so it is hardly surprising that social movements opposing militarization have developed global linkages of solidarity as well (Benitez-Rojo 1997; S. Davis 2015; Lutz 2009). Second, these movements are characterized by strong discursive and normative challenges to state-supported (especially U.S.) narratives of national security. In place of these dominant narratives, these groups focus on the security of local communities and civilian bodies (Hyndman 2004). Third, in addition to ideological claims for human security, self-determination, and decolonization, these globe-spanning movements frequently employ direct action occupations that challenge states' jurisdiction within particular spaces. These groups are not just for peace as an ethic of interstate behavior. They also challenge the use of specific land and seascapes for use as military bases, bombing ranges, and maneuver areas. Using direct action tactics that involve illegally occupying spaces, they directly intervene in the governance of space and the performance of military construction, operations, and circulations. In short, they challenge state sovereignty. I will analyze these activist tactics because they have, in several instances, led to successful outcomes for social movements when antimilitarization groups have blocked the construction of a new base, closed an existing base, or reduced a base's operations (S. Davis 2015).

The activism occurring in Henoko, Okinawa, can be effectively described using contemporary geographic theories that examine social movements as assemblages. In the 1980s and 1990s social movement researchers applied the insights of assemblage theory to stress how solidarity and collective identities within new social movements were constructed through the interaction of participants (Melucci 1995; Routledge 1996). In contrast to representations of social movements as networks that are the *result* of linkages between people with similar structural social positions (like class or ethnicity), researchers emphasized that newer social movements are *assemblages* constructed through active *processes* of personal interaction and the circulation of discourses and emotional connections (Fominaya 2010). As Kris Olds and Nigel Thrift put it, "[Assemblages] are not therefore to be thought of as subjects but rather as 'something which happens'" (2005, 271; see also Anderson and Harrison 2010).

More recent scholarship has built on this idea of social movements as assemblages and emphasized two major points. The first is that these assemblages are *translocal* in character. The second is that the processes that make up these social movements are not just discursive, ideological, or representational but also include material practices. The contention that these social movements are translocal directs researchers' attention to the fact that there is no a priori privileging of either the local or the global as the origin or key scale at which these assemblages are organized. These are not local struggles scaling-up or global organizing structures manifesting action in a local place. Instead, the assemblages of activism are constructed *through* the process of relating across space. Referring to McFarlane's work on social movements, David Featherstone adds, "This stress on 'relational processuality' . . . foregrounds the ways in which social/political processes are generated *through* relations between sites rather than configured through 'internal relations' in sites" (2011, 140; emphasis added). I would explicitly add that neither is it configured through a larger external framework or network. Instead, the assemblage is literally constructed through the *creation* of an active constellation of translocal articulations.

This is an important point to remember when we try to examine why connections are made and where to locate causality within the construction of these translocal movements. As Manuel DeLanda (2006) puts it, an assemblage is characterized by "relations of exteriority" in which components within it have "capacities," but these components do not have essential natures defined by the positions they may take within an assemblage. Drawing on DeLanda, a later study by Anderson and colleagues further explains, "While other modes of thinking relationally view entities as syntheses, where 'the linkages between its components form *logically necessary* relations which make the whole what it is', assemblage theory views relations as *contingently obligatory*" (DeLanda 2006, 11, cited in Anderson et al. 2012, 25; emphasis added). In other words, components of an assemblage stand in *possible* but not *necessary* collaboration (Alvesson and Sköldberg 2017, 55). There is no destiny or inevitability to the formation of any given assemblage, but there are still reasons for the connecting—even if contingent and temporary. In the case of the island of Okinawa, for instance, it is currently a component in multiple assemblages: the state apparatus of Japan, the military base network of the United States, circuits of tourism from mainland Japan and China, and so on. It is not, however, naturally a part of any of these. The assemblages Okinawa finds itself in are historically constructed, and we would expect them to continue to shift in the future, just as they have in the past. This perspective implies that contextual factors—logics of capital, Euclidian distance, violent domination, preexisting social similarities, historical inertia, and so on—may encourage/discourage/influence components to construct particular assemblages, but they do not *determine* them (Dittmer 2014). Also, it means that components can detach from existing assemblages to join or construct others, but that the agency to do so is neither wholly determined from the outside nor from within the component. As Anderson and colleagues put it, "The implication of assemblage thinking is that causality is located not in a pre-given sovereign agent, but in interactive processes of assembly through which causality operates as a nonlinear process" (2012, 29).

The second major point emphasized by contemporary assemblage approaches to social movements is that the articulations in assemblages are not just constructed through the sharing of discursive information but are also created by the circulation of material practices and the shared embodied visceral states of participants (Bosco 2007; Clough 2012; Featherstone 2012; Hayes-Conroy and Montoya 2017; Hayes-Conroy and Martin 2010; Müller 2015; Pain and Smith 2008). There are many forms these material practices take, but to focus the discussion I return to the example of kayakers transgressing the boundary of the landfill area in Oura Bay. There is a whole collection of practices that inform this style of occupation. First, many sites of antimilitarization activism are on islands and seashores. This geographic fact has made necessary a particular suite of techniques for activist occupations that are suitable to near-shore environments. The tactic of "boating in" to a body of water to stop military activities has been used in a variety of ways, from Greenpeace sailing into nuclear testing sites in Alaska (1970s) and French Polynesia (1990s) to fishers protesting military maneuvers in Puerto Rico (1960s–2000) to Hawaiian activists kayaking to Kaho'olawe Island to stop naval bombardment (1970s–80s).

These tactics were shared with Okinawans (and Okinawans have come up with and shared their own innovations) through written accounts but also, crucially, through in-person visits (Chan 2008; S. Davis 2015). Many of the people I interviewed in Okinawa had traveled to other militarized sites, such as Hawai'i, Puerto Rico, the Philippines, the Marshall Islands, and South Korea. Similarly, people from those sites have made solidarity visits to Okinawa. It is not just discursive information, however, that is being shared through these visits. Much of the learning is experiential. Activists are not just *watching* protests in other sites: they are also participating in them. They are learning practices such as how to cut fences, how to steer kayaks through rough seas, how to safely chain oneself to scaffolding in the sea with scuba gear on, and how to deal with police responses. Furthermore, during these visits activists are also constructing bonds of solidarity through the simple practice of putting their bodies in shared emotional and visceral states (Hayes-Conroy and Hayes-Conroy 2013). As I will expand on in chapter 4, many interviewees reported that some of the most important moments in informing their activist practice were emotional experiences that occurred when they visited other places (and could compare the militarization of their community with another) or when they shared highly visceral experiences with activists from other locations (such as the excitement and adrenaline rush of a protest action, or even the simple sharing of food with others). Several interviewees also noted that through these experiences they felt less alone in their struggles and more likely to take part in bolder protest actions. Looking at protest tactics as a product of this larger assemblage emphasizes that both the material practice of sea occupations *and* the associated two-way solidarities are produced together *through* the translocal articulation of ideas, emotions, and political actions (Brown and Yaffe 2014; Featherstone 2011). Furthermore, this tells us not only how the material processes of activist occupation are developed but also something about the larger sources of power that lie behind the actions. In short, thirteen people with kayaks did not make up this tactic; they should therefore not be considered to be alone in the sea.

From Protest to Sovereignty: Assemblages, Apparatuses, and Regulative Principles

While the view of social movements as performed translocal assemblages tends to emphasize the contingent, ephemeral, and deterritorializing aspects of these movements, there are ordering and unifying processes that solidify the collective identities of activists and give these movements some consistency, stability, longevity, and capacity for the territorialization of power (Melucci 1995). After all, many social movements have maintained their focus and activities for decades, even if they are reproduced through the amassed interactions of thousands of people spread across time and space. Viewing assemblages as active processes or as happenings does not mean they only exist when there is some kind of visible political action or act of civil disobedience. The "relatings" that underpin the assemblage of social activism seen in Okinawa are still quite active between protest actions in ways that are subtle but also critical for their operation. To better understand this, it is useful to consider some theoretical approaches for reconciling the ordering tendencies within social movements with the openness and contingency that is connoted by describing social movements as assemblages.

The first useful approach is the concept of "regimes of living" suggested by Stephen Collier and Andrew Lakoff to analyze how disparate elements can combine to organize social action (2005). They describe "regimes of living" as "situated configurations of normative, technical, and political elements that are brought into alignment in problematic or uncertain situations" (31). Using the example of the "protestant ethic," they discuss how a package of normative positions can be a "foundation and justification" that travels and guides social action when there is a perceived need to address a crisis or urgency—that is, when the situation does not match the ideals (32).

This idea of regimes of living shares much in common with Foucauldian theorizations of apparatuses (*dispositifs*) that examine how states deploy techniques of governance guided by certain ordering ethics—or *regulative principles* (Foucault 2007; Lemke 2001). While there is certainly debate over *why* apparatuses attempt to govern in certain ways—and whether there are grounding reasons for regimes of governance (capital accumulation, protection of state sovereignty, discipline and control, efficiency, economy, etc.)—it is hard to argue against Foucault's insistence that "there is no power that is exercised without a series of aims and objectives"—even if those calculations scale upward from the microlevel of everyday life (1978, 95).

Deleuze elaborates on this idea that there are certain ideals—and also certain social loci—that frame and guide the operation of an apparatus. He claims, "If from then on we try to define the most general characteristic of the institution, *whether or not this is a State*, it seems to consist of organizing the relations which are *supposed* to exist between power and government, and which are molecular or microphysical relations around a *molar agency*: 'the' Sovereign or 'the' Law, in the case of the State; the Father in the case of the family; Money, Gold or the Dollar in the case of the market; God in the case of religion; Sex in the case of the sexual institution" (1988, 76; emphasis added). He makes three points that deserve elaboration: that governance exists outside the boundaries of the state, that there are relations that are "supposed" to exist (which denotes ordering normative principles), and that there are certain "molar agencies" that center the imperatives for governance for different institutions (law or sovereign for the state, money for the market, etc.).

Taking the first point, while apparatuses are frequently associated with the workings of states, it is critical to consider that "states were the product, not producers, of 'apparatuses of security'" (Legg 2011, 129). Or, as Deleuze puts it, "There is no State, only state control" (1988, 75). Even though Deleuze refers to "state control," he shows how attempts at control and governance arise from the distribution of power relations that saturate the spaces of everyday life and that occur *outside* the state and exist *prior* to their capture by states (1988; see also Deleuze 1992a). In other words, there are apparatuses outside of states—including social movements—that attempt to govern social action and practice effective sovereignty over space. Social movements, then, are best characterized not as entities that *resist* (state) governance, but as entities that *are themselves apparatuses of governance.* As we will see later in this chapter, when these apparatuses of governance attempt to territorialize their ideals, it is hard to characterize what is being constructed as anything but an attempt at sovereignty. Therefore, antimilitarization social movements and the states they oppose are similar *forms* of governance striving for sovereignty, only with different regulative principles.

So how do we square the two conceptualizations of social movements presented thus far? How are social movements both assemblages and apparatuses? If Deleuzean assemblages are more spontaneous, processual, and deterritorializing, and Foucauldian apparatuses are more associated with ordering structures, how can social movements be both? The best way to reconcile these aspects of social movements is summarized in Stephen Legg's assertion "that apparatuses be considered a type of assemblage, but one more prone to (in the sense of anticipating, provoking, achieving and consolidating) reterritorialization, striation, scaling and governing" (2011, 131). In this way apparatuses are seen as somewhat assemblage-like in that they are flexible, shifting, and performed happenings. This position is also supported by Stephen Collier's work, which emphasizes the shifting and processual nature of apparatuses by pointing out that they are not as static or as epochal as they are frequently represented but instead involve shifting topologies of power that constantly modulate between techniques of sovereign power, disciplinary power, and biopolitics to produce desired effects (2009, 99; see also Deleuze 1992b).

The case of kayakers occupying the sea space off the coast of Okinawa is thus an example of a social movement "prone to . . . re-territorialization, striation, scaling and governing" (Legg 2011, 131). The kayakers can therefore be usefully analyzed as an apparatus attempting to supplant state power in place and alter material circulations and relationships. In short, even when not making rhetorical claims to formal sovereignty, protesters *practice* effective sovereignty (Day 2005; Featherstone 2012; Fernandes 2013; Routledge 1996, 2015; Zibechi 2010). By occupying particular places, these social movements are not just local groups reacting to and *resisting* state power and projects. Rather, these are groups organized as translocal assemblages that are attempting to territorialize and *produce* forms of governance and security that are focused on different "molar agencies" and framed by globally circulating regulative principles (such as community security, environmental protection, and self-determination) that run counter to those organizing state governance (national security, economy, and militarized deterrence).

Militarization, Opposition, and Competing Securities

At this point it is useful to dig a little deeper into this idea of regulative principles and the way they organize these different apparatuses of sovereignty. These regulative principles are important not just because they demonstrate the values and aims of an apparatus but also because they are what allow an assemblage of sovereignty to actually function across space (whether we are talking about social movements or states). Assemblages may be made of innumerable threads of ideas, material practices, bodies, and whatnot, but it is the regulative principles that orchestrate the operation of the composite entity. In this section I use the example of antimilitarization activists, but this is only a single example of a much larger process that holds assemblages together and allows coordinated action across space.

In the case of antimilitarization activism, the central regulative principles in play are ones that run counter to the values of national security frequently espoused by militaries and so-called realist geopolitical thinkers. Antimilitarization social movements prioritize regulative principles that include environmental protection, a belief in the peaceful settlement of international disputes, an articulated desire for political self-determination/decolonization, a concern for human health in the spaces of everyday living, and attention to the ways that militarization particularly affects women via increased levels of sexual violence and exploitation (Lutz 2009). As exemplified by the name of one transnational organization, Women for Genuine Security, these groups contend that security should be conceptualized not as national security but as a genuine security that focuses on how to make individual bodies, rather than states, healthy and secure (Booth 1997; Hyndman 2004; Loyd 2012). This shift in perspective on just what is being secured involves a shift in who security is for—from the state to individuals—as well as a shift in the scale of concern from the national/global to the local/body.

To return to Deleuzean discussions of power, there is an alternative "molar agency" that underlies the different regulative principles of security. From the perspective of genuine security it is not the injury done (or benefit to) the sovereign, the law, or the dollar that determines the correctness of social actions but rather the effects on *the body*. In the case of the militarization of Okinawa, for instance, activists are not concerned with the effects of militarization on the security of the U.S. state, or on the security of economic trade through the straits of the western Pacific, but with consequences for bodies in Okinawa. What do the jet and helicopter noise, the fear of assault, the environmental contamination, and the loss of land and seascapes do to bodies living on the island?

Bodies, while the targets of these threats, also then become both the active agents resisting the apparatuses of militarized security as well as the touchstones on which the rightness of the processes and policies of militarization are judged. The body should not be imagined as a separated and individuated body but rather as a relational body produced in its social and environmental context. The body is a locus of broader relationships as well as located in a stream of temporal processes of production and reproduction. Protecting its health demands not just a protection of individuals but also a safe social and environmental milieu—a milieu that is threatened by military activities in the spaces of everyday living. Taking the precepts of liberalism literally, activists call for the protection of the sovereignty of bodies rather than the sovereignty of states. This resonates with Foucault's discussion of ruptures in the valuation of life and shifts in governance in his statement, "What was demanded and what served as an objective was life, understood as the basic needs, man's concrete essence, the realization of his potential, a plentitude of the possible. Whether or not it was Utopia that was wanted is of little importance; what we have seen has been a very real process of struggle; life as a political object was in a sense taken at face value and turned back against the system that was bent on controlling it. It was life more than the law that became the issue of political struggles" (Foucault 1978, 145).

Through this lens of protecting bodies and milieus these social movements see military bases and their associated environmental and social impacts not as providing security but as assaulting it (S. Davis 2015; Lutz 2009; Woodward 2004). These quests for differently defined forms of security are central to the contentious politics currently occurring in Okinawa and in other militarized places. Scholar-activists in critical security studies and feminist geopolitics have produced a substantial number of case studies and theoretical interventions explaining and supporting this person-centered view of security and the associated critique of militarization (Booth 1997; Dowler 2012; Dowler and Sharp 2001; Enloe 1990, 2000, 2007; Fluri 2012; Hörschelmann and Reich 2017; Loyd 2012; Lutz 2009, McCormack and Norimatsu 2012; Santana 2002; Shigematsu and Camacho 2010). Furthermore, antimilitarization groups in the Asia-Pacific region have explicitly articulated that this counternarrative about a body-centric security is a critical foundation of their politics.

A good example of this can be seen in the activities of the Inter-Island Solidarity for Peace group that formed in 2014 with members from Jeju, Okinawa, and Taiwan. The objectives of the group extend beyond blocking the construction of specific military projects in the region to the promotion of other modalities of security in Asia and the Pacific. The group's vision is that the most effective long-term strategy to contest the construction of bases in the region is to promote the development of a different system of international relations in East Asia. While the group focuses on supporting opponents of militarization on the nearby islands, it also has a broader aim of cultivating more transnational connections and creating more peaceful relationships between the islands on the edge of East Asia. Inter-Island Solidarity for Peace optimistically and explicitly articulates the principle that nonstate actors on small islands, when linked in solidarity, can create "another kind of geography" for the whole region. At the group's second annual Peace for the Sea camp in 2015 in Okinawa (the first was in Jeju in 2014, the third in Taiwan in 2016, the fourth on Ishigaki Island in 2017, the fifth again in Jeju in 2018, and the sixth in Kinmen, Taiwan, in 2019), it issued the following communiqué that demonstrates its view of the recent U.S. shift of more military resources to the area but also addresses its vision for more peaceful geographies in the region based on the construction of a different kind of social assemblage:

> We fully understand that this shift [the U.S. military pivot toward Asia] will not bring about greater human security but will instead yield the conditions for a far greater risk of war and tremendous environmental destruction. We further recognize that these changes have been fueled by the global weapons industry, which reaps enormous profits from increased military tension and conflict, while ordi-

> nary people and the wider ecosystem suffer the inevitable consequences. We cannot leave this work to political leaders and governments, which largely answer to corporate interests and the military-industrial complex. We challenge the prevailing assumptions behind the current configuration of geopolitics that takes for granted the precedence of nation-states, military interests, and capitalist accumulation. We will instead create another kind of geography. Through our Peace for the Sea Camp and similar projects, we are already creating alternative political communities based on a sustainable economy, the ethics of coexistence, and our shared responsibility to preserve peace. (quoted in Paik 2015)

The values, promoted by groups such as Inter-Island Solidarity for Peace, have a broad circulation that extends far beyond antimilitarization and anti-imperial activist groups, or specialized academic circles. When social movements like those in Okinawa attempt to mobilize through appeals to values such as environmental protection, women's welfare, healthy communities, ideals of social justice, or a distaste for warfare, they are attempting to seek support by aligning their movement not just with the values of radical activists or academics but also with values that have millions, if not billions, of adherents across the globe. In fact, the ethic of protecting bodies in their relational milieu is a regulative principle within global circulations of progressive politics even if it is not always explicitly articulated using such terminology.

Because we all have bodies and can viscerally identify with others when those bodies are harmed, such appeals have a powerful force in attempts to get sympathy and political support for people in acute crises like those in Okinawa. However, it can also be an important glue for the production of larger transnational movements. When we see images of refugee boats capsizing in the Mediterranean, a mother putting a mask on a child before she goes out into the contaminated landscapes of Fukushima, a Syrian father mutilated by bomb shrapnel, children being torn away from their parents while crossing the U.S. border, or a Laotian teen being fitted for a prosthetic leg after stepping on unexploded bomb, we can read these as symptoms of larger structural wrongs because of the effects they have on bodies. The fact that we can identify and empathize with the visceral experiences of bodies subjected to physical and psychological pain—whether through direct violence, the degradation of their everyday lived environment, or forced separation from those for whom they feel affection and love—can serve as a common basis for solidarity and constructing new global political movements despite the important differences that result from the way social constructions of class, gender, and race imprint on our individual bodies (and the ways different bodies are socially valued; Butler 2010). The body here functions as a boundary object that can organize solidarity, collaboration, and mass action despite the differences between our perceptions of, and experiences within, bodies (Star 2010). While Jacques Derrida posits that our solidarity with those who are suffering could bind together a "new international" of leftist politics via a common *rejection* of the politics of nation-states because of the suffering they cause (see, for instance, the discussion in Campbell and Schoolman 2008, 301), an emphasis on the regulative principle of nurturing the relational body can change the focus around which larger movements are formed—from an emphasis on what a new larger politics could *reject* to what it could *promote*.

In this example from Okinawa, for instance, local activists seek to show that the building of a military base in their community is a localized manifestation of broader negative social processes (i.e., militarization and colonialism), but also that the activists are working to promote a governance in Okinawa based on the widely held principles of peace, respect for local public opinion, human health, and environmental protection. The regulative principle of protecting bodies therefore becomes not just an abstract ideal for resistance but also a rallying point of what should be around which a productive political program can coalesce and grow (Connolly 2017; Hardt and Negri 2004).

In the case of the confrontations between kayakers and the Japanese Coast Guard, therefore, the battle is not just over an outside project intruding on a local seaside village. Nor is it just a dispute over the establishment of sovereignty over Oura Bay by competing would-be governing entities. Crucially, it is also a battle between two globally circulating assemblages of sovereignty that are attempting to territorialize their regimes of living and regulative principles that relate to (and define) security in starkly different ways (Collier and Lakoff 2005). While people opposed to the new base in Henoko see construction as something that will bring environmental ruin, assaults on health, and threats to the security of bodies, military planners and political leaders in the United States and Tokyo have represented Henoko (and Okinawa as a whole) as a critical site for the deployment of military assets to enhance the national security of Japan and the United States, as well as to protect global supply chains and trade routes (Collier and Lakoff 2009; Cowen 2014; see also Pasternak and Dafnos 2018 regarding the larger trend of state fear of Indigenous assertions to jurisdiction interfering with supply chains). As Masamichi Inoue notes, the U.S. Department of Defense declared in 2005 that "the stability and prosperity of the Asia-Pacific region is a matter of vital national interest affecting the well-being of all Americans" and that the militarization of Okinawa is crucial for maintaining that stability (2007, 133). In this context, "security" is clearly a multiple and contested concept. If base construction is stopped in Henoko, it could be viewed by protesters and promoters of critical security approaches as a victory for self-determination, environmental protection, community health, and social justice, while simultaneously viewed by U.S. military planners and their allied counterparts in the region as a dangerous destabilization of systems of deterrence in Asia.

Territorializing Ideals: Competing Sovereignties in Place

There are thus different normative positions on security affecting politics in Okinawa, and here I will address the way those positions animate different attempts at governance. I begin with an examination of the social movement tactic of land and sea occupation as an attempt at territorializing governance (i.e., creating sovereignty through attempts to produce jurisdiction), and follow this with a discussion of how this tactic is similar to the practices and spatialities of state sovereignty. While social movements and states may have different levels of capability to govern space, I discuss similarities in the techniques and spatial practices that both use.

The account of the kayakers in Henoko that began this chapter describes a form of activism bent not just on rhetorically challenging power but also on territorializing an alternative regime of power in space. The phenomenon of nonstate actors territorializing power has, of course, not gone unnoticed by geographers and other social scientists (Routledge 1996; Rose-Redwood 2006). In particular, anarchist-inspired theorists have long appreciated how power is territorialized through direct action and occupation (Day 2005; Ince 2012; Springer 2014). While there has been a lively debate over the benefits of promoting an anarchist agenda within geographic scholarship (Clough 2012; Clough and Blumberg 2012; J. Hayes-Conroy 2008; Harvey 2015; Springer 2014), it is hard to deny that social movement tactics that stem from the anarchist tradition are a prominent element in contemporary activism and are worthy of attention. The label and banners of anarchism are not at the forefront of the organizing or rhetoric of either the Okinawan or global networks of antimilitarization activism, but principles long championed by anarchists, such as egalitarianism, self-determination, direct action civil disobedience, mutual aid, and nonhierarchical organizational structures, saturate both (S. Davis 2015). In the case of the tactics of occupation highlighted here, much political thought and action in the anarchist tradition—though certainly not all—is antistate but not necessarily anti*governance*. While anarchist theorists and activists have largely eschewed taking *state* power, the dual-power approach popular in anarchist and autonomist circles aims to marginalize state power through the wresting away of spaces from state control and then constructing spaces of alternative nonhierarchical governance (Day 2005; Bookchin 1998). This is also a popular and effective tactic for political change in many places, especially in Latin America, as exemplified by groups such as the Landless Workers' Movement in Brazil and the Zapatistas in Mexico (Fernandes 2013; Holloway 2002; Zibechi 2010).

The sociologist Richard Day characterizes this tactic of supplanting governance through occupation as a practice of "newest social movements" (2005). Day suggests that social movements can be categorized by the way they engage with state power. Day characterizes old social movements as those groups—such as socialist or anticolonial political parties—that seek to capture the state through either electoral or revolutionary means. New social movements are groups that aim not to take state power but rather to change social conditions through pressuring the existing state to comply with political demands. By contrast, the newest social movements are those that do not see the state as a site to capture or as an appropriate institution to redress grievances. Instead, newest social movements see the state as an inherently corrupt organ that must be resisted and supplanted rather than as a legitimate arbiter of social rights.

The categorization of these groups into "old," "new," and "newest"—while useful for understanding the different political and spatial strategies used by social movements—is problematic in two senses. First, it implies (inaccurately) that these strategies belong to particular epochs, as if old social movements did not still exist (or are somehow out of date), or state-avoidance or producing spaces of alternative governance had not been occurring for centuries (Scott 2009). Furthermore, it also obscures the fact that most social movements frequently use all three strategies in varying combinations to achieve their aims. In the case of Okinawa, for instance, in addition to the newest social movement tactic of blockading and occupation, there has been engagement in the old social movement tactic of electoral politics. This is evidenced by the election of antibase governors Takeshi Onaga in 2014 and Denny Tamaki in 2018, as well as a referendum in 2019 in which 71 percent of voters cast ballots opposing the new base in Henoko (the results of the referendum were seen as nonbinding by the U.S. and Japanese governments and have thus far been ignored by both). New social movement tactics have also been critical components of the campaign against bases in Okinawa, such as when massive protests and rallies (some with more than ten thousand participants) have been held over the past several decades in Okinawa, Tokyo, and other sites around the world.

Despite some of the problems with Day's terminology, however, it illuminates how different tactics and relationships to the state exist in social movement strategy. In addition, it shows how occupation and the territorialization of an assemblage of alternative governance are incorporated into contemporary activism. Protests like the ones in Henoko are making an earnest attempt to wrest the governance of a space away from state entities (or at least to permanently affect what goes on in the space by forcing states to use the space differently). These protests are using strategies of nonviolent resistance in which people are withdrawing their consent to be governed by either the Japanese state or the occupying U.S. military force. They also take it one step further (Sharp 1973; Ackerman and Kruegler 1994). While the protesters use techniques of noncooperation that demonstrate a lack of willingness to accept Tokyo and Washington's edicts, and therefore serve to undermine state power in Okinawa, the kayakers in Okinawa attempt to move beyond noncompliance by also attempting to imagine and *produce* an alternative governance through the creation of a substitute territorializing apparatus bent on enacting effective sovereignty over the contested space in Oura Bay. Similar to Paul Routledge's discussion of land occupation in Bangladesh, occupation in militarized areas "promises the reconfiguration of physical space . . . in order to articulate emergent forms of sovereignty . . . and transform social relations of power and reproduction" (2015, 13).

As Routledge emphasizes, however, the tactic of taking space and occupying it has a more complex relationship to state power than simply state avoidance or supplanting the sovereignty of the state. Routledge notes that in Bangladesh, although land occupation may appear to be a project of autonomy from the state, the precarious economic and social position of the occupiers often leads to campaigns to achieve state recognition to solidify claims, stop attacks by police and "goons," and create security for their occupied sites. In contrast to rigid formulations of how social movements interact with states, in Okinawa the occupations have this same complicated relationship to state power. In many ways they are attempting to challenge state sovereignty and supplant governance in Oura Bay and block the operation of state-sanctioned military construction. However, the occupations, "sit-ins-on-the-sea," and blockades also serve as tactics to create leverage and gain recognition for grievances so that state power can address them. As Andrew Cumbers points out, even in radical activism that seeks to challenge traditional regimes of property and governance, the state still remains an "important terrain of struggle" (2015, 72).

In the case of Okinawa, the relationship between activists and state power is multifaceted. Even within a single protest action there are multiple relationships to the state being experimented with and performed. In the single protest act by the kayakers it is difficult to decipher the extent to which the action is seeking to supplant the state or seeking redress from the state. One reason for this is that there is a diversity of opinion among the protestors themselves as to why they are taking the action. Interviews and discussions with protesters in Henoko revealed that concerns ranged from environmental damage to dugong (an endangered sea mammal) habitat to Okinawan political sovereignty vis-à-vis Japan and/or the United States to noise issues from the military operations to beliefs in pacifist international relations. There were also differences of opinion as to appropriate tactics and strategies, as well as differences in belief as to whether the U.S. and Japanese governments will ever willingly halt construction.

Not only is there diversity within the social movements, but multiple state institutions are also involved. When people talk about "the state" in Henoko, Okinawa, just what institution is being referenced? The U.S. government? The Japanese government in Tokyo? The Okinawan prefectural government? The municipal government in Nago? These different entities are sometimes arranged in ways in which they symbiotically push the base construction forward, while at other times they are at loggerheads. In addition, even when the head of one of these institutions favors one outcome for Henoko, other individuals *within* the bureaucracies oppose them. This is exemplified by the downfall of former Japanese prime minister Yukio Hatoyama, who opposed the base and was undermined by both the U.S. government and the defense establishment in Tokyo (Norimatsu 2011). It is also shown by how Okinawa governor Hirokazu Nakaima was trounced in local elections after bowing to Tokyo and altering his stance against the base. Even in the government that has been most steadfast in promoting base construction, the United States, powerful U.S. senators (John McCain, Jim Webb, and Carl Levin) have objected to the whole scheme of transferring Marine Corps functions to Guåhan and Henoko. They have instead supported moving Futenma's operations to the existing U.S. Air Force Base in Kadena, Okinawa. This multivalent and shifting terrain of the state is one that proponents and opponents of the new base are engaging with strategically in complex ways. In some instances, they are asserting activist autonomy from some state institutions—and radically appropriating and performing governance in space against state power—while simultaneously asking other state institutions for redress.

The protests in Okinawa therefore have a complicated relationship to state power that we could categorize as "more-than-state" politics. Direct engagement with the state (via electoral politics, legal actions in the courts, etc.) is happening, but the social movements are also trying to undermine the state in more indirect ways by trying to challenge its jurisdiction in a strategic space (which undermines state sovereignty) and by trying to influence the broader social contexts in which the state tries to make decisions (by trying to turn public opinion against the state by framing the new base as something that destroys environments, perpetuates violence on- and off-island, and exacerbates an already unfair burden on the people of Okinawa). If we think about the state here as an assemblage, the activists are attempting to alter its operation by altering the threads that influence and construct it—both in the islands of particular place-based struggles over rightful jurisdiction as well as in the ocean of the larger social context.

The Common Political Spatialities of States and Social Movements

So how can one theorize the spatiality of these social movements that occupy spaces and strive to govern them yet also have these aspects of engagement with existing states? It is necessary to return to the idea of the regulative principles that motivate the activism. In the Okinawa case, the goal of the social movements is quite clear: blocking the construction of the new base in Henoko. This goal does not exist strictly because of local concerns but also because building the base violates the globally circulating ethical principles of personal security, environmental protection, self-determination, and alternative visions for international relations. The actions to block the construction are about more than stopping a base—they are also meant to block the territorialization within the community of a state-sponsored way of life informed by militarist national security ethics. In place of the state-sponsored regime, social movements attempt to construct a different regime of governance. The protests in Okinawa are not merely cases of airing grievances or pointing out wrongs. They are attempts to give an alternative regime the force of sovereignty—to territorialize it and give it teeth (McCormack 2011)

From this perspective, sovereignty over space is about making real the world envisioned by the regulative principles. If that is best achieved through pressuring existing state structures, then that is one pathway. If not, these structures are supplanted. Who has *formal* sovereignty over a place is not as crucial as whether the regulative principles of a certain ethic are territorialized. It is therefore not of *primary* concern whether or not elements of existing state apparatuses are used to achieve these goals (although activists often articulated a lack of trust that state institutions could support ethical ways of life that run counter to traditional forms of governance and national security). Even though these movements have interactions with states, and sometimes even ally themselves with some branches of them, tactics such as land and sea occupations allow activists to engage with states outside state-formulated procedures. Even if occupation is not *necessarily* a state-supplanting tactic, it is engaging with the state on terms not dictated by the state (the way elections, court fights, or legislative actions might). Occupations, therefore, are powerful tools to *either* modify the behavior of an existing state or, more radically, supplant the state's effective sovereignty—either briefly or for longer durations—in favor of a governance structure that will enact a different regime of governance.

It may be tempting to discount the importance of social movements like the ones in Okinawa because of the small spaces they occupy. After all, what is the real threat to the power of the United States to have a shoreline occupied here, or to lose a single military base there? The smallness of the spaces of occupation might be insignificant if they really were mere isolated specks in vast continuous swathes of state power, but the example of antimilitarization activism discussed here suggests other ways to conceptualize the spatial deployment of both social movements *and* state power.

It would be misleading to think of spaces that are wrested from state control as being isolated, disconnected, or local. Instead of seeing activist occupied sites as merely autonomous islands and state-ruled areas as vast, unbroken seas, it is more accurate to think of both as interconnected archipelagos of sovereignty. As explained above, the activist occupation of Oura Bay is not a local or isolated action. The occupation of the bay is a bubble of alternative governance manifested out of a latent global substrate of shared experiences, solidarity, and regulative principles of governance. It is connected materially, discursively, emotionally, and normatively to other struggles and individuals around the globe. In short, the occupation in Henoko is a contributory part of a global assemblage of alternative sovereignty as well as an expression of it.

Occupations in Henoko may be islands of alternative governance, but they are immensely connected ones. There is much that can be learned about these kinds of political islands of sovereignty by examining recent scholarship on geographic islands that emphasizes that islands are not as isolated as traditional Western representations of them would lead some to believe (Chandler and Pugh 2018; S. Davis 2015; DeLoughrey 2017 Hau'ofa 1994; Roberts and Stephens 2017). Geographical studies in the Pacific and Caribbean, for instance, testify that far-flung geographic islands are intensely connected to each other and to surrounding continents via "submarine" solidarities, diaspora networks, circular migration, kinship connections, and shared histories of enduring and resisting colonialism (Benitez-Rojo 1997; DeLoughrey 2007; Lilomaiava-Doktor 2009). Furthermore, recent analyses of island geographies emphasize that islands (of either the geographic or political sort) are relationally constituted in an assemblage-like way to other islands to such an extent that it makes little sense to consider them as isolated spaces (Stratford et al. 2011).

As the concept of translocal assemblage explicitly contends, the islands of alternative governance produced by activists are also highly linked spaces. In this manner, the global antimilitarization protest movements share a similar spatiality as the Occupy Wall Street protest movement that erupted in 2011 in that each site of occupation and protest is linked by common (though by no means entirely consistent or ideological homogeneous) political ethics as well as shared networks of material, emotional, and rhetorical mutual aid that crisscross national spaces and reach across borders as well (Sparke 2013). As the recent literature on assemblage theory and social movements suggest, this view of the spatiality of social movements seems to fit a variety of contemporary and historical case studies of solidarity from contemporary Tibet (Davies 2012), apartheid South Africa (Brown and Yaffe 2014), and the U.S. Civil War (Featherstone 2012). In short, occupations and territorialized spaces of alternative governance do not need to be spatially contiguous to be connected or wield power.

It would be limiting, however, to view this archipelagic conceptualization of power as being in *contrast* to spatialities of state power. Instead, it is in contrast to older, inaccurate conceptualizations of state power and sovereignty. Jonathan Pugh (2013, 2016), Elaine Stratford and colleagues (2011), and Engin Isin (2007) persuasively argue that researchers ought to adopt "archipelagic thinking" when considering not only islands but continental political units as well. They argue that all places are produced in relation with each other and are held together by systems of governance that reach out to link *noncontiguous* spaces. Stratford and colleagues use the examples of Canada and Australia to demonstrate how even large political entities are actually made up of thousands of geographic islands of various sizes (2011). This view of state power as inherently archipelagic is even more obvious in the cases of the United Kingdom and United States (especially when the overseas military territories of both are taken into account).

Engin Isin's work (2007), however, takes this one step further and shows that this archipelagic view of the spatiality of power even applies to contiguous land areas. Isin contends that what are often thought of as states or empires are networked *virtual* entities that are actually performed and enacted from particular microterritories of human interaction—what he refers to as the "city"—and then linked via assemblages in an archipelagic manner. Isin states, "It is imperative that we think about actual and virtual spaces through the forces that create and assemble them. Juridico-political spaces such as regions, states, empires, leagues and federations are effects of the city created as virtual bodies rather than being solid and permanent. . . . The assemblage of the state as a space is realized through borders, controls, walls, checkpoints, taxation, education, passports and other real means and effects but the state as an actual entity does not exist. . . . [Instead,] the state is enacted and invented through the city" (2007, 221).

This view of the state as an assemblage-like archipelago of territorialized sites (border stations, capital buildings, military bases, etc.) held together by human practices enacted in place and organized by specific regulative principles is of course not very different spatially from the aforementioned characterization of social movements. The performance of an apparatus of state governance is not done everywhere across a national space. Rather, it is performed in a hopscotch manner within and outside national territories (Painter 2006). In the case of the U.S. state, this is very clear. The state has a strong presence and capability to govern in certain sites (within the Pentagon, at border checkpoints, in heavily policed city centers, and even in places outside its formal sovereign territory, such as within the perimeter of a foreign military base or on an aircraft carrier floating in the Indian Ocean), but there is a lot of space in between those sites where effective sovereignty is absent or diminished. In other words, this discontinuous geography of where states are able to territorialize power, and where they cannot, returns us to the topological view of space mentioned at the conclusion of the introduction (which will be expanded on in chapter 2). Certain sites are more connected and more distanced from effective governance regardless of the Euclidian distance from centers of power or whether their coordinates lie within formally recognized borders. Similarly, the effectiveness of social movements has a topological spatiality of its own as well.

State power, then, is not deployed in a different manner than occupying social movements or other actors. It is an archipelagic apparatus, driven by regulative principles, striving for governance through the *continual performance* of occupation in noncontiguous but topologically linked spaces. This similarity in the spatialities of governance between state and activist groups is also demonstrated by the malleability of the term *occupation* itself—and the moral color that term takes on when applied to different actors. For instance, the primary meaning of the word *occupy* in military colonies refers not to an activist tactic but to state-led colonialism. Many residents of Okinawa, Hawai'i, Guåhan, Puerto Rico, and other militarized areas see themselves as already occupied. This was demonstrated when the Occupy Wall Street affiliates in Hawai'i had to wrangle with how to translate the rhetoric of the Occupy movement into their existing framings of Hawai'i as already occupied by the United States. In the case of Okinawa, activist attempts to occupy Henoko can also easily be seen as attempts to deoccupy it from United States and mainland Japanese control. Pointing out the similarities in the territorializing spatialities of occupation by both social movements and states is not arguing that social movements have the same *ability* to govern a given space as established states. Thirteen kayakers in Henoko do not have the same ability to affect the world as the U.S. government and its military forces. However, the *manner* in which they attempt to deploy power in space—to construct sovereignty—is quite similar.

Conclusion

Thinking of occupying social movements as apparatuses of governance driven by alternative sets of regulative principles can create theoretical openings for the analysis of political action across a variety of scales. For one, it suggests the applicability of Foucault's rich work on apparatuses for the analysis of nonstate political movements. Second, by viewing the spatiality of both social movements and states as archipelagic, researchers can better see where, how, and why certain regimes of power appear and become real in various spaces. Third, by analyzing social movements and states as operating and deploying power across space in similar ways, both scholars and activists can move away from the dichotomy of hegemony and resistance, and move toward examining political action as a competition between the effective sovereignties of actors, whether these be states, transnational corporations, drug cartels, networks of religious fundamentalism, cosmopolitan bourgeoisie, foreign-deployed militaries, or social movements.

From this view, social movements are not offering liberation per se. After all, liberation describes a lack—what one is free from—but says little about what social actions are supposed to be performed under an alternative apparatus of power. What social movements like the ones operating in Okinawa offer is the territorialization of alternative governance centered on the civilian body and driven by regulative principles of peace, self-determination, community health, cooperative international relations, and environmental protection. By operating in a manner that mimics the archipelagic spatialities of state and imperial occupations, these translocal social movements provide scholars and activists with a nuanced example of sovereignty, as well as a reminder not to sell short the transformative potential of social movements—even ones that appear small.

This account of Okinawa also reinforces the notion that sovereignty is constructed in space in an assemblage-like way. It affirms the position that sovereignty is a contested project and that there are competing state and nonstate apparatuses attempting to territorialize power. It also reaffirms the value of looking at space from a topological perspective. Sovereignty does not simply exist as an already constructed thing that is then brought to the space of Oura Bay. It is not constructed at a higher-scale and brought to the local scale in a top-down manner, nor does it arise from the local and travel upward. In keeping with more recent geographical critiques that question both the ontological existence of scale (and the epistemological value of invoking it), this case would support the idea that sovereignty does not flow from one scale to another but rather is produced via translocal articulations (Jones, Woodward, and Marston 2007; Painter 2010).

Perhaps the most critical point here, however—and one that connects conceptualizations of sovereignty most strongly back to assemblage theory—is that sovereignty here is shown to be an *effect* of the continuous *performance* of occupation that arises from the articulation of multiple translocal elements that combine within the space (Painter 2010). Effective sovereignty in Oura Bay therefore arises from the effects of the competing performances. As Joe Painter points out, the creation of territory as the construction of sovereignty within a given location is never solid and permanent but rather is "necessarily porous, historical, mutable, uneven and perishable. It is a laborious *work in progress*, prone to failure and permeated by tension and contradiction. Territory is never complete, but always becoming. *It is also a promise the state cannot fulfill*" (2010, 1094; emphasis added).

What this account of sovereignty in Okinawa emphasizes is that control over space is a fragile and shifting project. This is not to say that social movements and others who aim to challenge state occupation have an easy road to social change. Echoing Painter's contention that territory is "a promise the state cannot fulfill," the tenuous ability of social movements in Okinawa to halt construction of the new military base also demonstrates that activist attempts to reconfigure governance are works in progress as prone to failure as the activities of states. The view of sovereignty as an assemblage, however, does show the possibility of shifting the locus of action when aiming to construct alternative regimes of sovereignty. It shows that the beaches, the streets, the mountains, the kitchens, and the waves can be effective sites of struggle and change—just as much as the ballot box, the courtroom, and the flagpole.

In this chapter, I have challenged many of the traditional conceptualizations of how sovereignty arises, how sovereignty is dispersed across space, and who can wield sovereignty. However, in this account many actors on all sides of the struggle still appear to imagine political power as something that is relatively autonomous from economic and social influences—or at least something that can stand above and regulate them. The solution to imperial political sovereignty appears to be local political sovereignty and vice versa. There are important lessons here, and we should appreciate that the production of sovereignty over a territory can be accomplished in networked ways that break out of the current geographic containers created by and for the purposes of colonizers. However, there still lurks a decisionist view of sovereignty with connotations that establishing political sovereignty over a space, even at the microlevel, is *the* way to keep out the intrusion of imperial political and military meddling.

In the following chapters I will further analyze this view of power as well as the spatiality of competing assemblages of sovereignty. However, I will also complicate this view of political sovereignty by challenging the conceptualizations of it as autonomous or as ruling over other social processes. I will do this through changing my geographic focus to other locations in the Pacific region, as well as through a more detailed teasing apart of the transnational connections that influence and construct assemblages of sovereignty. Specifically, I have divided the coming two chapters into discussions of geopolitical factors and more-than-political processes in the region. Using some of the theoretical positions from this chapter, I expand on just how webs of connection, apparatuses of violence and military force, and the topological folding of the region's spaces by colonial political and economic processes, discursive representations, social networks, and differing ethics complicate traditional views of sovereignty as supreme and autonomous. Then, in the final two chapters, I attempt to explicitly articulate the political possibilities of this more hybridized way of reading the global terrain of power and sovereignty.

CHAPTER 2

Oceans of Militarization

Traditional Assemblages of Geopolitics in the Pacific

In the introduction and chapter 1 I attempted to undermine some of the traditional assumptions about sovereignty by discussing how power reaches across space, how it is deployed in specific local sites (such as Henoko, Okinawa), and how its operation is countered by other spatially discontinuous but overlapping apparatuses of power. Specifically, I analyzed the ways that both state and nonstate actors that lack *formal* sovereignty can still wield *effective* sovereignty over a site. These analyses, however, only partially address the tasks I outlined at the start of the book: namely, to think through the paradoxes of invoking sovereignty as a political tactic, to imagine alternative conceptualizations of governance, and to promote novel political approaches that enhance equality, transnational solidarity, and self-determination. In this chapter and the following one, my goal is to examine the broader contexts in which competing sovereignties attempt to operate, and in which calls for sovereignty are invoked. The introduction and the first chapter examined how effective sovereignty is constructed in islands of local jurisdiction in order to show how the multifaceted strands of governance come together in a place. In this chapter, I turn to the oceans of regional and global constellations of power that structure the production of local systems of sovereignty.

I expand the view to a regional scale to examine more closely the contexts, or metasovereignties, in which local constructions of sovereignty are produced. The term *metasovereignties* refers to assemblages of social actions, discourses, and governance that condition and influence local sovereignties: that is, the governance that orders other governances (Larsson 2013; Lisle and Pepper 2005). While the language used here appears to suggest that this structuring occurs in a one-way, top-down fashion in which larger forces constrain or guide the local, that is far from accurate. It is critical to take a broad geographic view to understand how various agents construct governance in a given locale, but there are some dangers to using terms such as *metasovereignty*, *context*, and *terrain*. While these terms can be useful for discussion since they (along with commonly accompanying adjectives such as *larger*, *broader*, *regional*, and *global*) are familiar ways of representing different spatialities of power, there are some detrimental effects (both analytical and political) when they are used without some important explicit caveats. These terms connote that more regional (or global) political terrains are some kind of fixed, permanent given, or that they are somehow wholly constructed externally and that populations within the region have to accept this as a preestablished, unchangeable fact. Such a representation constructs a discourse that is analytically inaccurate, and also closes off crucial potential avenues for transformative political action. To counter this traditional perspective, throughout this discussion of governance and influence in the Pacific region I will draw on assemblage theory to stress that every place (no matter its size) is not only subject to *but also generative of* the relations that construct these larger terrains of power. Therefore the metasovereignties I discuss are, on one level, the context or field of potentialities from which site-specific island sovereignties in the region develop, but they are also something that *emerges* from, and is shifted by, actions on these islands. I argue that local constructions of sovereignty—whether in Okinawa, Oʻahu, Shanghai, Tokyo, New York, Lhasa, or Tahiti—are enabled and produced through connections within the larger milieus in which they sit, but these milieus are also partially constructed *from* these places as well.

Furthermore, these milieus are constellations of social and environmental processes that are much more than the machinations of any given state or even solely the result of what are usually considered political elements. In other words, local effective sovereignties arise out of connections not just to larger political structures (such as states, militaries, NGOs, social movements, etc.) but also to transnational economic flows, environmental influences, social interactions, cultural practices, and ethics. Accordingly, while this chapter emphasizes how military and political processes in the region shape the construction of island sovereignties, the next chapter focuses on what I refer to as "more-than-political" processes such as the shifting terrains of economic development, foreign aid, investment, tourist flows, and environmental conditions.

Throughout my discussions I follow a geosocial approach that examines transnational geopolitical and geo-economic processes from a situated perspective that relates how these regional and global processes construct, and are constructed by, individuals and communities in these island places. This perspective, put forward by Katharyne Mitchell and Kirsi Kallio (2017), extends the work of others in feminist geopolitics and stresses the importance of examining just how bodies are viscerally and emotionally affected by transnational connections, and how subjects then absorb, resist, and reconstitute those transnational processes. As Elaine Lynn-Ee Ho notes, the geosocial approach aims to understand "the constitution of subjects in transnational space" (2017, 2). The geosocial is therefore not a different *kind* of interaction per se—as if it were separate from the geo-economic and geopolitical. Instead it is a different way to theorize how the geopolitical and the geo-economic are structured across space in a topological way between and within subjects.

This approach is relevant since it illuminates just *how* people experience transnational connections in intimate ways. The geosocial approach allows us to consider how people in politically contested regions such as the Pacific construct local sovereignties as they confront the desires and actions of profit-seeking enterprises and imperial states. In short, it gives a better view of how people relate to (and contest) some apparatuses of sovereignty, while producing alternative ones that contradict the premises of imperial politics or capitalism. As Mitchell and Kallio put it, "We believe that the key intersecting relationship between the free market desires of unimpeded capital circulation and political desires of territorial control—or more bluntly, the grand macro narrative of the logic of capital and the logic of territory, can be nuanced and augmented with the addition of this third, co-generative axis of the geosocial" (2017, 6).

My choice, then, to divide my discussion over this chapter and the next into categories of "political" and "more-than-political" influences in the region should not be construed as an attempt to section off or reify these processes into types. Instead, it is a narrative device to disentangle and discuss these various influences. Deciding what counts as political, economic, or other involves making some analytical cuts through what are actually entwined and hybridized practices and interactions. My rationale for dividing the discussion this way is to highlight the political importance of interactions and processes that are frequently not labeled "political" as such. For instance, when examining how sovereignties are constructed in Pacific places, the patterns of Chinese investment and spending in the Pacific, or the immigration and educational linkages between islands and larger countries on the margins (discussed in chapter 3), are just as important for understanding what influences political allegiances, dependencies, and resistances as regional militarization and formal political relationships (discussed in this chapter).

Geographically, in this part of the book I will discuss how sovereignty is structured across the whole Pacific basin, but I will focus particularly on the ocean spaces surrounding East Asia and the island groups politically affiliated with the United States in the central and western Pacific such as Hawai'i, and the Caroline and Mariana Islands in Micronesia (see map 1 in the introduction).[1] By doing so, I look at the exercise of power over oceanic and island spaces that national laws and international law (and many geopolitical scholars and practitioners) have treated as spaces qualitatively different from continental landscapes. In addition to marine seascapes, this region also includes islands that great powers have long represented as too small to have their own formal sovereignties, and which, to this day, have been denied formal self-determination. In other words, states and other actors have viewed these areas as somewhat exceptional in terms of how formal sovereignty ought to be applied. The deployment and exercise of power here has therefore occurred in some unique ways. Because of this, an analysis of the regional politics here—while important in and of itself to the people both in the island Pacific and the surrounding landmasses—can also reveal facets of how sovereignty operates *in general* that can be more difficult to tease out in other contexts.

Sovereignties at Sea

While geopolitical concerns over sea spaces have traditionally focused on oceans as security buffers and transit surfaces, there is much more going on today in the seas around Asia. The seas are rich fisheries and sites for potential energy and mineral extraction (Thang 2012). They are also spaces where novel logics of governance are being experimented with and applied (Gray 2018; Steinberg 2018). To be sure, the application of state power to ocean spaces is not a new phenomenon (Campling and Colás 2018; Nolan 2013; Smith 2018; Steinberg 2001, 2018; Wirth 2016). Similar to the extension of state power over land spaces, there has been a long-running comparable colonial process that has aimed to change vast oceanic spaces from a "wilderness of waters" into known, legible, apprehendable, and governable social spaces (Nolan 2013; Scott 1998; Smith 2018; Steinberg 2001). People in coastal environments (in cultures both ancient and contemporary) have, of course, always imbued marine spaces with meanings derived from observation and lived experience. These experiences have allowed near-shore users, fishers, and mariners to understand the sea in order to identify dangers, catalog resources, navigate, and even claim ownership over watery spaces (McCormack 2011). During the eighteenth- and nineteenth-century era of Euro-American exploration, however, a truly global cataloguing and mapping of the world's oceans was undertaken in newly encountered ocean spaces (Smith 2018).

In the scientific/colonial endeavor to know the oceans, a general pattern can be discerned in which people first developed the technologies that enabled them to travel into these new spaces that were initially considered unowned, ungoverned, and filled with unknown opportunities and dangers. Later these ocean spaces were made legible and knowable through the (sometimes fantastical) anecdotal stories of voyagers as well as through more systematic studies that measured and mapped the ocean environments around the globe (Smith 2018). Through this increased knowledge, the ocean spaces became more legible to those searching for business opportunities (traders and whalers, for instance) as well as the navies of countries seeking to protect their mercantile interests. This combination of an ability to reach into a space and come to know it allowed states to project power into ocean spaces far outside their formal land borders and near-shore waters.

This ability to see into and project power into a sea space, however, should not be confused with *controlling* that space. Reach and legibility may be prerequisites for effective sovereignty, but they do not in themselves denote an ability to govern a space, adequately manage it, or keep others out of it. Just because someone can physically sail a ship through a part of the ocean, or plant a flag on a section of seabed (or plant a flag on the moon, for that matter) does not mean they actually govern that space—either formally or effectively. These are all expressions of an ability to reach, an announcement of a shift in the topology of space, but not necessarily the territorialization of an exclusive jurisdiction (Allen 2016; Pasternak 2017).

In colonial histories of terrestrial landscapes there has often been a progression from reaching into a space, knowing the space, making claims over it, and then incorporating the space into formal sovereign territory. Some have then assumed that this process can be applied to sea spaces as well. Alfred Thayer Mahan (1890), for instance, is perhaps one of the best-known theorists who in the nineteenth century argued for viewing sea power according to the ability of one nation to control sea spaces *at the expense of others* in a similar vein to terrestrial sovereignty. The opening of his influential 1890 opus *The Influence of Sea Power upon History, 1660–1783* noted, "The profound influence of sea commerce upon the wealth and strength of countries was clearly seen long before the true principles which governed its growth and prosperity were detected. *To secure one's own people a disproportionate share of such benefits, every effort was made to exclude others*, either by the peaceful legislative methods of monopoly or prohibitory regulations, or, when these failed, by direct violence" (1; emphasis added). In practice, however, achieving exclusive sovereign power over a sea space is tricky. Ocean spaces are particularly resistant to effective or exclusive governance due in part to the constant motion and flux of the water and its contents, the ever-shifting nomadic movements of the ships that ply the waves, the migratory species beneath the surface, and the vast extent of the watery territory (Havice 2018; Steinberg 2018; Steinberg and Peters 2015). These facts, however, have not deterred state actors from trying to impose control over ocean spaces or from representing them as being under the complete control of one sovereign power or another.

Certainly it is true that in the contemporary era more and more of the oceanic environment is legible and reachable. When one considers the extensive mapping of the seafloor, the exploration for benthic minerals and offshore petroleum deposits, the tracking of fishing stocks (and the greater ability to track the movements of the associated fishing fleets),[2] the ability of modern submersibles to reach the greatest depths of the Mariana Trench, and the newer ice-free accessible areas of the arctic, it is clear that more of the oceanic environment is accessible to the minds and machines of humans than ever before. The increase in legibility of, and reach into, the ocean realm has led states to follow the script of terrestrial colonization and *attempt* to capture, manage, and incorporate sea spaces under their sovereign power. States, for instance, have long claimed sovereignty over territorial waters within roughly twenty-two kilometers of shore as well as economic rights over resources within exclusive economic zones (EEZs) that extend over 370 kilometers out to sea. More recently, states, international bodies, and NGOs have attempted to manage even larger swathes of ocean environments through seabed claims and massive marine protected areas (Gray 2018; Zalik 2018).

It would be wrong, however, to imagine that sea spaces are undergoing a linear and teleological process of transformation that will inevitably result in the eventual enclosure and domination of the sea by state power. First of all—as I have argued throughout the book—even in terrestrial spaces state sovereignty is never the finished and complete process that states wish it was (and traditional conceptualizations of sovereignty would suggest). Instead, as Philip Steinberg (2018) argues, sea spaces are in a dynamic frontier state, but one that resists closure or incorporation. Rather than seeing a frontier space as merely the soon-to-be-incorporated, Steinberg emphasizes that ocean frontiers are spaces caught in dramatic tensions of closure and *opening*. In Deleuzean terms, the oceans are spaces in which practices of both territorialization and deterritorialization are constantly occurring. They are dynamic realms where increasing legibility creates an arena into which whole apparatuses of exploration, science, infrastructure development, and military maneuver operate. These may all be apparatuses of closure, but these "frontier machines" can operate only in the liminal spaces that sit *between* the poles of the wild unknown and the (elusive) realm of the completely controlled.

The key point here is that the western Pacific Ocean is an area increasingly subject to surveillance, intense exploration activities, military maneuvers, and sovereignty claims of various kinds that attempt to increase the ability of states to delineate, control, manage, and seek profits. While there are certainly historical antecedents to this process, it is striking that there is now such an intense focus on seas that were, for centuries, mostly regarded as unknowable or incapable of being subject to state sovereignty (Havice 2018; Nolan 2013; Peters, Steinberg, and Stratford 2018; Smith 2018; Stavridis 2017). That said, these spaces are also ones that *resist* closure due to their material attributes (liquidity, currents, depths, storms, etc.), as well as the existence of multiple counter-narratives that shape the oceans as political objects: narratives that include international legal doctrines regarding them as international waters with rights of freedom of navigation, environmentalist ethics, doctrines of private neoliberal capital extraction, and Indigenous conceptualizations of ownership and responsibility (Jackson 1995; McCormack 2017; Steinberg 2001). So while it may be tempting to look at how sovereignty has functioned on land and then apply it to the sea spaces that are increasingly being claimed in different ways, there is actually more that can be learned by moving in the other direction. Rather than looking at the territorializing of sovereignty in the sea, what if we consider how closure and sovereignty are *challenged* in sea spaces to better understand how contested and contingent territorializing projects such as invoking sovereignty or establishing spheres of influence really are across the whole region?

Island Sovereignties in Topological Space

In regard to the islands of this oceanic region, external powers have long represented them as if they were hybrids of a sort: part terrestrial, part oceanic, part deserted, and part Indigenous spaces (S. Davis 2015). Would-be colonizers have treated these island spaces, like oceans, as frontiers lacking internally constructed, Indigenous sovereignties. In some cases, they are even portrayed by colonial and military actors as spaces *incapable* of having Indigenous sovereignties (Shigematsu and Camacho 2010; Immerwahr 2019). Therefore, the whole island Pacific region is one deeply shaped by occupation and imperialism. Also, it is not just *legacies* of colonialism that we must consider. Instead, formal colonialism and occupation are widespread *present* realities across the region. Whether we are talking about unincorporated territories such as Guåhan, commonwealths such as the Northern Marianas, *collectivités d'outre-mer* (overseas collectives) such as French Polynesia and Wallis and Futuna, or incorporated/occupied archipelagos such as Hawai'i, there is nothing *post*-colonial about the contemporary Pacific (Clement 2019).

Because there is still a popular mindset (both within and outside the apparatuses of powerful states) that portrays the islands of the region as incapable of self-governance, external powers have had a tendency to represent the realm in ways that invite intervention and occupation. As I have discussed in an earlier book (S. Davis 2015), outside powers have viewed the Pacific as an anarchic no-man's-land where empires compete for influence.[3] Commonly this has involved overt military conquest, but, in its aftermath, it has also involved attempts to influence local allegiances by trying to convince people (frequently the *agents* of colonization themselves as much as the victims of colonization) that the imperial administration is there to protect people from the supposedly dastardly representatives of competing foreign powers (Shigematsu and Camacho 2010). In other words, the British made claims to protect islanders from the French. The Japanese promoted protection from European colonizers. The Americans then claimed to protect the region (in turns, over time) from the dangers of the Spanish, the Japanese, the Soviets, and, now, the Chinese. These justifications are important because they serve (historically and today) as mechanisms to justify the operation of an imperial sovereignty reaching into Pacific places whose legitimacy is clearly not derived from any kind of mandate derived from people *within* the region.[4]

There are many effects of this colonial competition over supposedly nonsovereign space, but the aspect I want to follow here is that the Pacific continues to be treated by external states not so much as a home to Indigenous inhabitants but as a stage on which to compete with *each other* militarily, politically, and economically. This is part of the context of the region and something people within it must consider when they are constructing their own sovereignties and struggling for self-determination. While there have been a number of foreign militaries operating here over time, I focus this chapter on the contemporary operations of the United States and China. While Russia, Japan, Taiwan, Australia, New Zealand, Vietnam, the Philippines, North Korea, and

South Korea are all important military players in the region, the United States is currently the most powerful naval and air power in the Pacific, while China is the largest rising military competitor.

While I stress in the coming chapters that military operations represent only one of multiple threads that make up the milieu of governance in the Pacific, it is clearly a very important one. This is not only because the ability to project military violence plays a part in the construction of both effective and formal sovereignties but also because the infrastructures created for military purposes deeply affect local communities and environments. Furthermore, militaries have been powerful agents that construct the topological spaces of the Pacific. As mentioned briefly in the introduction, it is valuable to examine the vast oceanic spaces of the Pacific through the lens of topology because it is a region in which infrastructures of connection and the resulting *functional* distances are frequently of much greater importance than Euclidean distances. As John Allen notes, "Power works by placing certain possibilities within or beyond reach. Reach, as I have stressed, when understood topologically, is more about presence than distance, something that can be folded in or stretched out by powerful actors to make their presence felt" (2016, 11). Through this process of reach, Allen argues that "power relationships *actually compose* the distances enacted" (7; emphasis added).

In the Pacific, militaries have been active agents in the production of much of the existing infrastructures of connection in the region (Bélanger and Arroyo 2012, 2016). In this way, we can view militaries—and the resulting airfields, ports, and base networks—as assemblages that reach across space and change the geography of where they can project military power. Furthermore, it is not just relationships of functional proximity that are created but also relations of remoteness as some places are cordoned off and disconnected. This can be seen in the way that nuclear test sites and military training ranges are *made to be* remote, but also in the way historical connections between nearby islands are limited and severed by political barriers (such as Guåhan from the rest of the Mariana chain, American Samoa from Samoa, or Bougainville from the Solomons). This rearrangement of the spatiality of the region affects military actors and also shapes the very topological space of the region that others must navigate. The construction of ports for naval coaling stations in the 1900s, the development of Guano Islands, the construction of airstrips and ports throughout the region during World War II, and the building and maintenance of modern military bases—these infrastructures have all affected island capacities for *nonmilitary* interconnection in the present day because they are frequently repurposed and reoriented.

For example, Won Pat Airport in Guåhan was originally built by the Japanese military in World War II, but it was then repurposed to be a U.S. Air Force—and later U.S. Navy—airfield as part of the U.S. project of bolstering its military position in the second island chain. It later became a civilian airport and now brings over a million tourists to the island—mostly from China, South Korea, Japan, and Taiwan. As I show in the next chapter, these tourists and their spending then act to pull Guåhan into closer relationships with nearby Asian countries in ways that complicate the U.S. military effort to maintain the island as a "tip of the spear." Also, the airport has become a locus through which migration is facilitated—between Guåhan and Hawai'i, between Guåhan and the mainland United States, as well as from other parts of Micronesia to Guåhan and the United States. This quick example alludes to the idea that infrastructures, which are designed to facilitate certain kinds of processes, do not *intrinsically* favor the processes for which they were intentionally built or the actors that originally built them. They merely create *capacities* that can be shifted to other kinds of connections that may facilitate other projects that condition different kinds of political potentialities.

Furthermore, I define the term *infrastructures* here in a broad way. It is essential to examine the "hard" infrastructure of runways, hangers, docks, buildings, and undersea fiber-optic cables, but it is also critical to look at the "soft" infrastructures that facilitate (or block) connections. These soft infrastructures include formal political statuses, visa requirements, patterns of aid and investment, tourism flows, airline timetables, import/export restrictions (such as the U.S. Jones Act), educational linkages, employment opportunities, and chains of migration. Soft infrastructures may be more difficult to see since they are not as visible as the artifacts of hard infrastructure in the landscape, but they are every bit as important for shaping patterns of mobility in the region. Also, as with the hard infrastructures across the Pacific, militaries have been key players in developing and maintaining these soft infrastructures.

If militaries have been shaping the topological spaces of the region, how are they making certain places more proximal and some more distant, and for what purposes? As discussed in chapter 1, militaries are apparatuses shaped by their own regulative principles—many informed by conceptualizations of national security for their own state. In the case of the United States and China, each has attempted to construct and maintain particular topologies in the region aimed at protecting their national security and political influence. In the case of the United States this has involved maintaining hard infrastructures such as military bases across the Pacific, but it also includes maintaining soft infrastructures that allow the military system to function across the region with less potential for interruption. Examples of this would include the colonial political statuses of Guåhan and American Samoa; the Compact of Free Association (COFA) agreements with Palau, the Federated States of Micronesia (FSM), and the Republic of the Marshall Islands (RMI); visa and immigration regulations for the Northern Mariana Islands; the diplomatic pressure the United States puts on Japan and South Korea to build new bases in the face of local opposition; and agreements the United States has with many Pacific nations that include provisions for strategic denial that exclude other militaries from these territories. In the case of China, they have engaged not only in building their own bases—and even, in the case of the South China Sea, constructing new islands to put them on—but also in forging new relationships of political, educational, and economic cooperation with island nations across the region that they hope will enhance their security and influence (Brant, Jiawei, and Cave 2016)

In the cases of the U.S. and Chinese militaries, both outside powers are aiming to shape the milieu of the region according to their own purposes. I detail these topology-shaping projects not just to give a view of the more traditional geopolitics of the region but also to inform activist projects to change this larger milieu. If, after all, we want to see a milieu in the Pacific that facilitates self-determination and decolonizing solidarities, we need to understand what the topological milieu currently looks like and the logics of the distant but powerful state agents that are still trying to construct the region for their own purposes. In other words, we have to examine certain kinds of military interconnections that situate how sovereignties in the region have been constructed and how more locally responsive sovereignties might be constructed in the future. Going back to the metaphor of thinking about constructing new apparatuses of sovereignty by looking at both islands and the ocean, this analysis is designed to analyze processes of dueling colonialisms, as well as to generate ideas for how self-determination can be carved out in this context and how the larger milieu can be constructed differently.

Tips of Spears, Chains of Islands, and Specters of Aggression: U.S. Geopolitical Considerations in the Pacific

In late 1941 and early 1942 the islands defending the thin U.S. linkages across the Pacific were quickly and easily overrun by the Japanese military. The east-west line of U.S. political possessions in the Pacific that had facilitated the

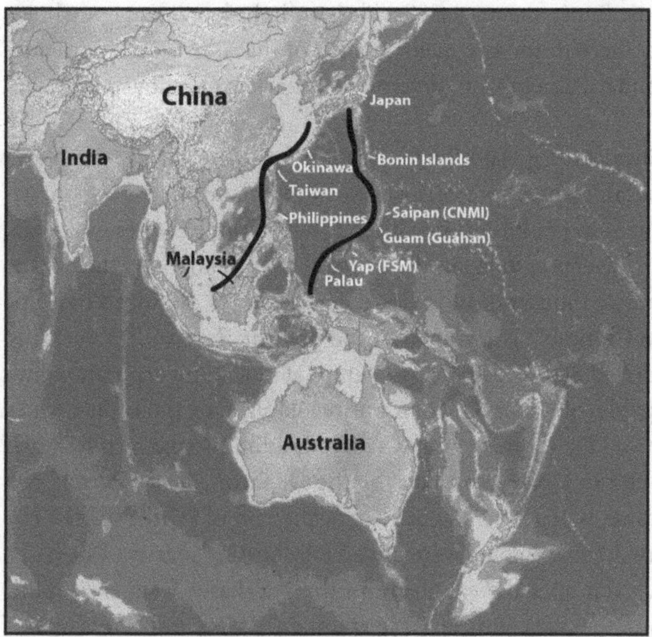

MAP 3. First and second island chains. Map by the author.

United States' connection to Asia was isolated and surrounded by the (at that time) Japanese-administered islands in the Caroline, Marshall, and Northern Mariana Islands. The U.S. possessions of Guåhan, Wake Island, and the Philippines quickly fell to imperial Japan, and the U.S. bases in Hawai'i were effectively attacked in December 1941. After the war, U.S. military planners were determined to maintain a more robust defense of U.S. connections to Asia and to not allow such a scenario to happen again in any future conflict with an Asian power. In a speech to congress in 1951, general Douglas MacArthur advocated that to contain Asian powers and block any advance across the Pacific, the United States should maintain not just a narrow east-west connection to Asia via a few island groups (Hawai'i, Guåhan, Philippines) but two continuous north-south defensive chains of islands in the western Pacific. These lines of defense in the Pacific would be along the first and second island chains (map 3). As with any chain, these defensive lines were only as strong as their weakest link. American military strategists therefore insisted that all points along these chains (especially key links of the first island chain, such as Taiwan and Okinawa, but *all* the other islands as well) must be held and fortified at all costs. MacArthur articulated this clearly when he said, "The holding of this littoral defense line in the western Pacific is entirely dependent upon holding all segments thereof; for any major breach of that line by an unfriendly power would render vulnerable to determined attack every other major segment" (1965).

This geopolitical strategy laid the foundation for the reestablishment and growth of American colonial projects across all the islands in the region. After the war, Okinawa was administered directly by the United States until 1972, and then after its reversion to Japan the United States maintained the dozens of bases with tens of thousands of military personnel (as discussed in chapter 1). From the Chinese Civil War until the present, Taiwan has been defended by the United States against any attempt at violent incorporation into the People's Republic of China. Guåhan was recolonized by the United States after liberation from the Japanese and was directly administered by the United States—first by the U.S. Navy and later by the Department of Interior. The Philippines became independent shortly after the end of World War II, but the U.S.-supported governments were amiable to hosting massive U.S. bases until the 1990s. Even after the expulsion of the U.S. bases from the Philippines in the 1990s, the two countries have maintained close military cooperation (though they have been strained during the recent presidency of Rodrigo Duterte). Across Micronesia the United States established bases and made political agreements to maintain U.S. influence in the region. In sum, the forms of control may have been different on different islands, but the end results have largely been the same: keeping these islands in the U.S. military orbit. MacArthur, no doubt, would have approved.

Even though the island chain strategy was formulated in the early 1950s in an era when the only way to attack the United States from Asia was by numerous amphibious assaults across the Pacific, maintaining these island chains in the U.S. realm is still imagined as crucial for contemporary U.S. military strategies. Many U.S. strategies for conflicts in Asia still depend on maintaining domination over both island chains. United States military strategies such as air-sea battle and archipelagic defense (Krepinevich 2015), as well as offshore control (Hammes 2012), assume the United States will have the ability to contain a hostile Chinese military to the west of the first island chain, while the United States holds all of the second island chain in order to have freedom of movement and sea lines of communication (SLOCs) into and out of the battle space. Strategists such as Thomas Hammes (2012) also note that U.S. control over both island chains would allow the United States to effectively strangle shipping into and out of China's eastern seaboard—and thereby force the Chinese government to capitulate without any kind of full-scale invasion or attack of mainland China. To the United States and allied militaries, a loss of political control over *any* of the islands in the western Pacific is a threat—not just because it undermines the actual strategies for a conflict with China in the Pacific but also because it would undermine the stable political geographies on which U.S. strategies have been imagined over the past seventy years.

Ropes That Tie Up the Dragon: Chinese Military Considerations in the Pacific

When we think about strong forces that shape the practice of governance in islands across the region, U.S. militarization has been a fairly consistent topology-shaping assemblage that islanders have had to consider and respond to. From the perspective of advocates for more islander political agency, it is "the devil you know." The threads of external influence in the Pacific region today, however, are more complex than the relative stability of unchallenged U.S. hegemony over the American Lake that characterized the period from World War II up to the early 2000s (Hayes, Zarsky, and Bello 1986). The multipolar political reality of the Pacific today presents both challenges and opportunities for the islands in the region. In this section I consider how one kind of new influence has been reshaping the political landscape of the region, namely, the rising military and political strength of China. In the next chapter I will focus on China's growing more-than-political influences in the region—such as economic investment, government aid, tourism initiatives, and cultural exchanges—but in this chapter I want to first discuss China's military, security, and infrastructure initiatives in the Pacific (as well as the reactions to them by the United States and their allies) to better understand the new emerging security architectures being constructed in the region.

In this section then, I begin with a discussion of the areas closest to Asia and then telescope out to view the Chinese government's growing influence and attention to areas further out in the Pacific. Beginning in the seas adjacent to China, it is well known that China has been increasing its military capabilities and has become more assertive in making territorial claims in the South and East China Seas (Krepinevich 2015). China's disputes with Japan and Taiwan in the East China Sea over the Senkaku/Diaoyu Islands, and with the Philippines, Vietnam, Malaysia, and Brunei over the Paracel and Spratly Islands in the South China Sea, show how very small islands can have a geopolitical importance that extends beyond the value of what resources might be on or around them. Though the Spratly Islands may have substantial fossil fuel deposits beneath the surrounding sea floor, and there are considerable fish harvests to be had in the sea, the competing territorial claims also demonstrate that the ocean spaces, and the small islands in them, serve other purposes for surrounding powers.

On one level, the states of the region treat these sea spaces as security buffers for their populated territories. Part of the rationale for states seeking control over a sea space is merely to keep other potentially threatening forces further away. For instance, the Philippines would view any Chinese military outpost on Scarborough Shoal in the South China Sea (a few hundred kilometers from Manila) as a grave security risk (Jennings 2017). What is more critical, however, is that the waters of the South and East China Seas are "logistic spaces": conduits for the movement of trillions of dollars of energy supplies and manufactured goods (Bélanger and Arroyo 2012; Cowen 2014; Chua et al. 2018). Stephen Collier and Andrew Lakoff's (2009) concept of "vital systems security" is a useful term for understanding the value of these seas to the surrounding states. Simply put, even though some states and international institutions may consider the seas near Asia to not be the territorial waters of anyone (and therefore not under the formal political sovereignty of any state), they are the spaces that host the incredibly important processes of trade, energy transport, and communication that are vital for the functioning of many contemporary states and their economies. If we accept that Japan, China, South Korea, and other states in East Asia currently *must* import energy supplies, and that their export-oriented economies would be devastated by long-term disruptions of trade, then we see that these transnational systems of movement are indeed vital for their security. The problem, however, is that many parts of those systems are not within the territorial boundaries of any one state (such as when energy or trade moves through the South China Sea). This creates a conundrum for state power. While state power is ostensibly supposed to be confined to a given territory, if many of the processes that enable that state to survive occur outside of it, then there are a few options to pursue—all of them with consequences.

First, a state can rely on external actors to secure those parts of vital systems that are outside its territory. China, for example, could choose to rely on an international rules-based order in which trade policies are somewhat stable and transnational freedom of navigation is promoted and secured by others (most notably by U.S. military power). This is, in effect, what Japan, South Korea, and many other countries have done over the past several decades. What if, however, there is a lack of trust in that international order, or a feeling that the order is disadvantageous to a particular state? Or what if there is a belief that the military guarantor of the system (i.e., the U.S. military) *might* decide to cut off those vital flows and connections that go through international spaces? In the case of China, these doubts are apparent. Given the existence of U.S. strategies such as air-sea battle, archipelagic defense, and offshore control, this should scarcely be surprising. After all, cutting off vital flows of energy and trade into the eastern seaboard of China in the event of a disagreement with China is what most of these publicly announced U.S. military strategies *specifically advocate*.

If there is a lack of trust that others can reliably secure your vital systems as they operate in, and transit through, international spaces, what other options are there? There are several possibilities, all of which China appears to be attempting to implement. First, you could try to go around potential blockades by developing alternative routes that avoid the eastern seaboard of Asia. Some of China's new regional infrastructure projects that seek to connect China to the west could certainly be seen in this light. There are many reasons for China's new "One Belt, One Road" projects (also known as "Twenty-First-Century Silk Roads," the "Belt Road Initiative," and "Six Corridors, Six Roads") that seek to build connections by land through Central and Southeast Asia, and by sea through the Indian Ocean: a need to invest capital internationally, a desire to tap into energy supplies in central Asia, the appeal of increasing trade with Africa, and political desires to better integrate western China with the east through development and greater connectivity (Blanchard and Flint 2017; Leverett and Bingbing 2016). It is also, geopolitically, a good project to make China less vulnerable to the American strategies of blockade and containment in the Pacific. In addition to constructing alternative routes for energy supplies and commerce, the One Belt, One Road projects are also hedges against the threat of vital systems interruption because the key nodes and hard infrastructure (ports, roads, pipelines, airports, etc.) are built with Chinese capital, largely owned by Chinese firms, and in some cases protected by Chinese military assets.

The construction of these alternatives to the west, however, does not necessarily make China content with the situation in the seas to its east. The fact remains that much of China's vital energy supplies and trade flow through the eastern seas dominated by the U.S. military but also by smaller, though well-equipped and modern, allied militaries such as those of Japan, South Korea, the Philippines, and Vietnam. All of these could pose a threat to flows vital to China's economy.

Other than the construction of routes that provide a back door for trade and commerce, what other strategies could a state such as China pursue if many of their vital systems flow through international spaces guarded by potentially hostile militaries? For one, they could try to change the status of the spaces from international to within the realm of their own formal and effective sovereignty. This could be done in two ways. The first is by claiming that the international space is really an intrinsic formal territory of the state. The second is through military technologies and strategies that aim to develop effective sovereignty over the space. China appears to be trying both of these strategies in the seas around Asia—particularly in the South China Sea.

China has more assertively claimed formal sovereignty out to its Nine-Dash-Line. If this were accepted, it would revoke the status of the entire South China Sea as international and would instead make it part of China's intrinsic territory (Hui-Yi 2016). The claims that inform the Nine-Dash-Line are mostly historical, and other countries in the region (and the United States) dispute their legitimacy. China's claims to making the whole sea its formal territory were dealt a further blow when United Nations Convention for the Law of the Sea (UNCLOS) arbitration ruled against their claim in 2016.

The Chinese government, however, did not accept the UN ruling and has also been pursuing an additional strategy: building new islands in the South China Sea by dredging sand and other seabed materials onto shallow reefs. While China has been (justifiably) criticized for the environmental damage caused by these kinds of military-oriented land reclamation projects (Caroll 2017), it is far from the only country dredging up material to increase the size of an island for military facilities.[5] These new islands serve two functions. The first is symbolic or legal. By creating new land China is trying to bolster its claims to the territorial waters around it (22 kilometers from the shore) and to exclusive economic zones (370 kilometers from land) that are usually granted under international conventions. Most other countries, however, balk at the idea that these territorial distinctions count when an artificial island is constructed.

There is another reason for building these islands, however: they enable more military control over the sea space. Putting permanent structures and military facilities on these new islands enhances China's effective sovereignty by occupying these sites. China is not the only country with outposts on small outcroppings and reefs in the Spratly Islands. Vietnam, the Philippines, and Malaysia have many as well. Creating a new island gives China the ability to occupy a spot that the other states have not yet occupied. Furthermore, placing military assets on these new islands enables China to better counter other militaries in the sea space. While having more ships and air units over the seas is important militarily, having ground bases is also invaluable. Like U.S.-produced infrastructures in the Pacific, China's building of these new islands is a way to alter the topology of the space. It is a way to make some sites within the sea functionally closer to China both practically and symbolically.

While China is trying to counter other regional militaries, such as those of Vietnam and the Philippines, it is also trying to wrest effective control of the space from the U.S. military, which still regularly sails into this disputed sea to uphold the claim that the space is in fact international. "Freedom of navigation" exercises by U.S. ships and planes are routine (and also occur in other places in the world where the United States believes territorial claims are excessive) but have led to some confrontations and heated exchanges between the Chinese and U.S. militaries (Panda 2018).

Formal territorial claims and island building, however, are not the only ways that China is attempting to take more control over the logistic spaces off its eastern seaboard. It is also developing more means to gain effective sovereignty over the adjacent seas through the development of improved military strategies and technologies. These developments have, of course, not gone unnoticed by observers in the U.S. and allied militaries, but there have also been some significant misunderstandings as well. For instance, in U.S. policy circles one often runs across the term *anti-access / area denial* (A2/AD) to define an imagined Chinese strategy in the Pacific. The idea is that the Chinese People's Liberation Army (PLA) intends to "prevent other militaries from occupying or crossing vast stretches of territory, with the express goal of making the western Pacific a no-go zone for the U.S. military" (Krepinevich 2015, 2; see also Yoshihara 2014). Specifically, American strategists suggest, "If anti-access (A2) strategies aim to prevent U.S. forces entry into a theater of operations, then area-denial (AD) operations aim to prevent their freedom of action in the narrower confines of the area under an enemy's direct control. AD operations thus include actions by an adversary in the air, on land, and on and under the sea to contest and prevent U.S. joint operations within their defended battlespace" (Krepinevich, Watts, and Work 2003, ii). This view suggests that China has an articulated strategy to deny the United States and other countries access to these seas, which are, of course, important spaces for the vital systems of China *but also* for Japan, South Korea, the United States, and many other interested powers.

This is one of the complicated facets of looking at these sea spaces through the lens of vital systems security. Namely, these are spaces considered vital to more than one state, since many of them rely on the same kinds of flows through the same space. All of the states have a vested interest in the flows continuing, but they do not necessarily trust the other players to secure those flows. If China distrusts the United States, Japan, and other allied militaries to be the guarantor of these flows, this is matched by other powers' distrust that China and the PLA should be the guarantor of the security of this important logistics space.

The question is, just because China is becoming more *capable* of denying the United States and its allies access to the seas around Asia, does that mean it actually has the *intent* to do so? Many Western observers seem to think so, but the problem with attributing an aggressive "anti-access / area denial" geopolitical strategy to the Chinese government and military is that some scholars have recently questioned whether it really exists, or if it is merely a projection of Western geopolitical fears. There are multiple layers to dig through to understand the concept of A2/AD and its connection to Chinese military strategy. First, even though the term "anti-access / area denial" is widely used in U.S. policy and strategic documents, many analysts point out that the Chinese do not use that term but instead use the term *counterintervention* (Yoshihara 2014). However, other scholars have dug further and found that neither A2/AD nor *counterintervention* are terms used by the PLA or Chinese government to describe military strategy (Erickson and Wuthnow 2016; Fravel and Twomey 2015). Given the importance that American policymakers and military planners place on countering this so-called strategy, it is somewhat astonishing that there is credible evidence there is no such strategy. It is worth quoting Fravel and Twomey at length on this crucial point:

> Chinese writings on military strategy and operations rarely if ever mention the concept of counter-intervention. Despite the frequent use of the term by outside observers—who attribute the concept to Chinese sources—the Chinese military does not use the term to describe its own strategy. When it does discuss related concepts of "dealing with" or "resisting" a third party's military intervention, it mentions them as a sub-component of one of the core campaigns or scenarios that drive Chinese planning, such as an armed conflict over Taiwan, not as an overarching strategy. . . . The concept of counter-intervention could be expressed in Chinese in three ways: "fan ganyu" (反干预), "fan ganshe" (反干 涉), and "fan jieru" (反介入) could all translate as anti- or counterintervention. Yet, most authoritative writings on defense policy, military strategy, and military operations by Chinese strategists do not use any of these terms. They do not appear in any of the white papers on national defense, which are authored by AMS [Academy of Military Science] for the Ministry of National Defense and have been published biannually since 1998. The 2011 edition of the PLA's official glossary of military terms does not contain an entry for any of these terms. . . . The People's Liberation Daily is the official (daily) newspaper of the Chinese military. No term

> for counter-intervention appears with any frequency on its online database archive. A moderate number of references use one of the three variants of the term to characterize U.S. (and Japanese) *perceptions* of Chinese strategy. Retired Maj. General Luo Yuan, for example, uses the term "fan jieru" (反介入), *but only as a way to characterize the U.S. view on China.* That same term (反介入) is also becoming the preferred way for Chinese strategists to translate the U.S. concept of "anti-access / area denial" (A2/AD), but only as a way to describe U.S. views. Ironically, some U.S. analysts then attribute "fan jieru" to Chinese sources even though *it is a translation of the U.S. concept* and not part of the Chinese military's lexicon. (2015, 172–76; emphasis added)

While it is certainly true that China has been increasing its technological ability to harass and deny dominance to U.S. military operations in the western Pacific, this is not the same as proclaiming a plan to drive out the United States or allied countries. Capability does not necessarily imply intent. It is inaccurate (and destabilizing) to state that there is an urgent need for a robust U.S. military presence in the western Pacific to counter an imminent, articulated Chinese threat, because that threat appears to emanate more from the geopolitical imagination of actors in Washington than it does from Beijing.[6] Even though there does not appear to be a grand strategy on the part of China to close off access to the common sea spaces of the western Pacific, the same cannot be said of strategies *articulated* by American and Japanese strategists that speak of doing precisely that to China. Thomas Hammes talks explicitly about how the United States could deploy tactics that *aim* to "cripple China's export trade" (2012, 5). Meanwhile, others speak of Japan using their own version of A2/AD to block China from the region and play on "China's deeply embedded fears of being denied access to the global commons" (Yoshihara 2014, 7). In short, the scholarship on these strategies throws serious doubt on the idea that China is *the* country threatening the economic and political stability of the western Pacific. Instead, what appears to be happening is that China is adding its own military forces to the mix of (hyper)militarization in the region where there is no paramount power dominating the seas. As emphasized throughout this book, sovereignty is never as simple as one power having total control over a space or it being in the sphere of influence of one state *versus* another. While I argue that this is the case for land areas, it is even more readily recognizable in sea and island spaces, since they have traditionally been viewed as outside realms of formal sovereignty. Perhaps it is obvious to state, but the seas of the western Pacific have no master, and control is not in the hands of either this state or that. Instead, multiple militaries jostle and overlap. This is a space where different powers attempt to occupy old islands and new, and where states also try to project power and construct exclusive territoriality over the sea. It is quite apparent, however, that governance of the sea spaces around Asia is not either/or but rather follows the Deleuzean logic of "and, and, and . . ." in which the more military units each country adds, the more muddled, uncertain, and insecure the governance of the space becomes.

While there is certainly a lot of attention on the South and East China Seas directly next to Asia, people have been paying less attention to what China's geopolitical visions and military strategies are for areas further out in the western Pacific on the "first and second island chains." While not as many studies examine Chinese conceptualizations of the islands further out in the Pacific, the fact that these islands are so important to U.S. military strategies means that Chinese planners certainly consider them as well. As Andrew Erickson and Joel Wuthnow (2016) have pointed out, Chinese policymakers see the more distant first and second island chains as "springboards and benchmarks" that serve as geographical markers of how Chinese influence is (or could) spread into the Pacific, but also as American "barriers" that constrain China (see map 3). Therefore, the U.S. presence there is a latent threat. As the PLA official Zhaolun Ding put it, the island chains of the western Pacific are like "ropes for tying up the huge dragon of China" (quoted in Erickson and Wuthnow 2016, 11).

What, however, could China hope to do about the U.S. control of these island chains that currently seems so entrenched? While China does have armaments such as the Dong-Feng 26 missile (dubbed the Guam Killer) that can strike U.S. bases in the first and second island chains with nuclear or conventional weapons, this does not diminish the military dominance of the United States along the chains themselves. If the Chinese state wants to gain more military or strategic control of these island groups, this would seem to require a long-term campaign of soft power projection, political persuasion, and investment. This is indeed happening (as the next chapter details), though it is less clear if eventual military domination is an intended outcome.

Security in the Western Pacific from the Inside Out: Contesting Colonialism in the Trust Territory of the Pacific Islands

While the militaries of the United States, China, and others project strategies onto the islands of Asia and the western Pacific, one has to ask what the people who live on these islands get out of being the stage on which these military dramas are set. It is one thing to view the islands in the Pacific and the rim of Asia from the perspective of the security of China and the United States, but what about from the perspective of these islands themselves? After all, if a war does come to the region, the history of places such as Okinawa, Guåhan, O'ahu, and the Philippines demonstrates that being the site of another power's military installations does not keep you safe from being attacked. Rather, it makes you a target for attack and for massive civilian casualties. Even when a war is not occurring, the militarized islands of the region must bear the burden of the environmental and social consequences of hosting U.S. military facilities and training ranges—including the continued lack of formal sovereignty in the name of maintaining U.S. political dominance (Lutz 2009). Strategies such as offshore control may be smart strategies for Americans (especially compared with the idea of attempting to fight a ground war in China), but the only way to enable them is to accept several deeply problematic underlying assumptions. Namely, that the continued colonization of Pacific islands such as Guåhan is appropriate *indefinitely*, that warfare on and around these islands populated by millions of civilians is an acceptable battle space for a war between two outside powers, and that China's destiny—as well as that of the island Pacific—is to be forever subservient to American power and interests rather than equal partners in security at the edge of Asia.

While plans for the Pacific hatched in the United States and China have been getting considerable attention these days, there is, of course, a long history of alternative perspectives on Pacific security and governance that come from *within* the Pacific region and are directed at enhancing the security and political agency of the people within it. While there are many contemporary projects that counter colonialism and external militarization in the Pacific, it is worth digressing here to look at just how colonial relationships in the region have been resisted fairly consistently since the victory in World War II granted the United States extensive formal sovereign power over wide swathes of the region. At the war's end, the United States had a far larger military presence in the region than any other power. Furthermore, the war's battles, bases, logistical chains, and military infrastructure projects had radically altered people's lives through dislocation, destruction, and labor migration (Poyer, Falgout, and Carucci 2001). In Hawai'i, increased militarization and martial law during the war solidified the U.S. hold on the unincorporated territory in the postwar years. Guåhan was liberated from Japanese forces and reverted back to its U.S.-affiliated colonial status. Many other Micronesian islands that had been under Japanese administration (Palau, the Marshalls, the Carolines, and the Northern Marianas) were made into the Trust Territory of the Pacific Islands (TTPI), which was officially under UN control but administered by the U.S. Navy until 1951 and the U.S. Department of Interior thereafter.

The TTPI, which lasted from 1947 until its dissolution in the 1990s, was designated a strategic area whose trusteeship could be terminated only by the UN Security Council (not the General Assembly). From the beginning the United States treated these islands as areas of strategic denial, sites for military bases, and sacrifice zones for nuclear weapons testing (S. Davis 2015). The United States blocked attempts for formal sovereignty and, unlike the island experience under Japanese administration, purposely hindered economic development in the islands by disallowing any foreign direct investment (even from the United States) for the better part of three decades (Hanlon 1998; Hezel 2003; Mulalap 2017; Peattie 1992).

While formal sovereignty was denied during this time period, people across the islands engaged in political debate and asserted political agency in a number of ways. For one, in many of these islands traditional leadership structures remained intact and worked parallel to newer ones imposed by U.S. administrators. Additionally, islanders used ostensibly advisory political bodies (such as the TTPI's Territorial Advisory Council, which later became the Congress of Micronesia) to engage in debates with each other over development policies and political status as well as to advocate for more sovereign control over the land and sea spaces of the region (Hanlon 1998; Hezel 2003).

During the time period of the TTPI, political figures engaged in arguments that are still relevant for understanding some of today's debates over political sovereignty, development, and interconnection throughout Micronesia. First, then as now, there were substantial internal differences within island communities over the importance of tradition, modernity, and affiliation with outside powers. Just as Joël Bonnemaison noted in the history of Vanuatu (1994, 2005), there were schisms throughout the TTPI time period in Micronesia between islanders favoring more Western-style development and those weary of it. Second, there were different visions of what future political statuses vis-à-vis the United States should look like. Should islanders strive for complete independence, incorporation through statehood, or some kind of quasi-independent status such as free association or commonwealth? Third, there were questions about what the spatiality of a postcolonial governance structure should look like. Should *all* of the islands of the TTPI—which encompassed an enormous area with many different linguistic and cultural groups—negotiate together to secure a common state after trusteeship? Or should different island groups go their separate ways?

These questions were articulated in debates throughout the 1960s and

1970s, and these differences of opinion came to the fore during the negotiations for the end of the trusteeship in the 1970s and 1980s. As David Hanlon (1998) has highlighted, during the TTPI era delegates to the Congress of Micronesia would articulate their politically taboo positions about fears of colonialism, modernity, tourist-objectification of their cultures, and discrimination through descriptions of dreams. Hanlon describes a dream Charles Domnick told to the Congress of Micronesia when he was a representative from the Marshall Islands in 1970:

> In his dream, Domnick beheld a vigorous economy driven by American money, protected by American laws and bureaucratic regulations, and beyond Micronesians' control. Every home had a television set on which families could watch news reports of riots in Micronesian schools. . . . The only feasts now celebrated in Micronesia were carried out at tourist hotels for the amusement of foreign visitors who, in addition to viewing the bastardized spectacle, ate Polynesian food, drank exotic tropical drinks, and listened to Hawaiian tunes strummed on ukuleles. . . . Domnick's dream, then, was one of development and dispossession—legally justified, bureaucratically regulated, and commercially driven by foreign, essentially inaccessible and hence uncontrollable forces. Agreements of free association had given way to territorial commonwealths and ultimately to total absorption by the United States. What made this view of Micronesia's future so horrific was a memory within Domnick's dream, a memory of earlier, once-considered alternatives to development that had promised greater self-determination and independence." (1998, 140–41)

In contrast, another Micronesian leader, Timothy Olkeriil, talked of his dream of

> a strong, united Micronesian nation comprising the six major districts. It was a model Pacific nation, a neutral state with an initial protective treaty with the United States to provide for its security and defense. At the conclusion of the thirty-year period of that treaty, Olkeriil dreamed, the treaty or compact was terminated, and the various military leases over Micronesian land and water were not renewed. This new Micronesia was no longer dependent on U.S. government monies, but had a viable, self-sufficient economy based on marine and coconut products, ocean mining, and controlled tourism. The nation's duty-free status helped it to become a major financial center of the Pacific, with a progressive economy directed by Micronesians themselves. (Hanlon 1998, 141–42)

The hopes and fears articulated in dreams such as these influenced views on development, connection to foreign metropoles, large infrastructure projects, and later negotiations with the United States for ending the trusteeship. The Congress of Micronesia, even though its decisions lacked the force of formal sovereignty, was able to advocate local positions regarding development, international connection, and the governance of local resources. For instance, the congress passed resolutions demanding that foreign direct investment be allowed in the TTPI, and the territorial administration relented on the ban on investment in 1974. The Congress also passed a resolution in 1977 to establish local management and ownership of ocean resources in the EEZ of the TTPI (Hanlon 1998).

Agreements and joint declarations notwithstanding, there were also substantial differences of opinion among people living in the TTPI regarding development and future political status. For instance, there was a significant controversy and schism within Palau over the development of a megaproject in the 1970s. Iranian and Japanese interests proposed building a "superport" on Babeldaob Island in order to skirt Japanese environmental regulations (Hezel 1978). This proposal generated factions within Palau (and beyond) both for and against the massive project (Shuster 1998). One of the most prominent early supporters of the project, Palauan politician Roman Tmetuchl, later turned against it. As Shuster writes, "Tmetuchl, as a nationalist, realised that a superport financed and built by foreigners would reduce Palauans to a minority in their own land. A concentration of energy at a port in Palau would certainly be controlled by the US Navy and Japanese industrial interests which would render Tmetuchl, or any other Palauan leader, politically impotent" (1998, 41). This is a very astute point that transcends the debates about aspirations for formal political sovereignty in the region, as well as larger issues about sovereignty in general. Namely, if there is something within your formal sovereign territory (terrestrial or marine) that is highly valuable to a more powerful entity, then you likely will not really have sovereignty over that space. In the face of both external environmental and political opposition, as well as the change of heart of early supporters such as Tmetuchl, the superport plan ultimately unraveled and was never built.

The schisms within the TTPI were not limited to differences of opinion within island groups but also occurred between the vastly separated areas of the TTPI. This was most noticeable in the process of how various island groups split and negotiated their own statuses with the United States as the trusteeship came to an end. The people who favored a united post-TTPI Micronesia were foiled in their attempts to keep all the island groups together. Eventually the TTPI dissolved into the current political units of the Micronesia region: the Republic of Palau, the Republic of the Marshall Islands, the

Commonwealth of the Northern Marianas, and the Federated States of Micronesia. There were many reasons for this—such as cultural differences, the vast distances separating the island groups, and concerns over whether taxation and spending would be fair based on political units or population—but one reason that heavily influenced the talks between the U.S. and Micronesian delegates had to do with prospects for income hosting U.S. bases. As Francis Hezel notes, "When the U.S. military first publicly presented its future land requirements in Micronesia during the Fifth Round of the Status Talks in July 1972, it specified Palau, the Marshalls and the Northern Marianas as those districts where it wished to acquire or retain the use of existing land and harbor rights" (1978, 206). This information, coupled with Saipan's early moves to negotiate status separately from the rest of the TTPI, led to the fracturing of the TTPI as island groups with potential military base income moved to contain their share in a smaller polity. The remaining parts of Micronesia (Yap, Chuuk, Pohnpei, and Kosrae) then remained together to form the Federated States of Micronesia.

As the negotiations over political status proceeded between the United States and these different regions, each region had its own unique issues that angled it toward different post-TTPI political arrangements. The Northern Marianas ended up with a commonwealth status that ties it more tightly to the United States (similar to Puerto Rico's commonwealth status), while the Marshall Islands negotiated a Compact of Free Association that also tried (but largely failed) to address the injuries and environmental damages of the nuclear testing era. Like the Marshall Islands, the FSM also negotiated a Compact of Free Association, which gives it formal sovereignty but with many strings attached, such as external oversight of U.S.-funded government budgets and exclusive U.S. military access to the islands and sea spaces. Palau also opted for free association, but their path included debates—internally and with the United States—over Palauan desires to keep the area free of U.S. nuclear weapons. The insistence that the land and seas of Palau be a zone without the storage or transfer of nuclear weapons blocked U.S. acceptance of the COFA from the early 1980s until 1994, when Palauan voters finally accepted a COFA without the nuclear-free provision. The internal debates in Palau over its relationship to the United States (and its nuclear weapons and military) were fierce and included the assassination of president Haruo Remeliik in 1985 (Aguon 2008). Meanwhile, Guåhan—with its large U.S. military presence—sat in the middle of this region but was never part of the TTPI and was never afforded the chance to negotiate a new political status. Furthermore, as I discuss more in chapter 3, Guåhan became a slice of U.S.-dominated territory to which migrants from COFA countries could migrate, but the local government was never adequately funded to absorb any of the costs of this substantial stream of new arrivals.

This brief review of the TTPI time period is important to consider for two reasons. First, it shows that many of the differences of opinion that still permeate politics and international relations in this area have deep roots. Contemporary political questions in the western Pacific about sovereignty arrangements, the desire for connections to external powers such as China or the United States, and support for or opposition to large-scale infrastructure projects (military or commercial) are influenced not only by the actions of external powers but also by long-running debates over development, modernity, the value of tradition, political status, cultural identity, and the proper scale of governance and solidarity *within* the region (Underwood 2019).

Second, this history highlights the assemblage-like nature of the spatiality of political units that wield formal sovereignty. These islands had their own spatialities of political, economic, and cultural connections before Europeans ever sailed into the area and labeled it Micronesia. The Spanish then grouped the islands together in particular ways and for particular purposes, as did the Germans. After the Japanese Nan'yo era in Micronesia, the United States arranged the islands for still different purposes (Peattie 1992). Like the U.S.-designed TTPI, the current political units are assemblages held together by relations of exteriority in which the islands within them stand in possible, but not necessary, collaboration.

While colonizers and foreign administrators worked to make their new political assemblage real, Indigenous peoples of the region constantly deterritorialized the TTPI as they debated, promoted, and pursued their own desires for political agency, economic development, preservation of tradition, environmental management, and varied spatialities of interconnection and governance. This process was not one of a unified voice of resistance against a colonizer but instead a process forwarded and shaped by the many differences of opinion, schisms, and contradictions within the region. As assemblage theory posits, every assemblage (as, for instance, a state apparatus or an independence movement) is actually formed in a fractal manner by a multitude of smaller assemblages articulated together (DeLanda 2006). Island societies are themselves assemblages with varying opinions and factions—factions that try to gain control over how that island (as an assemblage) takes part in other wider assemblages through articulating (or not) with other larger projects such as U.S. military networks, transnational political affiliations, tourism systems and flows, global oil transshipment (in the case of the Palau superport), or environmental and social movements (such as a nuclear-free Pacific). When one of these factions is able to get the upper hand and direct the island territory (and its state) in a particular direction and toward particular articulations, those on island who oppose it and dream of other articulations are still there reaching out (and within) to block or alter these processes. In addition, external events and outside actors can throw unexpected wrenches into these local debates. In the case of Palau, for instance, two of the most contentious debates of the 1970s and 1980s became somewhat moot when the U.S. military decided not to base anything there (even after years of conflict over the nuclear-free provision) and when Iranian and Japanese interest in the superport project fizzled (Shuster 1998).

When we look at the establishment, and the dismantling, of the TTPI we can see something fundamental about the beginnings (and endings) of the current countries of Micronesia (and political units in general) as well as the construction and deconstruction of any collective entity. Namely, we can see that any given political assemblage is not necessarily an expression of some primordial cultural identity but something that comes together from innumerable threads and that social identity continually coevolves with and wraps itself into. As Foucault put it, "If the genealogist . . . listens to history, he finds that there is 'something altogether different' behind things: not a timeless and essential secret, but the secret that they have no essence or that their essence was fabricated in a piecemeal fashion from alien forms. . . . What is found at the historical beginning of things is not the inviolable identity of their origin; it is the dissension of other things" (1977, 142, 147). Micronesia as both a political and a cultural entity exemplifies this in its multiple constructions, deconstructions, reworkings, and shifting spatial manifestations. In addition, it is interesting to consider that what seems pretty evident in the context of Micronesia is of course true everywhere. Even the United States and China are semipermanent assemblages that have been constructed from elements that are not that entity—and they will likely one day dissipate and become the material for later hybridized assemblages. If we are defending the continuation of a particular assemblage (a state, a nation, a culture, an economic system, a social movement, or an institution), we ought to ask ourselves why. Does it create a world in line with the ethics we really value?

The malleability of political arrangements we can see in the history of this region should make us question the future stability of not just states in the Pacific but also states and institutions more generally. We should not assume that governance and influence in the western Pacific will stay static, either in terms of the forms of governance in these locales or of the spatial arrangements of the political entities. There are ample opportunities for many kinds of political shifts, as multiple COFA agreements are set to end in 2023 and the colonial status of Guåhan is constantly contested. The territorial boundaries of states are also still debated. For instance, the FSM appears to be particularly unstable in the wake of several Chuukese independence initiatives, and a potential reunification of Guåhan and the Commonwealth of the Northern Marianas (CNMI) is also frequently discussed. In addition, as the rest of this chapter (and the next) detail, there are many signs that the *external orientation* of the region—which has been intensively directed toward the United States since the end of World War II—is shifting as well. Anyone who assumes that the current political statuses, and the political map, of this island region will stay static has scant historical evidence to support that position.

A Pacific-Centered Future: Where America's Day Begins; or, Just Left of the Setting Sun?

Despite the history of opposition to foreign domination in this region, it is hard to deny that continued militarization and colonization have become part of the lived reality that shapes the communities and subjectivities of island inhabitants. In places such as Guåhan, the military bases, the circulation of personnel, and the operation of military units are woven into the fabric of everyday life. It is quite clear that militarized transnational relations deeply affect the production of the current everyday landscape, and even the fences around the bases have become part of the community in various ways (Alexander 2016). In addition, as CHamoru scholars and others have pointed out,[7] personal identities in places such as Guåhan are themselves constituted in relationship with the U.S. military as an institution—as participants, supporters, resisters, or a mix of these positions (Bevacqua 2010; Frain 2016, 2017; Mitchell and Kallio 2017; Na'puti 2019; Na'puti and Bevacqua 2015; Na'puti and Frain 2017; Perez 2014).

Furthermore, the fact that the U.S. state has viewed Guåhan, as well as the islands that make up the Northern Marianas, the Marshall Islands, Palau, and the Federated States of Micronesia, as vital to their military strategies in the Pacific has led to a series of intimate entanglements that go well beyond simply the imposition of military bases. Yes, U.S. colonialism is experienced as bombers taking off and ships and sailors coming into port. However, it is also experienced through the visceral reactions to events such as the North Korean threats to Guåhan in 2017 (Aguon 2017; Bevacqua 2017; Leon Guerrero

FIGURE 2. Mural for veterans in Guåhan, 2007. Photo by the author.

2017). It is also experienced through the functioning of the soft infrastructures constructed to keep Guåhan and the surrounding islands in the U.S. orbit. For instance, the ability to migrate to the United States, and the ability to join the U.S. military (which young people in the region do at rates much higher per capita than in the United States itself) deeply shape life in Guåhan and across the Micronesia region (Aguon 2008). Everyday life in the area is also affected by the consumption of American media and cultural products, as well as laws such as the Jones Act that restrict shipping and reinforce the importation of U.S. goods and brands. It is also affected by the prevalence of English as the language of school instruction, the implementation of U.S. educational standards (such as the reading of British and American literature in the high schools), and the opportunities local students have for higher education in Hawaiʻi or the mainland United States. The geosocial connections between these parts of Micronesia and the United States are plentiful and strong. They shape opportunities; they also shape perceptions of what is possible and desirable. Because of this, feelings and expressions of patriotism toward the United States are quite common in these islands (figure 2).

Still, despite these tight geosocial relationships with the United States that have been developed over the history of colonialism, there is a simmering discontent in the islands about remaining under the umbrella of U.S. power and cultural hegemony. Given the prevalent role of the military in shaping the kinds of interconnections to the islands, as well as the heavy impact that military activities have on the ecological and social environments, it is hardly surprising that much of the opposition to U.S. control is focused on challenging militarization. Of course, by challenging U.S. militarization (and the connected political colonialism) in these islands, local groups are challenging not only a powerful military but also a deeply held logic within U.S. military and policy circles that the militarization of these islands is absolutely critical to U.S. global security strategies. This adds another facet to political and military strategies in the Pacific region as a whole. It is not just a matter of China and the United States (and Japan, Russia, Taiwan, the Philippines, Vietnam, Australia, etc.) vying with *each other* in a contest for supremacy in the region. It is also a matter of smaller contests between the desires of competing would-be colonizers and local desires.

These smaller contests may not get as much attention as the great power contests, but they are quite critical for understanding what actually happens in the region and how military power and political influence circulate there. In short, it matters what people on these islands want. These local struggles, as shown in the example of Okinawa in chapter 1, absolutely influence where military bases and operations can happen and where they cannot. This has been true in the past, and it is still true. For instance, despite the best-laid plans of U.S. military strategists, the shape of the military network in the region is partially a result of local opposition. As of this writing in 2019, the shape of the U.S. military footprint in the region remains contested and fluid. Chapter 1 of this book looks at the situation in Okinawa, and chapter 4 looks more closely at the case of Jeju, South Korea, but these are not the only places in Asia and the island Pacific where U.S. military operations are contested and shifting. For instance, the plans to move thousands of Marines from Okinawa to Guåhan as part of the deal made in the 1990s between the United States and Japan are still moving more slowly than planned. Local opposition to these plans in Guåhan and the adjacent Northern Mariana Islands have slowed and altered the plan for a large military buildup. Specifically, many citizens on Guåhan balked at the potential social and environmental impacts of hosting over eight thousand Marines (as well as their associated dependents, as well as construction workers for the build up project).

There are two particular thorny issues that have affected U.S. plans to more extensively militarize the Mariana Island chain. The first has to do with where to put training ranges. If more combat units are going to be put on Guåhan,

FIGURE 3. Pågat, a proposed site for a military firing range blocked by activism on Guåhan, 2019. Photo by Tiara Na'Puti.

then the military insists that there must be nearby ranges available for live-fire training. While there are existing training facilities in the area, and the United States uses the island of Farallon de Medinilla (about forty-five kilometers from Saipan) as a bombing range, the military has suggested they would need to construct a new firing range on Guåhan itself as well as use all of Pagan Island and the northern half of populated Tinian Island (both in the CNMI) for live-fire training. On Guåhan, local groups and government agencies (such as the Historic Preservation Office) mounted political protests, lawsuits, and legal challenges that blocked the military's plans to put a new firing range in Pågat on the northeastern coast of Guåhan (figure 3). In response, the military devised new plans to use land on the northwest corner of Guåhan at Litekyan (a.k.a. Ritidian Point) for a firing range that would involve limiting access to the existing U.S. Fish and Wildlife refuge. This proposal, like the one for the use of Pågat, has also generated determined local opposition.[8] Likewise, local opposition in the Northern Marianas has slowed military plans to use Tinian and Pagan Islands as bombing ranges (Gelardi and Perez 2019; Hofschneider 2016).

While the environmental and social consequences of military training (and other base operations) are one set of factors that create opposition to U.S.

plans in the Marianas, there is also a second, related, issue: the perceived connection between militarization and the denial of formal sovereignty and self-determination. As many CHamoru scholars (as well as others) have explicitly pointed out, living on an island that distant powers view as critical for their own national security leads not only to the militarization of the island but also to the denial of political self-determination (Alexander 2016; Bevacqua 2010; Frain 2016, 2017; Na'puti and Bevacqua 2015; Na'puti and Frain 2017). Because an island is deemed to be crucial for the national security of a distant power, it gets militarized. In the case of Guåhan and the Northern Marianas, after their (re)conquest in the latter stages of World War II by the United States, they become the tip of the spear of U.S. military power in the region. They first became bases and staging areas to strike at Japan, and then later, as part of the second island chain, they became part of the imagined American bulwark against potential Asian foes such as Russia and China. Because of their importance to these military projects, the United States is reluctant to grant them any form of political autonomy that may threaten those military assets. Then, because of their colonial political status, the military begins to imagine these islands as welcoming sites for *further* militarization since they lack local sovereign governments that can contest it (S. Davis 2011). In other words, militarization and colonialism are mutually reinforcing.

This has been noticeable for quite some time, but it became more visible during the summer of 2017, when Guåhan became the target of North Korean missile threats. As noted in the introduction, the North Korean government portrayed militarized Guåhan as a threat that fell within the range of their missile technology at the time.[9] This episode of saber rattling between the United States and North Korea left many on Guåhan with the feeling that they were caught in the middle of a conflict that had little to nothing to do with the inhabitants of the island itself (Bevacqua 2017). Protesters on the island quickly linked their precarious security position with their colonial status and argued that what would make them safer was not more militarization but less militarization coupled with more local self-determination (Raymundo 2017).

This opposition to an increased U.S. military presence in the Marianas is instructive for looking at how power operates in place more generally. Yes, the U.S. military has an unmatched ability to project violent power. Yes, the U.S. government has formal political sovereignty over both Guåhan and the Commonwealth of the Northern Marianas. True, neither Guåhan nor the CNMI has any effective (voting) representation in either U.S. or international political institutions. And the U.S. military has well-articulated doctrines that frame what they want to do in the island chain. Still, this does not mean the U.S. military can easily execute their plans in the ways that they wish. As we saw in chapter 1, having an unquestioned superiority to project violence into a space, holding formal sovereignty, and denying local people representation in official governance structures does not necessarily confer effective sovereignty over a place when people in it are determined to oppose that power.

For instance, in the face of this opposition, the U.S. military had to tone down their plans for moving eight thousand U.S. Marines from Okinawa to Guåhan and get geographically creative with their basing strategies. These strategies have included basing more marines in O'ahu, modernizing training facilities in Pohakuloa on Hawai'i Island, and deploying a 2,500-strong rotational force of Marines in Darwin, Australia. It also means continually looking for openings for more military ties with old allies (such as the Philippines) and potential new ones (such as Vietnam, where the aircraft carrier U.S.S. *Carl Vinson* performed a historic port call to Da Nang in early 2018). Despite these changes and challenges—and the recent tweaks to military operations and the U.S. base structure in the Pacific—the first and second island chains still remain colonial spaces militarily dominated by the United States. The question is, however, with substantial local animosity toward continued militarization and colonization, how long will it remain that way?

Conclusion

If we take the perspective of the inhabitants in the islands in this region, what are we to make of the islands' positions in the midst of this maelstrom of geopolitical visions and military maneuvers by continental powers? It is fairly clear from the above discussion why the United States and China find the region important geopolitically, but what would islanders gain politically by staying under the American political/military umbrella or by shifting their allegiance toward China? After all, being in one military orbit or the other does not really protect residents so much as put them in danger of being caught in the middle of a great power conflict fought in and around their homelands. It could be argued that Chinese political domination and colonialism could be worse than the American variety, but we should not underestimate the negative effects of U.S. rule in the region—considering that Guåhan still has no formal choice about political status, as well as the legacies of nuclear weapons testing in the region. It would appear, then, that there are few military or geopolitical reasons for islanders to throw their support toward one potential hegemon or the other. If anything, an analysis of the geopolitical situation demonstrates that a nonaligned, independent island Pacific would be the best option for avoiding warfare between a more assertive China and a United States whose foreign policy seems to be increasingly reliant on military posturing. Also, more formal and functional independence would provide more opportunities for self-determination and human security. Of course, to get it, they would have to struggle against a United States that is likely to tighten its colonial grip rather than let go of its long-held national security strategies involving the occupation of the island Pacific.

A key point in all this is that despite these great power contests over the region, these islands are not intrinsically part of any particular larger assemblage of empire or sphere of influence of one power or another. The islands of the western Pacific are not somehow naturally part of the American realm simply because the island chain doctrines deem them to be. Just as stars in the sky can be arranged into various culturally imagined constellations, so too can islands be imagined by different actors to be parts of different chains or silk roads. From an assemblage view, these islands have capacities to be linked to any variety of geographically larger systems and projects, but they do not have to be (DeLanda 2006). Furthermore, the islands are not wholly dominated by any one project (such as U.S. militarization) but already are participating in multiple projects that differ both in kind (political, economic, social, ecological) and spatiality. The hard and soft infrastructures that the U.S. state has constructed in the region produce a certain field of potentialities and make certain orientations (toward the U.S. sphere) more appealing and give them a kind of inertia. However, as demonstrated by the fact that the islands of Micronesia are an object of military contestation today—and have seen four competing formal colonizers come and go over the past 125 years—the systems of relations in which these islands take part are both geographically fluid and impermanent. Simply put, the future of the islands is uncertain and is not going to be wholly dictated by one outside military power or another. Yes, the desires of great powers will shape some of the context in which people in these islands will chart their futures, but there are more options available than simply being part of someone else's dream of national security.

CHAPTER 3

Against Spheres of Influence

Environmental, Economic, and Human Circulations in the More-Than-Political Pacific

The previous chapter made the case that we need to pay attention to the more spatially expansive contexts and currents in which local sovereignties are constructed, maintained, and contested. While the last chapter did this through a discussion of military concerns and political discourses and practices, in this chapter I want to expand this a bit to recognize how other processes are at work that shape local struggles over sovereignty and political agency. To continue the metaphor of "islands and oceans" (with "islands" as the sites at which jurisdiction is performed, and "oceans" as the contexts that structure its production), the ocean in which sovereign power is constructed is much more than an arena of competing states and other formal political actors. The context in which sovereignties are invoked, constructed, and reproduced is composed by much more than military and diplomatic maneuvers—or even processes we might commonly label as "political."

As noted in previous chapters, assemblage theory encourages us to think about the many factors affecting a particular place according to the logic of infinitely additive influences. In this chapter, I follow Deleuze and Guattari's prescription to analyze the production of places by examining how multiple influences weave together (the logic of "and, and, and . . .")—instead of making an either/or determination in an attempt to identify some kind of dominant influence. To do this, I follow on my discussion from the last chapter by maintaining attention on the island Pacific—especially Micronesia—but with a shift in the topical focus. In this chapter I explore how processes that might not necessarily be thought of as political are crucial for understanding how political sovereignties are produced and contested. Specifically, I explore how environmental processes, economic practices, patterns of migration, and geosocial connections circulate within the region in order to untangle how they affect the construction of local sovereignties as well as regional constellations of political power.

That influences aimed toward places across the Pacific are an amalgam of different kinds of processes (political, economic, environmental, etc.), and also originate from many different directions, demonstrates that influence is more-than-political. In addition, it also demonstrates that cutting up the region into foreign spheres of influence according to military or formal political allegiance is a mistake (both analytically and for the purposes of political praxis). The idea that an island's identity is defined as being within *either* the U.S. or the Chinese sphere of influence is still a common point of view as well as a potent part of the geographical imaginary of powerful state actors. For instance, U.S. government reports put out by the U.S.-China Economic and Security Review Commission are weighted with concern that every new engagement by China in the region is a threat to U.S. control (Meick, Ker, and Chan 2018). Lyle Goldstein, director of the China Maritime Studies Institute at the U.S. Naval War College, even goes so far as to suggest, "It is around these islands that the line of spheres of influence between the [United States and China] are being drawn. . . . The question is where does the line switch?" (quoted in Tobin 2019, 1). The problem is that this is an overly simplistic way of thinking about the spatiality of power.

From the perspective of the islands looking out, even if we look only at the overtly political realm, there is multipolarity everywhere. For instance, despite persistent representations of the Pacific as an American space or an "American lake" (Wilson 2000; Firth 1987; Hayes, Zarsky, and Bello 1986), the region has been—throughout history as well as today—a *contested* realm where multiple powers have exerted formal and effective political influence (S. Davis 2015). There have been multiple formal colonial administrators in many parts of the Pacific (and some places were even jointly administered by multiple colonial powers simultaneously, such as Vanuatu in the South Pacific, which was governed under the "condominium" between France and Britain). In addition to these plural formal colonizations, the region has also experienced many sorts of competing colonial *claims* (such as the Marquesas Islands, which have had U.S., Spanish, and French claims). Even today the island Pacific as a whole is a patchwork of independent countries as well as territories with various kinds of colonial ties to France, the United Kingdom, Australia, the United States, New Zealand, Japan, Ecuador, and Chile. Furthermore, if we expand our vision beyond formal political attachments and examine *other* contemporary circulations, such as economic investments, government aid, and geosocial influence (including patterns of migration as well as circulations of media imagery and cultural practices), the picture becomes even more complex and multipolar.

If we look at influence in place as unavoidably multiple (in terms of both kind and point of origin), then the idea of spheres of influence becomes misleading at best. This is not only because the concept is based on a paternalistic assumption that smaller places lack full political agency and have to be part of someone else's larger security umbrella, but also because influence within any space is *always* multiple, contested, and incomplete.

While Deleuze and Guattari's insistence that the number of influences that affect a particular place or event is essentially infinite, in this chapter I am circumscribing the rich tapestry of reality by making analytical cuts that, while broader than formal politics and militarization, still inevitably privilege some influences over others and leave some out altogether. If we take assemblage theory seriously, then we must admit that no analysis is ever total or complete. It would be impossible to write a chapter that catalogs every influence a place has experienced. My goal here, then, is not to give an exhaustive account of every influence in the region but rather to explore *some* influences beyond the political (as traditionally defined) in order to both direct our attention to how political sovereignty is conditioned by many more-than-political processes, and to encourage political actors to think about how political change can occur through channels we may not see at first glance as political. In other words, political change can be initiated through tactics of creating islands of occupation (as detailed in the introduction and the first chapter), as well as through attempting to shape the larger ocean in which states and other political actors are enmeshed.

There are of course many different agents currently attempting to shift the context of the region. Social movements and Indigenous groups seeking self-determination are ones I emphasize in the latter chapters of the book (and I looked at militaries and states in chapter 2), but in this chapter I focus on how the Pacific is shaped by environmental conditions—or "more-than-human" actants (Whatmore 2002)—as well as by primarily economic agents such as capitalist investors and tourists/consumers. I also examine the role of human migrations and circulations within the region. I analyze these different influences to emphasize how these agents (intentionally or not) rearrange the political milieu of the Pacific.

Through these discussions of environmental processes, economic practices, and patterns of human mobility I hope to accomplish three things. First, I want to give a more nuanced picture of the context in which political statuses and struggles in the region have been, and continue to be, performed. Second, by highlighting the way influences emanate from multiple sites within and outside the region (from the United States, China, Australia, etc.) and how those influences come in different forms, performed by different kinds of agents (corporations, states, tourists, migrants, and nonhuman environmental actants), I want to show how political possibilities are conditioned by all sorts of influences we might not immediately label as "political." My goal is to show the importance of considering these in order to better understand contemporary colonialism and Indigenous struggles for self-determination, as well as the shifting terrain of current competitions for hegemony between so-called great powers both within and outside the Pacific region. Lastly, I hope that this analysis of the more-than-political processes that condition political struggles can be useful to activists working for decolonization, local political agency, and social justice. As I explicitly address in the chapters that follow, social movements in this region have been pursuing strategies that recognize the importance of shifting the larger environmental-economic-social context in which political contests are taking place. I hope that my analysis and discussion in this and the following chapters contributes to this project of illuminating potentially novel avenues for effective activism.

The Environment as Political Agent in the Anthropocene Pacific

The environment plays a key role in influencing political decision making. This is true everywhere, of course, but it is particularly evident and observable in the island Pacific. From the active volcanism present in Hawai'i, Tonga, Vanuatu, and other locales to the effects of tides, erosion, and sea level fluctuations on islands across the region, the power of geologic and climatological processes to affect life is ever-present. This dynamism has inspired island mythologies and traditional philosophies of governance as well as more contemporary theorizations. Epeli Hau'ofa's (1994) perspective of the Pacific as a large and expanding realm, for example, was developed after an epiphany he had while traversing the growing grand volcanic landscapes of Hawai'i Island. Other perspectives, such as seeing the islands of the region as an archipelago *connected* by the sea and its rhythms, rather than separated by them, stem from observations of physical patterns and processes. Political ideas such as thinking archipelagically, tidalectics, submarine solidarity, and aquapeligos also come from living in and observing island realms in the Pacific as well as the Caribbean and other island spaces (DeLoughrey, 2007, 2017; Hayward 2012; Pugh 2016, 2018; Chandler and Pugh 2018; Stratford et al. 2011). Of course, my metaphorical construct of "islands and oceans" stems from this as well.

While the physical environment is an inspiration for political thought, the environment is also a powerful actor in its own right that shapes politics and the operation of sovereignty (while also being shaped by it). Environmental processes are key components of the milieu that influences the production and operation of sovereignty. Returning to an assemblage theory view of the world, the environment is not something separated off from human actions; it both affects human societies and is affected by them in numerous ways. The severing of the environment from the human realm is a categorizing exercise that involves making artificial distinctions and separations in an attempt to make real an ideology that imagines dichotomy and distinction where there are plainly many sorts of interaction and mutual influence. While Bruno Latour (1993) posits that this distinction between the social and natural is a foundational idea of Western modernism, he also points out that maintaining this illusion is a project fraught with contradictions and difficulties. As Sarah Whatmore (2002) notes, it is better to think of environmental conditions not as a realm outside the reach of human activities and processes but rather as the realm of the more-than-human. Using the terminology *more-than-human* is useful as it denotes that human actions have affects in this realm but that their influence is only one thread among many.

For instance, if we were to look at a given coral reef environment offshore of an island in the tropical Pacific and explain how it came to its present state, there are many processes that go into constructing the resultant entity. The rocky substrate, the currents, the availability of sunlight, the pH of the water, the water temperature, the existence of competing and symbiotic organisms—these all play a part in influencing its construction. Also, nearby human factors, such as population numbers, dredging, fishing methods and intensity, the importation of invasive species (intentional or not), and conservation planning (or lack of it) will also directly affect its form and health. Furthermore, human activities that originate in distant places—whether climate shifts caused by the burning of fossil fuels, overfishing by roving fleets, or the accumulation of plastic, chemical, and radioactive wastes in the ocean—can influence some of the natural processes listed above. In this way the reef is a more-than-human construct (McCormack 2017). This returns us to the philosophy of "and, and, and . . ." in which the reef, as much as any more obviously human construct, is a form that is born from an assemblage of processes.

Researchers, philosophers, leaders, and citizens in both Indigenous and Western contexts have long noticed this dynamic of interconnection (even if some Western theories of modernity are built around dichotomous bifurcations of the world into human and nonhuman realms). In the contemporary era, the interconnections are even more obvious as human processes become more intense and affect planetwide climate systems. This is particularly demonstrated in the scholarship that posits that we are now living in the Anthropocene era in which human activities have had such an impact that our existence will leave a mark in the geology of the planet via processes such as our accumulated solid waste, changes we make to the atmosphere, and mass species extinction from habitat destruction (Dalby 2014; Deloughrey 2017; Pugh 2018).

One of the key points of the Anthropocene literature is that, regardless of the mark humans leave for future geologists, the physical environment cannot be realistically considered a natural or passive backdrop for human action, or a prepolitical influence on human societies. Politically, the idea of an Anthropocene environment forces us to recognize that, increasingly, the physical environment we encounter today, and will find in the future, will be—at least partially—the result of social and political choices. The pH of tomorrow's oceans, the sea surface temperatures of the twenty-second century, and the frequency and geographical distribution of the next decade's tropical cyclones will be determined in part by human decisions today. In the island Pacific, environmental change, and sea level rise in particular, represents a challenge to governance and management in many places and is an existential threat to entire atoll nations. This is a region where people are acutely aware that not only will today's political decisions and social practices change tomorrow's environment but that even the current widespread belief that islands in the region are going under has concrete political ramifications today. For instance, the threat of future inundation of Pacific atolls affects how willing local governments and international donors are to undertake infrastructure projects (both military and civilian), as well as how governments and citizens consider issues regarding migration in the region (Bélanger and Arroyo 2016; Keown 2017; McNamara and Gibson 2009).

While human activities and political decisions clearly have an effect on the environmental conditions in the region, I want to emphasize that the reverse is also true. The environment—even when considered as a more-than-human artifact of the Anthropocene—influences and structures the practices of sovereignty and governance. As assemblage theory would emphasize, neither the natural nor the political realm is primordially causative; rather, both are mutually influencing and coconstructing. One could then conduct an analysis of human-environment relationships by centering environmental processes and tracing out the linkages to non-human and human influences (as exemplified by the above hypothetical coral reef example), or, as Hawaiian concepts such as ea (discussed in the introduction) assert, we can look at human governance and the operation of sovereignty by tracing out the human and nonhuman influences that order its construction. Just as nature can be thought of as more-than-human, the operation of political sovereignty is more-than-political. The important point here is that neither realm is autonomous. Just as it is no longer tenable to believe that nature is something primordial outside the realm of human influence, the practice of governance in a space—sovereignty—cannot be imagined as something autonomous that merely governs and orders natural and social processes. Governance, then, is not a state-led, all-powerful process of ordering. It is, at best, a mechanism that attempts to manage the relations between dynamic human and nonhuman entities and processes in which the governors are themselves situated.

As I have emphasized throughout this book, this means that states and other agents trying to practice sovereignty are far from monolithic centers from which power emanates but are rather agents embedded in larger contexts that must shift as the contexts around them shift. Dynamic earth processes and environmental conditions are one set of factors that affect governance. This is evident in the political effects of drastic natural disasters, such as how the Managua earthquake of 1972 affected Nicaraguan politics; how the eruption of Mount Pinatubo hastened the closure of U.S. military bases in the Philippines in 1991; how Hurricane Katrina affected U.S. politics (Braun and McCarthy 2005); how the Indian Ocean tsunami reconstructed politics, land use, and economic inequality in the region (Klein 2007); how the triple disaster in Fukushima Japan in 2011 affected Japanese politics (Davis and Hayes-Conroy 2018); and how Hurricane Maria in 2017 intersected with years of government austerity programs in Puerto Rico to hamper disaster response and reconstruction (García-López 2018). As many political ecologists have noted, however, even slower and more subtle shifts in the environment, such as drought, climate change, soil salinization, and erosion, have important political effects (Robbins 2011).

Despite the evidence that governance is a situated practice deeply affected by more-than-political processes (such as environmental ones), representations of sovereignty as autonomous are still widespread and continue to inform both statecraft and activism (as discussed in the introduction). While traditional theories of sovereignty may define it as supreme, unitary, autonomous, and mutually exclusive, there are political philosophies that recognize the ways sovereignty, as a practice, is structured *in relation* to the environment. This is perhaps most obvious in the discussion (also in the introduction) of how Hawaiian conceptualizations of governance emphasize that political sovereignty arises from the land (ʻāina) itself rather than from the political (or even human) realm (Goodyear-Kaʻōpua 2014).

I present this discussion of the way environmental processes intertwine with practices of governance not just to point out that the environment influences governance, and not even merely to suggest that the locus of sovereignty exists outside of the state or the traditionally defined political realm. Instead, I want to reiterate the point from assemblage theory that sovereignty, like any social process, has *no single definable locus* from which it springs. Shifts in governance can occur because of shifts in other nonpolitical and nonhuman realms (realms that, I should add, are themselves affected by still other processes). The practical value of this perspective is—as I will clarify in the two chapters that follow—that many kinds of political changes are possible through directed action in realms that we might not necessarily think of as political but that influence state action. In the following sections of this chapter, however, I first want to present further evidence demonstrating how other more-than-political processes shape the operation of sovereignty in the Asia-Pacific region and beyond.

Geosocial Circulations

Looking at environmental influences directs our attention to different geographies of power than those that are made apparent by looking at formal arrangements of political sovereignty or the placement of military installations. In many cases, examining these other processes shows how geographies of influence in the Pacific are much more complex, multipolar, and overlapping than might have been implied by the depiction of militarization in chapter 2—and certainly more complex than the idea that there is a definitive boundary of some sort that cuts across the Pacific and separates one foreign power sphere of influence from another.

While I will spend much of this chapter discussing the ways that more-than-political influences counter or erode formal political sovereignties and spheres of influence, it is first valuable to examine how they can also bolster colonial relationships. In some cases, many of these more-than-political processes follow patterns that are channeled by formal colonial relationships and also reinforce those colonial relationships. For instance, New Zealand is the largest aid donor in its politically affiliated territories of Niue and the Cook Islands, and Australia is the largest donor to Papua New Guinea, while the United States is still currently the largest aid donor to U.S.-affiliated Micronesian states. Also, much of the migration for work or education in the Pacific region still occurs between former (and current) colonized and colonizing countries. For example, much of American Samoan and Micronesian outmigration is to the United States, while citizens of independent Samoa tend to take advantage of connections and legal structures that make New Zealand an attractive option (Lilomaiava-Doktor 2009).

These particular social circulations have tended to reinforce relationships between colonies and metropoles, and are facilitated by both the hard and soft infrastructures that have been created throughout the colonial era. While the hard infrastructures put into place (such as the docks and airports) continue to allow connection, these hard infrastructures have certain capacities and can allow connections to happen in many different ways—not just toward the former colonizing power. The soft infrastructures, however, are much more critical for channeling numerous potential circulations into and out of island nations in particular ways and according to particular circumscribed geographies. For instance, political agreements put into place during and after formal decolonization have worked to encourage some kinds of circulations, discourage others, and direct flows toward certain destinations.

A good example of how political agreements channel circulations, even after formal decolonization, can be seen through an analysis of the Compacts of Free Association (COFAs) signed between the United States and the Federated States of Micronesia (FSM) and the Republic of the Marshall Islands (RMI) as the Trust Territory of the Pacific Islands (TTPI) dissolved.[1] These COFAs, negotiated by the United States separately with the FSM and the RMI, both originally came into force in 1986, were extended and amended in 2004, and will end in 2023. While there are some differences in the COFAs, there are also many similarities. For instance, both COFAs have a list of provisions that not only facilitate continued connection between the island countries and the United States but, it could be argued, facilitate *more* connection to the United States than in the earlier TTPI era. For instance, provisions in the COFAs that allow RMI and FSM residents to travel to, live, and work in the United States without the need for a visa has led to a tremendous wave of migration from these countries to Guåhan, Hawai'i, and the U.S. mainland. This has led to some of the highest outmigration rates in the world. Crude net migration rates in the 1990s and early 2000s for FSM hovered around −25 per one thousand citizens, and near -30 for the RMI.[2] Also, the COFAs provide U.S. funds for the FSM and RMI governments, but with U.S. oversight, so there were strings attached that gave the U.S. Department of Interior some say over government spending. The COFAs also stipulate that the waters and lands of the two countries are spaces of "strategic denial" where the U.S. military has unfettered access but other nation's militaries are not allowed. Furthermore, the COFAs allow FSM and RMI citizens to join the U.S. military, which they have done in large numbers (Aguon 2008). The COFAs also made the FSM and RMI part of the territory administered by the U.S. postal system, Federal Aviation Administration, and Federal Emergency Management Agency. In other words, alongside nominal political independence, the COFAs set up a variety of conduits that integrate the RMI and FSM more fully into U.S. political, economic, military, and cultural spheres. As Marshallese move to Honolulu for jobs, as Yapese students go to the University of Hawai'i campuses for schooling, as Chuukese move to Guåhan to be near families that have already migrated or to be closer to better schools and health care, and as high school graduates in Pohnpei join the U.S. military, the ties between the United States and Micronesia grow stronger through a plethora of social connections that are quite durable over time.

These connections are important not only because they represent economic or educational opportunities that RMI and FSM citizens are taking advantage of but also because they serve to bolster the geosocial connections between these island groups and the United States. In short, these connections are geopolitically important, because through these circulations and interactions affinities to the United States are developed, and in some cases accepted and desired. This can be seen, for instance, in the way that these programs and connections to the United States were actually advocated for by RMI and FSM parties during the COFA negotiations, and in the way that their potential ending when the COFAs terminate in 2023 is a source of great anxiety among some in the islands (and among the large U.S.-based diaspora). Also, despite the grave concerns many island residents and leaders have about the anti-immigrant rhetoric and climate change denial policies of the Trump administration, this did not stop the leaders of the FSM, Palau, or RMI from meeting personally with Trump in May 2019 or from declaring that the COFA states and the United States "jointly reaffirm our interest in a free, open, and prosperous Indo-Pacific region. We recognize our unique, historic, and special relationships, and reaffirm our countries' commitments to the Compacts of Free Association, resolving to continue our close cooperation in support of prosperity, security, and the rule of law" (Johnson 2019).

Being associated with American-ness, even while maintaining a cultural identity associated with one's own island or nation, is quite common across the region. In short, there is a patriotism toward the United States in the region, especially in Guåhan, but also even in the nuclear-battered RMI. Furthermore, the use of English as the language of instruction in the schools of the FSM and RMI, the opportunities for chain migration into existing Micronesian communities in the United States, and even the way American cultural products (from music to movies to sports teams to social media platforms) are cool in Micronesia—all serve to Americanize island societies and tie the islands more strongly to the United States geopolitically even as U.S. military dominance, political engagement, and economic power wanes.

The Decline of U.S. Influence in Micronesia

While these geosocial processes serve to more tightly bind Micronesia to the traditional hegemon in the region, there are other processes and circulations chipping away at this connectivity to the United States. This is especially true when we look at more contemporary shifts in patterns of government aid, investment, development projects, and tourism. Keeping our focus on Micronesia, for instance, can illuminate not only how soft infrastructures still bind the region to the United States but also how long-standing connections are eroding and being replaced by connections to other places. This erosion of U.S. influence is due to several factors: local animosities toward U.S. policies and actions, the perceived withdrawal of U.S. economic assistance and engagement in the region, and the availability of other (non-U.S.-focused) economic opportunities.

There may be support from some for the Americanization of Micronesian societies, and feelings of affinity and patriotism toward the United States may be widespread, but there is plenty of animosity toward the United States in the second island chain as well. Guåhan, for instance, may be the site of some of the highest per capita enlistment rates into the U.S. military, and may host Liberation Day parades whose patriotic theming rivals any mainland Fourth of July, but it is also a place with staunch opposition to U.S. policies. This is evident in frequent protests over Guåhan's colonial status and militarization. While some of the protests in 2017 were mentioned in the introduction, the opposition to colonial domination has bubbled up throughout the time period of U.S. governance—as well as in eras of Spanish and Japanese colonialism (Na'puti and Bevacqua 2015; Perez 2014; Rogers 1994; Lutz 2009). There are many long-running historical processes that stoke resentment toward U.S. rule, including the denial of effective self-government, the confiscation of large areas of land for U.S. military use, and the restrictions on trade between the island and international destinations due to the U.S. Jones Act.

In other parts of Micronesia people also chafe at similar denials of full formal sovereignty, as well as the effects of current and past militarization. In the Marshall Islands, for instance, contamination from nuclear weapons testing in Bikini and Enewetak, and missile testing at Kwajalein Atoll, are not historical events but contemporary realities that affect everyday life. Whether it is the fact that much of Kwajalein Atoll is off-limits to Marshallese due to continued missile testing, or that many places on Bikini, Rongelap, and Enewetak Atolls remain contaminated with radioactivity, or that many believe the United States has not adequately cleaned up these landscapes or sufficiently compensated their inhabitants, the result is that many in the islands perceive U.S. actions as both damaging and immoral (Aguon 2008; J. S. Davis 2005b; Jose, Wall, and Hinzel 2015). These legacies clearly damage the reputation of U.S. power in the region and have an adverse effect on the desirability of depending on the United States politically, militarily, and economically. While the RMI and FSM generally support the United States in United Nations votes (even being among the lone supporters of the United States on globally unpopular votes critical of Israel), the RMI also brought forward a lawsuit against the United States for breaching the nuclear nonproliferation treaty (Simons 2016). Additionally, other recent political, economic, and social policies in the United States have hurt its standing in Micronesia. In particular, the fact that the United States has refused to sign, or has pulled out of, major international treaties on reducing carbon emissions has put it at odds with many Pacific leaders who see climate change as a key political issue (and life-and-death threat) in the islands (Pearl 2017).

Even when considering migration between COFA states and the United States there are aspects that hamper the production of tighter relationships between the islands and the United States. Namely, Micronesian immigrants face substantial discrimination in U.S. territories, and there is increasing concern that these circuits of migration may become more limited in the near future. While migration to the United States is an attractive option for many in Micronesia, it is far from easy. Not only are there the usual difficulties with relocation and navigating a new social milieu, but discrimination toward Micronesian migrants is rampant in many of the communities they move into (Jetnil-Kijiner 2017; Yamada 2011). While this racism is partially an individual and cultural response in immigrant receiving places, it is structurally exacerbated by language in the COFA agreements that states that the U.S. federal government will compensate local governments for the impact of COFA migrants. For example, the 2003 U.S. congressional act ratifying the COFA notes,

> There is hereby authorized and appropriated to the Secretary of the Interior, out of any funds in the Treasury not otherwise appropriated, to remain available until expended, for each fiscal year from 2004 through 2023, $30,000,000 for grants to affected jurisdictions to aid in defraying costs incurred by affected jurisdictions as a result of increased demands placed on health, educational, social, or public safety services or infrastructure related to such services due to the residence in affected jurisdictions of qualified nonimmigrants from the Republic of the Marshall Islands, the Federated States of Micronesia, or the Republic of Palau. (Compact of Free Association Amendments Act of 2003, 20)

This seemingly innocuous language has had some startling effects on amplifying racist characterizations of Micronesian migrants in Guåhan, Hawai'i, and Saipan. Because these cash-strapped local governments can get more funding from the United States if they represent and quantify the activities of COFA migrants in their jurisdictions as *costs*, there is a financial benefit for doing so. The amounts of money at stake are not unsubstantial. For instance, in 2017 the government of Guam (Guåhan) received $1.49 million, Hawai'i $1.28 million, and the Commonwealth of the Northern Mariana Islands (CNMI) $231,000 to cover the calculated costs of COFA migrants (Borja 2017). I personally sat in a meeting in Guåhan in 2011 at which the heads of Guåhan's government agencies sat around a table and reported quantified costs of COFA migrants: how much they were costing the schools, how much they were costing the police and correctional facilities, how much they were costing health care providers. The government then took these figures and widely publicized them in order to bolster their argument that they deserved more funding from the United States. While it is true that migration from COFA countries stretches already strained social services in these locales, it is also true that the continual depiction of this particular group of migrants as "people who cost" has a chilling racist effect that exacerbates discrimination toward Micronesian immigrants in U.S. territories. Citizens from RMI and FSM are, of course, aware of this, and it does come into play as another factor that creates social and political distance between the United States and the Freely Associated States.

The anti-immigrant turn by the U.S. government after Trump's election makes the already substantial difficulties and uncertainties faced by Micronesian immigrants even worse. The Trump administration's anti-immigration rhetoric and policies have concerned Micronesian leaders and citizens (Jaynes

2017). This was especially true when U.S. sources began discussing cutting off safety-net programs for all immigrants (which COFA country émigrés have historically used in relatively high numbers) (Hagiwara et al. 2015). The current rhetorical and political atmosphere in the United States around immigration certainly sends signals that people in COFA states should not count on maintaining rights to immigrate to the United States when the COFA agreements come to an end in 2023. Given the importance of circuits of migration for pulling the islands of Micronesia toward the U.S. orbit, making migration more difficult between the COFA countries and the United States has personal effects as well as important geopolitical effects. Anything that discourages or limits the attractiveness of migration to the United States serves to weaken U.S. influence in the region.

In addition to the potential effects on circuits of migration, the end of the compacts in 2023 have other potentially detrimental effects on U.S. influence in the region. Chief among these is that the United States' direct funding to the RMI and FSM governments will end. In 2016, 25 percent of the RMI's $123 million government budget and 33 percent of the FSM federal government's $103 million in spending comes directly from the United States through transfers associated with the compacts (GAO 2018).[3] In accordance with neoliberal ideologies that have been popular in the United States for decades, the COFA agreements are structured to promote the cutting of FSM and RMI government spending and to decrease the U.S. government's financial commitment over time. Each year between 2018 and 2023, the amount of U.S. compact money available to the RMI and FSM governments for spending goes down while payments to trust funds increase (GAO 2018). These trust funds are supposed to provide revenue to the RMI and FSM governments in perpetuity, but a 2018 report by the U.S. Government Accountability Office pointedly shows just how inadequate and unreliable trust funds payouts for government services will be. In particular, educational systems in the RMI and FSM, as well as state governments in the FSM, appear to be heading for financial cliffs. As the U.S. Government Accountability Office (GAO) report states, "Our updated projections for the FSM and RMI compact trust funds after 2023 indicate a continued likelihood that, given their balance at the end of fiscal year 2017 and current compact trust fund rules—the baseline scenario—the funds will be unable to provide maximum disbursements (equal to the inflation-adjusted amount of annual grant assistance in 2023) in some years; [and] *unable to provide any disbursement at all* in some years, with the likelihood of zero disbursement in a given year increasing over time" (2018, 31; emphasis added). In addition to the loss of direct U.S. funding, and the likely inadequacy of trust fund payouts, the COFA counties will also have to take over other U.S.-provided services in 2023 (postal service, aviation administration, etc.). Clearly this looming withdrawal of U.S. aid has critical implications for many aspects of everyday life in the RMI and the FSM—from education to sanitation services to law enforcement to public sector employment. The way the end of the compact is being engineered, however, does something else as well: it reduces the influence of the United States in the region. In a part of the world where there is little private investment coming in from U.S. sources, the diminishment of U.S. state aid represents a drastic decline of U.S. economic influence overall. If this is coupled with increasing restrictions to Micronesian mobility to and from the United States and its territories in 2023, then several of the fundamental structures linking the region to the United States will be undermined and diminished by the U.S. government's own hand.

What does this withdrawal of U.S. involvement in the more-than-political realm of Pacific relationships mean? In particular, what does it mean from the perspective of these islands? On the one hand, from a postcolonial perspective, this withdrawal of U.S. influence can be seen as a positive that can enable more self-determination in the region. On the other, this decline in economic aid (and potential limiting of immigration rights) is not something advocated by the islanders themselves but rather something the colonizing power is pushing through over many local objections.[4] This gets into tricky territory, where, as it has been noted in some island jurisdictions, local governments have been fighting *against* decolonization programs initiated by colonizing powers (Baldacchino and Milne 2009). This may appear at first glance to be a contradiction or paradox. If we view it from an assemblage perspective looking outward from the islands, however, it is easier to see that even choosing dependency is about trying to be able to choose *how* a place is connected to other places in ways that can confer some benefits, even if they come with limitations on formal sovereignty. In other words, effective sovereignty can be performed in order to *maintain* connections rather than to sever connections and produce autonomy—even if doing also comes with infringements on formal sovereignty.

Chinese Tourism, Investment, and Other Options in the Multipolar Pacific

If the United States is intent on diminishing its influence in the Pacific in all but the military sphere, what other options are there for people in these islands? What other influences, capacities, and potentialities for connection are available in Micronesia? There are many that have been historically available, and there are also new and shifting ones. First, the Pacific as a whole has more varied sources of influence than discussions of lines between U.S. and Chinese spheres of influence may suggest. Even though the region is rife with formal colonialisms and occupations that structure military, economic, and social relations towards particular foreign powers, this does not mean the Pacific is completely divided into separated imperial blocks. Instead, if we view the context of the region from a standpoint within it, instead of through the colored lenses of one external power or another, we find that the meta-sovereignty structuring relations is constructed not just wholly from one state but rather from a confluence of several competing actors and collectivities that try to project influence in different ways. This has many negative consequences, of course, such as the massive militarization in the region and the tenacity with which imperial powers still cling to continuing formal colonialism for reasons of national security. However, it also creates political opportunities.

While it may seem tempting to point to the United States as *the* imperial power in the region, this is far from the case both historically and today. Historically, the islands of Micronesia serve as a prime example of just how changeable global power can be over time. The Caroline and Northern Mariana Islands, for instance, were politically administered, in turn, by the Spanish, the Germans, the Japanese, and the Americans. In addition to the waves of successive colonizers in the region over time, every era has been marked by competition—sometimes to the point of war—between would-be colonizing states, between commercial enterprises (sometimes aligned with particular states), as well as between colonizers and Indigenous people. Today is no different.

In Micronesia, and even more so in the Pacific region as a whole, the situation today is more one of multipolar influence rather than unipolar American empire. Not only are multiple outside powers attempting to participate in this competition, but different states use different assets to exert influence based on their unique strengths, political objectives, and historical connections. The United States has focused on its military superiority and its immigration and educational connections in the region. China, however, has become more active in using its economic influence and aid. Other powers, such as Australia (the largest aid donor in the Pacific), Japan, Taiwan, France, Chile, the European Union, and New Zealand, all have a plethora of intensive projects that affect governance going on in various parts of the region.

Even though I noted above that projects in any given place tend to be dominated by initiatives that originate in the traditional metropole (New Zealand projects in the Cook Islands; U.S. projects in the FSM; Australian projects in Papua New Guinea, etc.), there are also projects that do not follow this colonial pattern. For example, the RMI and Palau have long partnered with Taiwan, and each gets a substantial amount of aid from that country (in exchange, of course, for support for international diplomatic recognition of Taiwan). The FSM has long hosted volunteers and development projects from Australia, Japan, the European Union, New Zealand, and other locales. It also receives aid from those countries as well.

A newer development has been the ascendency of China in the region, and it too is becoming a major influence in the Pacific. The FSM for instance, since it recognizes the People's Republic of China (as opposed to Taiwan), has received about $40 million in aid from China.[5] Furthermore, the large amounts of potential private investment and tourist spending emanating from China have recently redirected a lot of the FSM's attention away from the United States and toward China. This is not to say, however, that China is taking over as the hegemonic power in this part of the Pacific. The situation is more nuanced, multipolar, and interconnecting than that. From the island perspective, China represents another possibility for connections (which, of course, like connections to the United States, have the potential to be beneficial or threatening).

An event on the island of Yap is illustrative here. Yap, the state of the FSM closest to mainland Asia, was chosen in 2016 to host the 2018 Micronesia Games, a sporting event that brings together athletes from around the region. The island—like the FSM government of which it is politically a part—is somewhat cash-strapped, and so there was a need to raise funds. While the games are modest by most international sporting event standards, the infrastructure of Yap was strained by the event, and the cost of hosting the games was estimated to be $48 million. Therefore in 2016 local organizers held a meeting on Yap to ask ambassadors from other nations to contribute to the event. Paul Lane, a former U.S. Peace Corps volunteer who married a Yapese citizen and then resided in Yap, said of the meeting, "The Japanese and Australian ambassadors pledged some help and the deputy Chinese ambassador brought a cheque book and simply asked, 'How much do you need?' No one from the U.S. even showed up to the meeting" (quoted in Bohane 2016).

This example of a fairly simple meeting to fund a sporting event on a small island can be unpacked to show innumerable threads of geopolitical, geoeconomic, and geosocial influence. First, the meeting is held in a territory that has a free association political affiliation with the United States. This alludes to the extended geopolitical reach of the United States into the region and Yap's strategic position that helps secure U.S. sea lines of communication (SLOCs) to the periphery of Asia. Second, we see the attention of the Japanese, Chinese, and Australian ambassadors. This demonstrates that other geopolitical players in the region besides the official metropolitan power express interest in the island. Third, we have two instances of spatially stretched geosocial connections present here, too. One is that one of the local participants in the meeting is an American who has married into the community thanks to his involvement in the Peace Corps. The second is that the meeting is about an event designed to bring people from across the Micronesian region together with the aim of creating a greater sense of social cohesion among islanders from an oceanic realm that spans an area roughly the size of the continental United States. The most obvious point from the story of this meeting, however, is that we see the new geo-economic influence of China in the region paralleled by an apparent American absence. As discussed, U.S. military planners may still be keen to keep the island Pacific in the American fold (Matelski 2016), but the pressures in Washington, DC, to reduce and eliminate U.S. economic aid to the region seem to override that in this example. Into this gap, Chinese aid and influence move in.

With China's increasing economic presence in the region, it is not just sporting event planners that are asking if the days of the Pacific as an "American lake" are coming to an end (Rodriguez, Losinio, and Carreon 2017). Part of the reason for this is that the Micronesia Games donation is far from the largest Chinese project in Yap right now. In 2011 the company Exhibition and Travel Group (ETG), based in Chengdu, China, announced plans for a megaresort in Yap. The original Paradise Island plan called for a multimillion-dollar hotel and casino complex with four thousand rooms that would drastically change the physical, social, and economic fabric of Yap. Exhibition and Travel Group is a well-financed company whose billionaire owner, Deng Hong, oversaw the construction of the New Century Global Center in Chengdu (one of the largest buildings in the world), and multiple large hotel projects managed by the British hotel company Intercontinental. The group's plans for Yap include expanding the airport to be able to handle forty-three direct flights from China per day (the airport currently gets less than five flights per week) and the expansion of the docks to accommodate larger cruise ships. The group estimated that the project would increase the gross domestic product of Yap one-hundred-fold and that the revenue would be used to build a lavish government building and a modern "Native-town" that would house all of the displaced Yapese.[6]

While it may seem fantastical to imagine that such an enormous venture could actually be profitable and sustained, there are a few factors that could make it work. First, Yap is relatively close to mainland China (about four hours by air) if the infrastructure is put in place to facilitate greater air travel and cruise ship traffic between the two. Second, Chinese tourists are now the largest (and highest-spending) segment of the international tourist market. In 2017 Chinese citizens made more than 130 million international tourist trips (Tan 2018). Third, some of the other more developed tropical destinations close to China are in countries that have contentious political relationships with China (such as the Philippines, Japan, Vietnam) or in U.S. territories (such as Guåhan and Saipan) where U.S. immigration and visa requirements serve as an impediment to Chinese tourists (though Chinese tourism in Guåhan and Saipan has increased substantially over the past decade, and Chinese tourism now represents a serious economic pull toward China in these places too). The Federated States of Micronesia, meanwhile, does not require a visa for Chinese tourists. Fourth, this project is imagined as a vertically integrated Chinese project in which Chinese capital funds it, Chinese citizens work in the resorts, Chinese airlines fly the routes, and Chinese tourists are the consumers. Exhibition and Travel Group has the expertise and connections within the Chinese tourism system to make this work, and the capital to actually build the project. Finally, the FSM and Yap state governments, as well as landowners who are signing leases with ETG, are hard-pressed to come up with alternative streams of income that could match the potential windfalls from this kind of megaproject.

As of 2019 the Paradise Island plan has been downgraded to one thousand rooms (to begin with), and the timeline for its construction has slowed considerably. Still, ETG has gained control over many large properties around Yap Island through long-term lease arrangements, and an ETG official I interviewed in Yap in both 2016 and 2017 stated that ETG still intends to move the project forward (figure 4). Like the superport megaproject in Palau in the 1970s, however, this current plan has created an uproar of opposition and created schisms in the community. Some in Yap worry about the dramatic environmental and social changes this kind of project would bring to a relatively undeveloped island of approximately eight thousand people. Those in the military and national security circles in the United States and Australia are concerned about the geopolitical shift this project may create. To military planners this kind of

FIGURE 4. Site of proposed ETG Paradise Island project, 2017. Maap, Yap. Photo by the author.

development represents a potential toehold of Chinese-owned and controlled infrastructure on the second island chain that could undermine long-standing U.S. military strategies in the Pacific (detailed in the last chapter). After all, some U.S. pundits say, an expanded airport or dock may be intended for tourist use, but the same infrastructure could be used by the Chinese military to extend its influence and operational capabilities far into the Pacific.[7] To some, this erosion of U.S. dominance in more-than-political realms such as economic development foreshadows a potential decline in the military realm in the region as well (Matelski 2016).

Whether the Paradise Island project in Yap comes to fruition or not, the fact that the project could be built (and could be successful) shows just how things have changed in terms of Chinese influence in the region. The existence of tens of millions of potential tourists from China (and their ability to spend vast amount of money), and the existence of Chinese companies ready and willing to invest millions in the region, and the fact that the South Pacific (though vaguely defined spatially) is one spoke in the new massive "One Belt, One Road" infrastructure project; all demonstrate that there are opportunities for China-oriented development to fill the gap left by the economic decline of the United States in the region (Leverett and Bingbing 2016; Blanchard and Flint 2017).

The expansion of Chinese outbound tourism in the region and the example of the Micronesia Games show in microcosm what is going on across the larger region in terms of shifts among global powers. It is not just in Yap (or the FSM as a whole) that these shifts can be seen. Chinese investment and tourism spending is becoming a key part of many Pacific island economies—even in territories such as Palau, the Commonwealth of the Northern Mariana Islands, and Guåhan that have formal U.S. political affiliations. In today's Pacific, this dichotomy between where official military and political allegiances lie, and where economic opportunities originate, demonstrates that spheres of influence are not at all clearly defined or mutually exclusive. Instead, in the Pacific there is a complex assemblage of overlapping, contesting, and entwining influences (some economic, some military, some cultural) coming from many different directions. This shows the importance of more-than-political factors for establishing or maintaining influence, and also shows how small places, and the people who live in them, can exert agency over global structures of power.

The Post-American Pacific?

Given this view of the Pacific as a realm of competing and overlapping influences, is it fair to say the era of U.S. dominance has ended? I believe it is, but this does not mean that U.S. influence is absent or inconsequential. What I believe the above analysis tells us is that the context of Pacific politics today is more about patterns of influence and attempts by various powers to construct hegemony rather than about empires per se. This may seem like a fine distinction to make, but I believe it is a critical one. As John Agnew (2009) has explained, *hegemony* is different from *empire* in that empire connotes a relationship of domination and forced subservience while hegemony is attained via getting other countries, or individuals, to want what you want. In other words, it is not that power is laid down or simply exerted by some actors onto others, but that it arises relationally through more nuanced, though still unequal, interactions.

This difference between looking at power as hegemonic versus imperial is critical in the current age because it is a time when the gulf between the two is so apparent. For instance, the United States is still the largest and most lethal military in the Pacific region, which suggests that it could still maintain imperial relationships of forced subservience. Maintaining hegemony in the region, however, involves having the clout, guile, diplomatic initiatives, soft power, and respect to attract enthusiastic supporters that want to get in on the projects you are leading (Nye 2004). The United States' ability to do this is clearly declining, and this offers opportunities (and dangers) to people living in the region.

While there are many analyses that give valuable insights into the political and economic causes of hegemonic strength and decline (Arrighi 2005; Harvey 2003; Khal and Brands 2017; Kennedy 1987; Wallerstein 2004), the past two chapters have focused more on *how* U.S. decline is occurring and on what that decline means for places within the Pacific that are the targets of its various political projects. There is value in examining these situated examples of how influence is contested in the region because it speaks to larger questions of how effective sovereignty or the establishment of a sphere of influence actually comes to be. It is not just who has the most capacity for violence but also who has the best capacity to gain *willing acceptance* and support for particular projects.

If we think about power not as something emanating from states but as something that is relationally constructed within particular places, we see that there are multiple sites from which power arises, and multiple actors that take part in its construction. Catherine Lutz's article "Empire Is in the Details" (2006) exemplifies this approach in claiming that wider international relationships of power and domination are created within quite intimate circuits of interpersonal interactions. Lutz contends that even global empires function only through the accumulated and coordinated actions that occur in thousands of local sites. While Lutz makes a compelling case for why we ought to care about the details when examining empire, it is even more critical to look at the details when considering shifts in influence and hegemony. This is because hegemony, by nature, is not just about hanging threats of violence over people's heads. Instead, it is about cultivating an understanding of what other, less powerful actors might want, allowing them to have some agency, and attempting to influence them. This is not to say that the construction of hegemony is altruistic or nonexploitive. Certainly, the art of hegemony works to a large degree by the hegemon limiting the agency of others (using both carrots and sticks) to a few options—all of which are acceptable to the hegemon. However, to get active support rather than mere acquiescence, the hegemon has to be able to offer something others want.

During my research I was reminded of this distinction between hegemony and empire when I happened upon two very different quotes on the same day. One was in a news article I was reading about a speech by Donald Trump:

> From this moment on, it's going to be America First. (Trump 2017)

The other was posted in a museum in Palau:

> I could see that he never used the strong hand where gentler means would serve, and rarely attempted to force his ideas on them. He preferred to make the leader of the natives feel that the suggestion had come from themselves and not from him; they were sure then to work with a will to carry out his reforms. (anthropologist J. Macmillan Brown, referring to Dr. Hermann Kersting, a district officer of German Micronesia in 1913; quotation displayed in an exhibition at the Belau National Museum in Koror)[8]

Both of these approaches are attempting to coerce, to amplify influence and power, but clearly each does so in very different ways. As the current state of world affairs demonstrates, the United States still has tremendous military power (especially in the Pacific), and its media and cultural productions are still globally popular, but on a wide variety of political issues the United States has substantially lost its ability to orchestrate international political agendas and to get other states "to feel that the suggestion has come from them."

As of this writing in 2019, the long-forecast decline in the legitimacy of American global leadership and hegemony is apparent everywhere. On the global stage, the United States under Trump has abandoned three critical pillars of what built U.S. hegemony after World War II: the promotion of a U.S.-coordinated global system of free trade, a rhetoric (if not the practice) of endorsing universal human rights, and its role as arbiter of international political agreements. As of 2019 the Trump administration has pulled the United States out of proposed free trade agreements such as the Trans-Pacific Partnership and begun an escalating series of tariff battles with its political allies. With its callous and racist anti-immigration policies and its departure from the UN Human Rights Council, it also has lost any sense of global moral leadership on human rights. And it has unilaterally pulled the United States out of multinational agreements on climate change and the Iran nuclear deal (a.k.a. Joint Comprehensive Plan of Action).

The consequences of these newer policies, on top of the disastrous policies and military misadventures of Trump's predecessors, are clear in many parts of the world beyond the Pacific examples detailed above. In the Middle East and Central Asia, the past decade's military interventions have not strengthened the U.S. position. Iraq is a fractured political quagmire after years of vicious fighting between the Islamic State and government-backed sectarian militias. A seventeen-year military operation in Afghanistan has still failed to secure the country. In Syria, the United States finds itself largely on the sidelines (diplomatically and militarily) while Russia, Iran, Turkey, and the Gulf States have far more influence.

This is not to say that the United States was a knight on a white horse in global politics (or Pacific politics) before Trump came into office. Projects such as the Trans-Pacific Partnership, after all, were designed to enrich the already wealthy and to amplify corporate power; the partnership offered next to nothing in the way of progressive change for most people living in the Pacific realm. Furthermore, in practice, the U.S. human rights record in Asia and the Pacific has been horrific. Whether we are looking at nuclear testing in the Marshall Islands, the long-term denial of formal sovereignty within the region, the war crimes of the firebombing of Tokyo and the atomic bombing of two of Japan's cities, or the millions of deaths caused by U.S. wars in Korea, Vietnam, Laos, and Cambodia, the diminishment of U.S. power is not something people within the region should be disappointed about. I am therefore not advocating for greater U.S. influence in the region or pining for the return of some kind of benevolent U.S. protection, which, from the perspective of these islands, has largely been a rhetorical fiction. Instead, I want to simply point out that despite the maintenance of U.S. military dominance, U.S. hegemony has unmistakably diminished in the Pacific. This change in context is important and sets the scene for various political possibilities. Also, if we look at the details of what is going on in the region, this change in the influence of the United States in nonmilitary realms is also undermining its ability to maintain its military dominance. As I aim to show in the next chapter, it is not just that other militaries are infringing into formerly U.S.-dominated spaces or that other states are becoming more influential. As this chapter and the previous one argue, this is already happening to some degree. Another important issue, however, is that residents of islands within the region are organizing to contest the continuation of colonial political relationships, as well as the building of new military infrastructures and the continued operations of existing ones. In the end, it may not be a military defeat that signals the end of U.S. social, economic, and moral dominance in the Pacific. Instead it may be the unraveling of U.S. social, economic, and moral legitimacy—an unraveling spurred in part by its own legacies and contemporary practices of colonialism, militarization, neoliberal economic doctrines, and immigration restrictions—that may lead to diminishing its military capacities and making them less politically relevant.

CHAPTER 4

Sharing the Struggle

Contesting U.S. Militarization and Constructing Transnational Solidarity in Global Social Movements

The previous chapters have sketched, in broad strokes, how transnational processes and influences interact across space and entwine in place. Part of the rationale for this analysis has been to show that the larger context of Pacific politics not only affects island locales but is also generated from these locales. In other words, there is no hegemony in the Pacific other than that which emerges through its operation within the Pacific. The islands of the region, and the people who inhabit them, are the sites where regional hegemony is constructed: by what is done to them but also by what they do. Therefore, when thinking about what orders the construction of sovereignties in places, it is misleading to ask, who rules these places? Instead, it is more revealing to ask, how is rule constructed in these places, how could that context be changed, and what kinds of connections ought we make? As Manuel DeLanda (2006) points out, each node in a political assemblage is not intrinsically part of some larger whole. Instead, an assemblage is literally made from the relationships of the nodes brought together within it. On one level we could say that a given island in the Pacific is not essentially part of anyone else's realm—be it American, Japanese, Chinese, or other. More radically, however, we could say that the construction of the connections between islands and other places or states are what literally construct the realm in the first place. Consequently, each place has capacities to attach, belong, or depart from larger assemblages and to then change the context.

In this chapter I examine how people in the Pacific challenge existing assemblages of colonialism and militarization, and how they forge new kinds of connections aimed at building a different political context in the region. To do this I dive a little deeper into the specific ways that Pacific social movements are constructed and maintained. If, as assemblage theory posits, connections are always in the process of becoming and being (re)produced across space, then it is worth looking at just what creates these connections and influences. While I have noted the importance of approaching the relationships across the Pacific region from a geosocial perspective, in this chapter I take to heart a core element of that perspective by presenting a more intimate view of the people involved in making the transnational connections that I have thus far discussed mostly in a more abstract way. To this end, this chapter focuses more on personal interviews with individuals involved in transnational anti-imperial and antimilitarization activism in the region. I have chosen to focus on these activists because these are actors who are directly and intentionally working on many of the issues I foreground in this book, such as militarization and colonialism. I hope, however, that through this discussion of how these particular people construct allegiances across space, readers will better see how, in general, people circulate ideas, bodies, and material practices to create political change. In short, in this chapter I try to get at just what it is that creates the glue that binds places and people together into larger assemblages of social change.

A Morning in Gangjeong, Korea

As the sun rises on a cold morning in Gangjeong Village, a man dressed in traditional Korean funeral garb stands in front of the gate of a new military base. He states that he is in mourning for the death of democracy and peace in Korea. Both, he says, have been killed by this new naval base on the south end of Jeju Island. The base—which is ostensibly a South Korean base but which also hosts American-made missile defense Aegis destroyers—has been the site of constant protests since its construction was announced in 2007. On this morning in 2014 the protests are highly ritualized. The assembled activists engage in one hundred prostrations while blocking traffic from entering or exiting the base. The protesters assemble in front of the gates. A group across the street with a microphone gives short speeches that are amplified through a loudspeaker. This is followed by the sound of a gong that cues the protesters to kneel, then lean forward, with their heads down and fingers pointing toward the offending base (figure 5).

Many of the protesters are Korean citizens from Jeju and other parts of Korea. There are, however, foreigners too. I am here, and there is also a contingent of a dozen Americans from the Seattle, Washington, area. All of us participate in the ritual as an act of solidarity. After the one hundred prostrations, the foreigners and local activists go to a communal kitchen for breakfast and

FIGURE 5. Protest in Gangjeong Village, Jeju, South Korea, 2014. Photo by the author.

then later return for a Catholic mass that is performed in front of the gate. This mass-as-blockade is more confrontational than the morning protests but also ritualized. As construction vehicles waiting to exit and enter the base accumulate, a phalanx of uniformed police appears from behind the barricades. On a megaphone they explain in Korean and English that the protesters are breaking the law and could be arrested and—in the case of foreign nationals—forcibly deported from South Korea. The threat of deportation is not an idle one. Dozens of foreign visitors have been forced to leave the country since protests began here. After the police announcement, the officers advance on the activists, who are sitting in plastic chairs. Two or three officers grab each chair, lift the protesters, and move them to the side of the road. After they clear the way, the police stand in a line to block the protesters from obstructing the gate while trucks flow in and out of the base. Then the police retreat back into the base and the protesters again move in front of the gate, sit in their plastic chairs, and continue the mass.

The protests have become smaller and less fierce than they were before the construction began. Starting in 2007, the announcement that the new naval base—which had been rejected by the two adjacent municipalities—was going to be built in Gangjeong sparked protests by thousands of villagers and activists (Gwon 2013). By 2014, however, the base perimeter had been established, and the base construction had reached the advanced stages. The new base in Jeju is relatively small in comparison to main operating bases on other islands in the Asia-Pacific region such as Okinawa, Guåhan, and O'ahu—as well as sites on the mainland of South Korea that host large and permanent concentrations of U.S. military units. While the base in Gangjeong is not a particularly large base, its location at the end of the Korean Peninsula at a dividing line between the Yellow and East China Seas (see map 2 in the introduction)—and a mere five hundred kilometers from Shanghai, China—makes the base particularly strategic (or threatening, depending on your perspective).

There has been a dance of sorts between military planners and antimilitarization actors that has caused the network of military bases in East Asia and the Pacific to shift and morph over the past decades (S. Davis 2015). The new base in Jeju is part of these larger fluctuations that are occurring not only at bases in other countries around the region but also in other parts of Korea as the United States concentrates its forces at Pyeongtaek and leaves older bases such as Yongsan in Seoul (Kim 2018; Man, Paik, and Pappademos 2019; Yeo 2010). Early in the struggle hopes were high among activists that base construction in Jeju—like base construction and operations in Henoko, Okinawa, and in Guåhan, Puerto Rico, and Hawai'i—could be delayed or stopped. Instead, the base was completed, and in the fall of 2015 it hosted its first visit by Aegis missile defense destroyers. As the base construction progressed despite the resistance, many residents started to shy away from the protests. In their place some committed villagers, determined activists from the mainland of Korea, peace-promoting Catholic clergy, and international visitors professing solidarity made up the bulk of activists still contesting the base (Gwon 2013; Yeo 2013).[1]

Like other communities hosting military bases in the region, now that the Jeju base has been built, political concerns and the negative consequences of day-to-day living next to the base continue to spark protests in Jeju. While military bases like Jeju's are ostensibly constructed to provide national security for the United States and their allies—as well as supply chain security for the movement of trade (Cowen 2014)—they are also sites of practices that undermine the everyday feelings of security in the communities that host them (Ireland 2010; Kirk 2008; Lutz 2006, 2009; McCaffrey 2002; Vine 2009, 2019; Warf 1997). As discussed in chapter 1, scholars of feminist geopolitics and critical security studies have pointed out that military bases such as these promote a security that appeals to so-called realist military and state-centric conceptualizations of security, while undermining the daily security of bodies that must endure the violence these bases project into distant warzones as well as dispense locally in the form of environmental contamination, noise, violations of local self-determination, and increased incidence of sexual assault (Booth 1997; Brown and Staeheli 2003; Dowler and Sharp 2001; Enloe 2007; Jones and Sage 2010). The more body-centric views of security that have informed the antimilitarization social movements working in Jeju and elsewhere, however, reject the imposition of bases within communities on two fronts: as violent instruments of war and power projection, and as institutions that locally create contamination, raise the risk of sexual assault, and commandeer land that could be used for food security, development, recreation, housing, and other purposes.

Building Activist Assemblages: Critical Consciousness and the Sharing of Struggle

Despite the fact that the Jeju protests were not able to stop the base from being constructed, the struggle in Jeju is an important one to consider because it was one of the foci of the international antibase activist community for many years. Like the protests in Henoko, Okinawa, discussed at length in chapter 1, the protests in Jeju have been carried out by a collection of people from many different places that move and interact across scales. This is not surprising given that the phenomenon they are fighting against (the militarization of communities) operates in many of the same multi- and trans-scalar ways. Following from the assemblage theory perspective, it would be a mistake to characterize the movements protesting in Gangjeong as either local movements with local grievances (environmental damage, lack of formal local political sovereignty, sexual violence) reaching out for external solidarity or local manifestations of reactions against global grievances (war, imperialism). These movements are simultaneously both (Loyd 2012). The protests in Gangjeong are better characterized as arising from a more complex geography that mixes local grievances, regional political tensions, and globally circulating ethics and activists (Gwon 2013). The protests in Jeju—like others in Okinawa, Puerto Rico, Hawaiʻi, and Guåhan—are translocal assemblages simultaneously manifested via both local and transnational processes (McFarlane 2009). It is therefore not a question of how movements scale-up (or down) to accomplish goals. Rather, as Colin McFarlane (2009) emphasizes, these movements are, in an *essential* way, already translocal and are from the beginning constructed from spatially stretched interrelationships. This view is supported by one Hawaiʻi activist, who said of organizing within the region, "We need to learn about each other's struggles and be transnational and transcultural *within* place" (personal communication 2014; emphasis added).

As discussed in chapter 1, being translocal is but one of the central principles of looking at social movements through the lens of assemblage theory. There are other important points about assemblages that deserve further exploration in order to understand how social movements arise and how they are sustained. The first point is that assemblages are best considered as existing as an actual *process* of interaction, not as a resultant formation created by interaction. Assemblages are therefore not just networks of fully made subjects interacting autonomously with each other because of some kind of shared geographic, ideological, racial, or class similarity. Instead, they are constructed and persist through the active comingling and sharing of ideas, but also of things, bodies, and material practices. Viewing social movements as assemblages stresses that the nodes (activists, places, and the movements themselves) are themselves constructed relationally through the performance of their translocal dialogues, relations, and actions. An activist as a subject, therefore, does not preexist her/his performance of activism, and a movement does not simply exist; it is performed.

As several scholars have pointed out, it is not so much that solidarities and transnational movements for decolonization, peace, and justice are constructed by merely connecting separated individuals that already hold similar values, but rather that solidarity actively emerges from translocal performances of care and shared experience (Brown and Yaffe 2014; Featherstone 2012). In this way, the interviewees in this chapter support the finding in the academic literature that collective identity in social movements is not preexisting between communities in similar circumstances. Instead, collective identity, critical consciousness, and solidarity are the *outcomes* of interaction (Fominaya 2010; Melucci 1995; Routledge 1996).

Another key insight of the assemblage approach to social movements is the ontological view that the material and discursive aspects of an assemblage are intrinsically tied together (Baird 2015; Davies 2012; Legg 2009; McFarlane 2009). Connections between activists are theorized to be not merely ideational but material, emotional, and visceral as well (Bosco 2007; Hayes-Conroy and Martin 2010; Hayes-Conroy and Hayes-Conroy 2013). As can be gleaned from the above description of protests on Jeju Island, activism is not just about dialogue and ideas. It is an intensely physical, emotional, and spiritual experience. The one hundred prostrations in the morning, the performance of the Catholic mass while being carried off by police, the dancing in the streets, the eating together afterward: these are not just the results of solidarity. Instead, the solidarity arises through these shared bodily performances. The point of these shared experiences is for activists to build a sense of common oppression not just through the sharing of information about militarism or colonialism but also through putting their bodies in shared emotional and visceral states. Simply put, activists posit that solidarities and translocal connections are built from a consciousness of shared oppression, and that a critical aspect of developing a consciousness of common oppression is cultivating it through the sharing of affective experiences—both pleasurable and fearful. This is something that organizers are very aware of and that they attempt to promote.

This brings the discussion to the other important aspect of the "translocal assemblage" approach, namely that the ontological view of a translocally connected world promotes an associated epistemic and pedagogical approach to the conduct of the activism itself. The contention that the world is ontologically assemblage-like encourages activist approaches that focus on the transnational connections and circulations and on how these work in concert with local actions. According to many of the respondents I interviewed for this research, these global networks of solidarity have been built through the process of developing in activists from different corners of the Earth a recognition that their oppressions are shared. With many parallels to Paolo Freire's *Pedagogy of the Oppressed* ([1970] 2000), activists invoke the idea that activism within—and solidarity between—militarized communities such as Gangjeong arises through the development of a critical consciousness (*conscientização*) in which people come to see the oppressions and contradictions of the larger context of imperialism and militarization within which all of their communities are embedded. This ontological position posits that processes of both oppression and liberation are therefore simultaneously, and inseparably, operating at local and global scales. Activists drawing on the principles of assemblage theory (sometimes quite explicitly referencing the academic work on these perspectives) hold that whether people are in South Korea, Okinawa, or the United States, they are all enmeshed and entangled in pervasive shared processes of oppression. This view encourages activists not only to emphasize the larger sociopolitical contexts of local grievances to bring about critical consciousness and enlist sympathetic supporters but also to direct their organizing to proactively and explicitly attempt to change those larger contexts (the ocean) that affect local grievances. In other words, social movement activities are constructed to do work at many scales simultaneously, even when the activities are focused on specific embodied affective and visceral experiences occurring in a particular locale.

Social Movements as Translocal Affective Experiences

While long-distance communication between activists in different parts of the world through social media and other internet technologies help translocal social movements cohere across space (Gillan and Pickerill 2008), activists in Jeju and other parts of the Pacific region emphasized the value of shared experiences that occur during in-person visits to each other's communities. Interview respondents repeatedly discussed how their consciousness of their own situation developed through experiences meeting with people in other militarized islands. This developed in these interviewees a critical consciousness of their own situation, and simultaneously constructed lasting bonds of solidarity with other people and places. In other words, the perception of oppression in one's own community was realized through comparisons with, and in relationship to, other people and landscapes.

Activists reported that they valued visits and travel not just so people could visit sites of struggle but also so that people from militarized communities could put their own militarization in context. An activist on Jeju opined that international travel and visits were important not just for other people to see what was occurring on Jeju but also for people on Jeju to go see what was going on in other places. She stated, "[We need to] get out of nationalism—get out of this box—people on these islands don't know much about each other. People here don't know how bad the base here will be, like in Okinawa. Solidarity [is] important just to know [we are] not alone—it's overcome by visiting. Visitors must come back and educate others in their home communities—sharing of that experience. As enthusiasm wanes [in Jeju, it is] important to still see the international presence. It impacts in a positive way" (personal communication 2014). Similarly, an activist from Okinawa involved in the protests in Henoko said this about her visit to Hawai'i, "Eye-opening was going to Hawai'i and seeing [the] same issues, but with more activism around it. [It encouraged me to] go to Henoko and bring food to people doing sit-ins on scaffolding in the sea [blocking construction of the military runway in Oura Bay]. Talking to those older people who were doing the action, when you visit them more often, you are less scared" (personal communication 2014).

As can be seen in these quotes, visits to other militarized sites are not just about sharing knowledge or information. They are also emotional experiences that embolden activists. This reinforces the point discussed above about the assemblage-like view of activism. Activists do not simply act across space as individualized nodes; activists as subjects—and their motivations for activism—are literally created through these translocal experiences. The sections of respondents' interviews that focused on visiting other sites were saturated with stories of personal transformations that occurred through the sharing of affective experiences. When activists were asked about the most important moments in their struggles, or in their personal histories of activism, most of the respondents reported translocal experiences that included moments of intense, almost overwhelming, emotion. One activist from Hawai'i who had visited the protests in Gangjeong talked much more during her interview about the dances in the streets, the food, and the comradery than she did about the politics of the base. Furthermore, when I asked an activist from Vieques, Puerto Rico, about his favorite moment in the struggle to end the routine bombing of the island by the U.S. Navy, I received an answer that had much more to do with a moment of personal connection created through the sharing of food. Even though the struggle in Vieques is seen in international activist circles as an important victory in which a small colonized island was able to oust the U.S. military, his favorite moment was not the announcement that the United States was leaving, or a direct action protest, but was instead about the sharing of faith and food with others in jail. He said, "In federal prison I had a really wonderful ceremony with a Dominican guy who was Jehovah's Witness, and a guy from Cameroon. The three of us—I had been doing a twenty-one-day fast [to protest the bombing]—so one day we did a wonderful ceremony in my cell where we ate crackers and honey. The Jehovah's Witness guy read something from scriptures in Spanish, the guy from Cameroon did a prayer in his native Bamileke language, and I said a small Hebrew prayer. And that was a neat moment" (personal communication 2014).

While many of the activists fondly recalled positive affective experiences as being important moments in their activist trajectories, some pointed to other emotional experiences that resulted from visiting other places. An Okinawan man reported that an important moment in the development of his activism came from visiting the United States and *not* seeing the same kind of militarization there as he saw on his home island. He stated, "After returning from [a visit to] the U.S., I saw planes landing at Futenma [Marine Corps Air Station in Okinawa]—I didn't see this thing in the U.S., but I see it here. I was mad. I had known it in my head, but then I knew it in my heart. I knew it was wrong, but I was used to it. That was my moment of connection between head and heart. [I was] Surprised. I had anger and a 'Eureka' moment" (personal communication 2014).

What has been the outcome of these shared experiences that result from visits? Have they cultivated a consciousness of shared oppression or lasting bonds of solidarity and mutual aid among these social movements? Respondents for this research repeatedly stated that they believe that they have. As one activist said, "Solidarity [is] only possible through experience. People must visit, not just read. Today's education is too nationalistic. [You need visits] to overcome issues like the Senkaku/Diaoyu [islands contested by China, Taiwan, and Japan]" (personal communication 2014). This emphasis on personal visits echoes what other researchers on the geographies of transnational activism have found: even though the internet has allowed for much more global communication, these virtual connections do not build trust and solidarity in quite the same way as the face-to-face sharing of experience (Gillan and Pickerill 2008). One Hawai'i activist contended that these visits enable people to come to care about distant places and to put more value on helping to protect them. He stated, "It's hard to fight for a place you haven't fallen in love with" (personal communication 2014).

While these visits may promote this love, and get people to contextualize local grievances, do these visits build mutual bonds of solidarity between activists? Recent geographic scholarship has emphasized that transnational activism can be fraught with inequalities because some activists (those that have the time and means to engage in this kind of travel) come from positions of privilege relative to other activists who are more place-bound (Cumbers, Routledge, and Nativel 2008; Featherstone 2012; Nicholls 2009). This can result in the perpetuation of relationships of domination within movements or make international visits to sites of protest merely voyeuristic vacations and power-laden interactions that reconfirm and strengthen international inequalities (Koopman 2011). It is important to appreciate that these social movements—some of which make strong claims to having nonhierarchical or horizontal organizing structures—still contain members with different levels of privilege based on race, class, gender, sexuality, mobility, nationality, education, and other axes of identity.

While there are clearly elements of inequality present within the movements, study respondents mostly reported that the benefits of the translocal linkages outweighed the negatives. In fact, many of the movements used these inequalities quite strategically. Some respondents pointed to the advantages of having visitors of different nationalities present at protests. As one resident of Gangjeong explained, "Police behavior is different when internationals are present" (personal communication 2014). This demonstrates a tactical use of the privilege that adheres differently to the bodies of international people who—in the case of Gangjeong protests—are subject to deportation instead of arrest, and who, if injured by police, could draw the attention of other governments and constituencies (see also Koopman 2011). That said, there still were some critiques of international support. One Korean activist, for example, said of Noam Chomsky's public support for the protestors on Jeju, "What is Chomsky doing besides saying things?" (personal communication 2014). An organizer on Vieques mentioned that they did have some problems with a small group from the main island of Puerto Rico that occasionally did not respect the larger organization's consensus on actions, and he also pointed out that sometimes visiting activists were referred to as "anti-mili-tourists," who observed more than participated. Overall, however, activists repeatedly stated that educating wider international audiences—and forging links with people from other militarized sites—is such a vital ingredient for success on local issues that it was still pursued despite the recognition of inequalities in transnational activism. The fact that the protest organizations in all of these places (Jeju, Okinawa, Vieques, Hawai'i, and Guåhan) actively cultivate these transnational relationships speaks to this. In Jeju, for instance, local activists spend a great deal of time and resources to cultivate relationships with foreign activists and to host them.

Interview respondents articulated a variety of reasons these solidarity relationships are valued. Some activists emphasized that solidarity is needed to spread the word of the struggle in the face of media disinterest or censorship. Another stated reason for building solidarity is to share tactics and strategies with other activists. Additionally, many participants spoke about the importance of building bonds of emotional connection with visitors and how this also raises the morale of activists. In the interviews for this research the importance of affective relationships seeped into almost all of the discussions, even when the conversation was on the subject of educating people about the struggles or the sharing of tactics with foreign activists. A quote from an organizer in Vieques demonstrates this well. On the advantages of building transnational solidarity he said,

> It's also about expanding promotion and knowledge. Bringing international [pressure] to bear, but it's also a sharing of strategies. In Vieques we had people from Okinawa and other parts of Japan—and many other places—and sharing with us strategies of struggles. Creating a theatrical display of the struggle, how to cut cyclone fence, how to bring in different segments of the society that often

don't mix together. [But also] The simple fact of holding up a sign that says "Stop bombing Vieques" in Okinawa, in Hawai'i, in the Philippines, in the Marshall Islands—and all of this has taken place—and in Korea—is important in terms of the spirit of the community in Vieques, as I'm sure it is in Okinawa. To see others in faraway parts of the world who know about their struggle, who care. *It brings a charge of energy.* It's a promotional boost. And international pressure is more important than just local or even national pressure. So just to have people calling in from other parts of the world is important. (personal communication 2014; emphasis added)

These sentiments were echoed in my interviews with activists in other locales. Hawai'i activists discussed how the tactics employed in Vieques and Okinawa informed what they did. Activists in Puerto Rico described how they learned a lot about how to do direct action on an island from the examples of protests in Okinawa and Kaho'olawe (Hawai'i). Activists on Guåhan reported that since the military expansion there was related to realignment in Okinawa, linkages with activists in Okinawa were especially politically valuable. Many activists in Okinawa also reported that they were inspired by the political activities of antimilitary activists in Hawai'i and that their campaigns for language revitalization and political independence from Japan are inspired by Hawaiian examples.

As did the activist from Vieques, people working in social movements in other sites emphasized that the value of transnational solidarity was not limited to promoting their struggle or sharing tactics. The emotional effects were also critical. As an activist from Hawai'i stated, "We learned from Vieques that you've got to do the mundane, the methodical—build your capacity, hold head above water, to be ready for the catalyst. Working when the tide is low versus when [there's] opportunity. [We learned from] how they utilized that moment. Brought together new local constituencies—the *energy* from direct action. People learned skills, *but also spiritually overcame a hesitancy. They overcame fear and the subservient relationship to power*. [We] saw that and could [also] see what Kaho'olawe meant for Hawai'i [in the past]—how can we get that *dynamic* again?" (personal communication 2014; emphasis added).

Conclusion

Translocal social movements have become increasingly important actors who can affect local, regional, and global political geographies. This is certainly true of antimilitarization social movements that have had a major influence on the spatial arrangement of military bases and training ranges around the world (S. Davis 2015; Lutz 2009; Vine 2019). However, it is also true of many other kinds of global social movements that focus on human rights, economic justice, and environmental causes (Brown and Yaffe 2014; Davies 2012; Featherstone 2012; Koopman 2011; Loyd 2012). It is therefore critical to consider the geographies of these movements and to better understand how they arise and how they cohere across space. In the case of the antimilitarization activism examined here, it is clear that transnational interconnections are a vital aspect of social movement activities, and that activists see international solidarity as a crucial ingredient that has contributed to political victories. In particular, activists reported that in-person visits by people from communities with similarly militarized circumstances helped produce translocal activist assemblages that bridged the vast distances between communities as far apart as Gangjeong on Jeju Island and Vieques, Puerto Rico.

Activists articulated that these visits and interconnections were important for sharing tactics, resources, and emotional support, but that they were also important for changing activist understandings of the context of their own local experiences with militarization. Visits and the associated sharing of experiences helped produce a sense of shared oppression that not only enabled people on distant islands to cohere into a transnational movement but also encouraged activists to see their local struggles as enmeshed in a larger context that called for translocal action. While one outcome of this was an emboldened activism stemming from a view that individual activists are not alone in the struggle, another was that their travel experiences also caused activists to reframe the scale of the problems they perceived in their communities. As evidenced by the responses of many of the people interviewed for this project, activists increasingly recognize the larger regional and global arrangements of the militarization that they oppose, and that solutions for peace could benefit from transnational action as well. In this way, these groups are drawing from—and adding new insights to—perspectives on the geographies of how peace is created and nurtured (Megoran, McConnell, and Williams 2016).

Another key point is that many activists in these social movements reported that this new "critical consciousness" of shared oppression—and the solidarity that springs from it—was effectively cultivated by the emotional experiences that occurred during visits as well as through the placing of activist bodies in common visceral states. In other words, effective translocal social movements are built not just from ideas but also from embodied discursive-material interactions. Activities such as dancing, rituals involving bodily movement, direct action occupations, and sharing food were reported as integral parts of developing solidarity. In this sense, critical consciousness was achieved through the dissemination or discussion of ideas as well as through more experiential and visceral forms of learning. Solidarity, then, is not necessarily something that precedes this visceral relating. It is a two-way relationship that emerges through performance rather than something that follows from preexisting similarities in political ideology. Put another way, what these activists report is that successful social movement organizing is not just about making an intellectual argument and spreading the word but rather about developing translocal performances that cultivate care and powerful emotional experiences. It is not so much that people care about others in these faraway places because they care about the injustices, as much as it is the other way around. As one activist from Hawai'i succinctly put it, "The relationships that are built are important—if you care about the people, you care about the grievances" (personal communication, 2014; emphasis added).

CHAPTER 5

Learning from the Contemporary Pacific

Assemblages, Ethics, and Strategies for Social Change

What does this book's review of politics, sovereignty, and social movements do for researchers, activists, and citizens that live within the Pacific region and outside it? The previous chapters demonstrate that these islands, and the waters that surround them, are dynamic environmental and political landscapes. How people in this region engage with that dynamism—and address the long-standing problems of colonialism, militarization, dispossession, and environmental degradation—can both inform and inspire political thought and action regardless of where on the earth we find ourselves. This is not to say that political actors on islands in the Pacific have figured it all out, or that they have been particularly successful in decolonization. It is also not to say that their tactics have been more exceptional than those deployed in other regions. Still, when one looks at how the different social movements on these islands operate locally and across space, it becomes quite clear that people in this region are developing radically innovative political theories and practices. People who are interested in affecting social change in their own communities can benefit from an examination of what these individuals and groups are doing.

In particular, an analysis of the actions and philosophies of these movements shows the political promise of new approaches to political change and social justice. While the previous chapters dove into the details of these approaches—and the larger political, theoretical, and cultural contexts in which they have developed—in this chapter my goal is to summarize some of the main points of that analysis to inform the creation of *actionable* political tactics. While I do discuss some of the implications of these Pacific examples for political theory and geographic understandings of the region, my main focus in this chapter is thinking through how the political thought and activism in these islands can inform and inspire struggles around the world for decolonization, social justice, equality, self-determination, and environmental protection. In this chapter, then, I purposely move out of the intellectual terrain of analysis and into a discussion of the value of the preceding analysis for political advocacy. This means this chapter is more speculative and future-oriented while also being less focused specifically on the Asia-Pacific region than the others. I believe, however, there is value for people who live outside the region to think a bit about how sovereignty functions in the Pacific (and to think about how Pacific social movements have operated), because the examples here can make clear both how sovereignty works in other places as well as how social movements can be more effective. In short, the situations I have been discussing throughout the book can, I believe, inform and inspire people working for social change around the world. To make this case, I first list the main points that I have gleaned from studying Pacific politics and social movements. I then go on to examine each of these points in turn and discuss how they can inspire future directions in political thought and praxis inside the region and out.

1. We need to stop framing struggles according to the binary of resistance and domination and think more about struggles as competitions between various would-be systems of governance. If sovereignty can best be thought of as an assemblage that arises through human and environmental relations rather than something that merely stands above them and organizes them, then creating new modes of governance comes from producing new relations. Rather than seeing decolonizing struggles as resisting state power, we should see struggles as being about the territorialization of different apparatuses seeking to govern according to different sets of ethics or regulative principles.
2. There is a popular set of globally circulating ethics that demands a form of governance based on the principles of protecting and nurturing all bodies as well as the associated healthy relationships between bodies and their broader physical and social environments. This set of ethics, or regulative principles, animates many social movement struggles, and it rejects the common state practices of governing through sacrifice and exclusion.
3. The territorialization of more ethical apparatuses of power can best be achieved not through elections, petitions, or protest but through the occupation of locales (the islands).
4. Governing apparatuses, whether they are states or not, are situated in larger assemblages of ethics, environmental processes, cultural norms, and material practices that facilitate or limit their operation (the ocean). These can be intentionally influenced or changed.

1. Forget Resistance: Moving from Opposition to Production

One of the key points that I believe comes out of an analysis of Pacific social movements is that resistance as an organizing principle of political thought, rhetoric, and action is deeply problematic. As seductive as calls for resistance may be in various political situations, I argue that they can also be dead ends that limit our ability to imagine and implement alternative futures. To be blunt, for analytical accuracy, and for developing more effective political practice, we need to transcend resistance as an organizing paradigm for political thought and action. For many people, particularly those who suffer from crushing oppression, resistance has been a valuable concept deployed to enable survival in the face of exploitive and violent processes of colonialism, militarization, occupation, imprisonment, and capitalist social relations. Resistance by itself, however, is only half a strategy.

I began this book with a comparison of two different calls for sovereignty in 2017: one by activists on Guåhan during the episode of escalating war rhetoric between North Korea and the United States, the other by white nationalists in Charlottesville, Virginia. Juxtaposing these two calls for sovereignty brings to light a number of ways in which thinking of them through the lens of resistance is analytically inadequate. On the surface we could see some similarities in these two struggles in terms of what they are resisting. Both are, after all, efforts to protect an imagined community by fighting against what is viewed as foreign influence over social processes (Anderson 1991). Yes, both groups may be resisting that which they view as foreign, but one of the valuable aspects of thinking about sovereignty as an assemblage is that since an assemblage is always something in process that creates and produces governance—something that is constructed and that creates material effects—it forces us to consider not what a political movement is *against* but what it aims to *produce*. While both groups called for sovereignty, the calls clearly imagined quite different forms of resultant governance. One sought to block the power of the U.S. state to continue its colonial control over an Indigenous people who have been denied full political rights within any kind of formal political apparatus for many centuries. The other promoted circumscribing a national space from international processes of capital, migration, and cultural influences in the name of reviving (what is imagined to be) the declining dominance of a racially defined settler colonist people.

If both of these groups get the increased sovereignty they ask for, what are the regulative principles that animate and guide a resultant apparatus of power? The most glaring ethical difference, of course, is the false equivalence white nationalists make between the social conditions of people who have been—and still are—colonized, dispossessed, and denied political self-determination through formal and informal processes of discrimination and their own perceived diminished dominance within the systems of wealth accumulation, political representation, and cultural production in which they continue to participate. Beyond that, what kinds of governance would these groups produce if they could? What might the resultant day-to-day life look like within their place (the island)? Also, how would the governing apparatus act in relation to other people and places? What kind of larger milieu (the ocean) might it aim to construct?

The presidency of Donald Trump in the United States certainly provides a glimpse of what kind of governance white nationalists are attempting to construct. It also shows how white nationalists in the United States have made the move from calls for resistance (against globalists, multiculturalism, the welfare state, etc.) to attempts to produce their desired place and milieu (island and ocean). Guided by regulative principles such as the valorization of evangelical Christian traditions, a strong belief in American exceptionalism, and a position that the United States should not have more immigrants or refugees in its national space, Trump has attempted to produce an apparatus of governance that fulfills these values. Though he is receiving opposition from both within and outside the U.S. state apparatus, he has been trying to reconstruct the national space according to these values through a variety of exclusionary and discriminatory processes: banning people from Muslim countries from being able to enter the United States, proposing to build a southern border wall, separating children from migrant parents and imprisoning both, and attempting to slash both government social spending and tax rates on the wealthy.

Trump has also been trying to engineer the larger world milieu by advocating an incredibly nationalist and atomized view of foreign relations and trade that may be an example of the territorial trap par excellence (Agnew 2017; Khal and Brands 2017). It appears that Trump not only believes in America First but expects other heads of state to be thinking only of their own formal sovereign territories as well. This is exemplified by what he said in 2017 in relation to Chinese premier Xi Jinping: "I like him a lot. I call him a friend. He considers me a friend. With that being said, he represents China, I represent the United States" (Yu-Lin 2017). The global political milieu (ocean) imagined by Trump, his right-wing political allies, and his white nationalist antiglobalist followers is one where international politics is a realm of national competition in which the only actors are states, and the strong states (assumed to be the United States) push around and get their way against the weak ones (assumed to be everyone else). Metasovereignty here is imagined to be an (overblown) ability of U.S. military might to check the ambitions of other states in a chaotic free-for-all world order.

What is critical here is that through this belief they also reproduce the milieu that they believe already exists, and that they also assume should exist and be perpetuated. It is a perspective that revels in nationalist exclusion, international competition, and conflict. One of the consequences of this view of international power politics is that, for better or for worse, it throws in the back seat (if not totally out the window) ideals that have been the guiding regulative principles of the global order of cultural, economic, and political integration since World War II, such as universal human rights and neoliberal globalization (Dillon and Reid 2009). Furthermore, it is not just Trumpians and nationalists in Europe and the United Kingdom who advocate for a political world that is a patchwork of very separate mutually exclusive sovereign countries. The Chinese government has also advocated a world order in which formal sovereignty is paramount and everything that happens within a country's borders is the business of that state—and nobody else's. These ideals were laid out in the Panchsheel Treaty that China signed with India in 1954 and include a frequently reiterated "Five Principles of Peaceful Coexistence": mutual respect for sovereignty and territorial integrity, mutual nonaggression, noninterference in each other's internal affairs, equality and mutual benefit, and peaceful coexistence (Nathan and Ross 1997). While some aspects of this are of course appealing to smaller countries (such as island states in the Pacific) who appreciate the way Beijing considers them to be, at least rhetorically and ceremonially, on equal footing with any other state, it is also a mindset that eschews any larger vision for global solidarity or for the granting of political rights to Indigenous or stateless peoples.

It is critical to consider just how this rise of nationalist mindsets—especially as deployed in Trump's attempts to fashion a more divided international milieu—affects many of the militarized and colonized places discussed throughout this book (such as Guåhan, Okinawa, Hawai'i, South Korea, and Micronesia). While in theory this nationalist perspective could lead to a greater respect for the sovereignty of all countries great and small, in practice it creates a justification for the continued colonization and domination of island states because the militarization of international relations is believed to be not only necessary but desirable. Colonialism put in service of nationalistic and security goals therefore becomes more necessary as these "small" or "weak" places become assets or leverage in the political battles between the larger states that "matter" rather than places that deserve the same kind of exclusive formal sovereignty with which more powerful countries are imagined to be naturally endowed. In short, even though there may be a switch in the global political milieu from neoliberal dreams of global integration to a more fractured world of nationalist rivalries, the logics of military colonialism may remain the same. While Trump's view that countries as independent "billiard balls" of sovereignty may appear to give some hope that smaller jurisdictions could be granted more autonomy, the fact that U.S. occupation and militarization in these island locales enhances the power of the U.S. state makes it unlikely that decolonization efforts will emanate from the American government any time soon. This is something that decolonization advocates will now have to respond to and confront.

While it is easy to see past Trumpian and white nationalist calls for resistance to globalists in order to focus on the kinds of governance they are seeking to produce (especially since they are controlling large portions of the U.S. state apparatus), it may not be as obvious that sovereignty-seeking decolonization groups in the Pacific, such as those in Guåhan, Okinawa, Hawai'i, and other sites examined in this book are also seeking to produce governance as well. As the preceding chapters detail, we can also analyze the actions of nonstate individuals and social movements as not just protesting or resisting colonialism and militarization. Instead, they also attempt to construct countergovernance in place and across space. One of the benefits of looking at sovereignty through the lens of assemblage theory is that it undercuts dualistic conceptualizations of power such as domination versus resistance or the "power-to" do something versus "power-over" others to make them do things (Holloway 2002). Instead, it forces us to view power and governance as *that which happens*: as actions performed, connections made, places transformed, and rules of the game that are created and enforced. In this view there are no types of power per se, only relations of power and actions that vie with each other to achieve different aims. From this perspective terms such as *resistance* and *freedom* say very little because they do not describe what it is that actually happens or what people would like to happen. Power, if thought about relationally, is not something one can be free of, and it can never be simply resisted or destroyed—it can only be countered by the production of other actual actions and practices.

The disadvantage of this perspective is that it undermines the idea that there are different forms of power, some of which are more moral than others (resistance being preferable to domination, power-to better than power-over).

However, this assemblage perspective has many advantages for both political analysis and activist praxis. For one, it prompts a more nuanced analysis of the terrain on which current social interactions and political struggles take place. The struggles of social movements are attempts not just to resist or protest but also to occupy and produce countergovernance in place (the island) and create new larger milieus (the ocean). In terms of serving as a theoretical template for future political struggles, there are also advantages to thinking of struggles as attempts to produce systems of countergovernance as opposed to just resisting or protesting what is. Thinking of sovereignty as assemblage forces us to imagine not just what we do not want but to imagine what we *do* want and how we ought to go about constructing systems of governance that can make our political desires real.

2. New Ethics of Governance: From the Health (and Wealth) of Nations to the Health of Relational Bodies

If we accept that there are no different types of power, only different kinds of relations that contend with each other to be made real and territorialize in place, we need to take a close look at the different ethics that animate competing apparatuses of power. A quote from Michel Foucault given in chapter 1 is worth reiterating here: "There is no power that is exercised without a series of aims and objectives" (1978, 95). I briefly discussed what those aims and objectives are for nationalists and powerful states, but what are the values—the regulative principles—that underpin attempts for countergovernance by social movements contesting colonialism and militarization in East Asia and the Pacific? Are these principles place-specific, or is there a larger pattern of common ethics that can be discerned by examining these multiple sites of activism as well as the activists that circulate among them?

I argue that there is a relatively coherent set of principles that are shared by these different social movement struggles that do more than resist the colonial, militarist, xenophobic, and nationalist impulses that are increasingly animating state apparatuses. Examining any one particular anticolonial or antimilitarization struggle in the region—such as in Okinawa, Guåhan, or Hawai'i—may give the impression that these struggles are David-versus-Goliath contests and that each is quite specific to a given context. If, however, we examine these struggles together (as I have tried to do in this book), something quite different presents itself. Looking at these social movements in tandem reveals not only how linkages exist between resistant struggles but also how these movements share widely circulating ethics of how governance ought to be produced and practiced. Like the movements themselves, these ethics arise in a way that is best considered as translocal in that they are neither essentially local values that spread outward nor global ethics that land in particular locales. Instead, these values are produced through embodied and emplaced experiences that mesh with more widely circulating discourses and ethics. They are hybrids of theory and experience that shift as they travel. They are also produced, as shown in chapter 4, through the visceral interactions of people as they move, meet new people, and experience new things. In short, the regulative principles that animate activist visions of countergovernance are, like the movements themselves, assemblages.

I want to sketch out the contours of the common ethics that are produced through these social movements because I believe the regulative principles themselves are a real political force. These principles serve to direct existing struggles, form one of the bases of solidarity between struggles, and are ideational kernels around which activism swarms. I also believe that if the common principles in these movements are more explicitly articulated, and promoted more widely, they can animate campaigns for more decolonial, inclusive, and just countergovernances inside the region and out.

I want to suggest that a central regulative principle across anticolonial and antimilitarization social movements is valuing the health of bodies. While I introduced this idea in the context of protests in Okinawa in chapter 1, I want to dig into it a bit more here now that I have discussed and analyzed other processes and contexts across the region. Valuing the health of bodies may seem to be a somewhat mundane and uncontroversial basis for both protest and governance. After all, few political actors go around clamoring for people to be *un*healthy. If, however, we examine the demands of groups such as these antimilitarization social movements that insist that we take seriously health promotion for all bodies, we quickly find that this position is quite a radical challenge to many traditional forms of governance. By expanding the notion that all bodies matter—not just American, Chinese, or some other particular nationality, but also those in Okinawa, Guåhan, Hawai'i, Yap, and elsewhere—it becomes hard to justify forced sacrifice for the good of others' national security or economic prosperity. This insistence that all bodies matter, and that their health is the touchstone to which good governance is judged, actually challenges modes of governance that valorize militarization, colonialism, nationalism, and capitalism.

Of course, the idea that governance ought to be arranged for the betterment of all bodies is not a new phenomenon. While there have long been nationalist and tribal ideologies that explicitly articulate that rights and protections ought to be extended only to members of some in-group of chosen people, there is also a long history of people making more universal claims that all of humanity is the in-group, and that all bodies are worthy of respect, protection, and nurturing. This idea is, for instance, a key facet of many popular religious texts that date back millennia. It also underpins the rhetorical claims of liberalism and principles of universal human rights. And it is a central rhetorical claim of contemporary state-led political and economic policies that insist that technology, free markets, militarized security, and progress are deployed for the betterment of all. In fact, the ethic of universal inclusion and human rights has become so central to political thought that even contemporary nationalist and exclusionary regimes must frequently at least give lip service to these ideals and disavow claims to racism—even as the material effects of their policies are designed to be disproportionately detrimental to outsiders.

As both Michel Foucault (2007) and Giorgio Agamben (2005) point out in different ways, modern statecraft has to some degree become an exercise in the way these two impulses—universal inclusion and nationalist exclusion—have hybridized and entwined rather than one overcoming the other. These theorists have discussed at length just how pervasively states and other apparatuses (even modern ones claiming liberal universalist values) sort bodies into categories of those that matter and those that do not. Agamben's (2005) work in *Homo Sacer* highlights how apparatuses of governance produce sacrificial bodies that are cast out of the body politic to the point that legal protections are voided and the bodies can be killed or "let die." His work emphasizes the way some bodies are protected through the exclusion of other less privileged bodies from the body politic. Foucault (2007), in contrast, emphasizes that the extreme marginalization of some bodies, even to the point of death, occurs not so much through a casting out from the body politic as from their inclusion within a larger population in which tolerable levels of suffering and death are calculable, expected, and even desirable.[1] While there are important differences between these two perspectives, they share in common a convincing argument that governing apparatuses, even liberal ones that rhetorically claim inclusivity and universality, sacrifice the health and well-being of all sorts of bodies in actual practice—such as those of migrants, colonized people, or people living adjacent to military bases.

What makes these contemporary social movements in Asia and the Pacific particularly noteworthy is not that they make rhetorical claims that all bodies should be protected and nurtured, but that they insist that governance should be actually practiced in such a way that the material effects match these ideals. Taking the precepts of liberalism literally, activists therefore call for the protection of the sovereignty of bodies rather than the sovereignty of states (Hayes-Conroy 2018). These social movements in Asia and the Pacific are demanding that people in proximity to military bases actually be protected the way (supposedly) liberal states say they ought to be protected. They contest the logics of (supposedly liberal) statecraft that makes rhetorical claims to inclusion, protection, and freedom while delivering material practices of environmental damage, economic profit extraction, and paternalistic colonialism. In order to effectively do so, however, they must not only point out that a hypocritical schism exists between rhetoric and reality but also actively confront and oppose the material practices produced by the state-centric logics of exclusion and forced sacrifice.

Because of the pervasiveness of practices of exclusion, marginalization, and sacrifice by most modern state apparatuses of governance—even those espousing liberal ideals of universal togetherness—the insistence by social movements that all bodies actually deserve health in practice is a radical position. If the health and well-being of people living next to military bases, abandoned nuclear testing sites, and live-fire training ranges were actually protected as well as bodies on Wall Street and the Pentagon, what kind of operations of everyday governance would have to cease immediately? What kinds of grand military strategies would no longer be viable? What kinds of profit-extracting enterprises would have to end? In short, the insistence that all bodies matter in practice threatens the foundations of most contemporary systems of economics and politics.

Valuing the health of all bodies and their milieu has become a key regulative principle that animates how social movements attempt to reorder governance. It also serves as a basis for the shared connections with social movements in other sites. Metaphorically speaking, this body-centric ethic guides action to change both the islands and the ocean as it serves as a catalyst that spurs local actions, links them together, and circulates into—and shapes—broader contexts. How, though, can this ethic get put into actual practice and dictate how governance in a place operates? If this ethic of protecting all bodies in practice is so antithetical to how actually existing states operate, how can it animate actual governance in places? Is it just a utopian ideal to be strived for and never attained? Or, to use the language of geographic theory, we could ask, can this ethic ever become territorialized?

3. Islands of Hope: The Promise of Counteroccupations and Territorializing Alternative Governance

When we talk about how to make these new ethics the basis of actual governing, we are talking about theories and tactics of creating social change. One of the more useful approaches for analyzing different social movement tactics is the work of Richard Day, which I introduced in chapter 1. Day's distinctions between old, new, and newest social movements are a useful shorthand for understanding the various approaches to activism and social change. Day categorizes activism into approaches in which old social movements aim to take state power by revolution or ballot box, new social movements petition existing states to govern differently, and newest social movements aim to occupy and decouple spaces from state control and govern them directly. As I have already discussed (particularly in chapter 1), many of the social movements I have been analyzing in this book use newest social movement tactics (as well as other tactics). It is therefore likely not surprising that in this section I want to expound a bit on just why forms of activism that include counteroccupation are effective approaches to making real an inclusive body-centric politics.

To discuss why counteroccupations are a promising strategy for social change, I first want to state that as both a researcher and an activist I am highly skeptical that existing state apparatuses are the best institutions for producing a system of governance that is animated by a body-centric ethic of universal inclusion. I understand that many scholars and activists look for possible avenues to challenge colonization via international law or the legal systems of settler states. For instance, there is work in Hawaiian studies, CHamoru studies, and among First Nations in North America that has endeavored to show that dispossession did not follow the legal frameworks of the colonizers themselves, and therefore, there are legal strategies (domestic and international) that can be pursued to rectify the situation (Bruyneel 2007; Goodyear-Kaʻōpua, Hussey, and Wright 2014; Hannah 2000; Louis 2017; Osorio 2014; Pasternak 2017; Rogers 1994; Simpson 2014). There is great value in these studies that demonstrate the hypocrisies of colonial domination and find new openings to fight against that domination. However, based on what I have seen in social movement organizing and action, I am interested in looking at a different suite of tactics that are less connected to legal strategies or existing state institutions.

Specifically, I am not interested in the ways in which the law can be used in struggles. Using the procedures of a legal system that was created in tandem with the establishment of systems of oppression and exploitation over a given people is unlikely to lead to the liberation of those same people. I am more interested in how regimes of law are established, undone, and replaced by others. After all, if there is one lesson that is quite clear from the colonial histories in Asia and the island Pacific, it is that colonizing systems of governance did not come to dominate these locales solely by working through existing Indigenous legal systems or by petitioning Indigenous governance structures to address the grievances of the colonizers. For the most part, Indigenous governance systems were swept away and replaced through occupation without much concern for the existing institutions or their proper procedures. Colonizers, for the most part, saw existing governance structures as illegitimate and they occupied spaces and put their own systems in place. I am suggesting that this kind of tactic, though in reverse, is what is needed today to undo these systems. The remedy to occupation is not resistance; it is counteroccupation. What is needed is a supplanting of the current system of governance by another one through counteroccupations that territorialize a system of governance with different ethics.

The usefulness of this strategy goes far beyond the context of formally colonized places. As most people are aware, systems of domination and exclusion saturate social life around the world. The above discussion of the racist, misogynist, and xenophobic proclivities of the government of the United States is but one example of this. Another example is the way that capitalist economics and property relations dominate one class over another around the globe. In other words, even though I am drawing from examples in heavily militarized and occupied islands, counteroccupation as a tactic can be quite useful in other places and political struggles in which people are interested in producing spaces of alternative governance.

As a tactic, counteroccupation is not specifically about the restoration of Indigenous rule; it is about changing the system of governance over a space. What that governance looks like depends on the objectives of the people performing the counteroccupation. This means, of course, that people can (and do) create counteroccupations and limit the effective sovereignty of a state in order to perform repressive, violent, and exploitive social relations that are even worse than states (Agnew 2017). Terrorist organizations, drug cartels, human traffickers, and hyperexclusive identity movements also territorialize certain systems of ethics through the occupation of space. There is no particular link between any specific set of ethics that underlies governance and the fact that occupying space is a fundamental aspect of how all governance works.

Because many of the groups that perform counteroccupations that defy state power have been violent and exclusionary, it may appear to some that the tactic itself is not the best way to promote values of inclusion, democracy, and equality. This position, however, has been countered in recent decades by groups such as the Zapatistas, First Nation occupations of traditional land, anti-WTO protests, urban squatter movements, and the occupations by antimilitarization groups in Okinawa, Puerto Rico, South Korea, and Hawai'i discussed in this book (Akaka et al. 2018; Estes 2019; McCaffrey 2002; McCormack and Norimatsu 2012; Pasternak 2017; Simpson 2014; Sixth Commission of the EZLN 2016; Wainwright and Kim 2008; Yeo 2010). In short, the activists discussed in this book lend further credence to the idea that occupations can be politically effective, nonviolent, and inclusive (in terms of both their local makeup and the way they reach out across space).

While these spaces of counteroccupation could be characterized as autonomous zones of either the temporary or permanent type (Bey 1991; Naylor 2017), I think the examples of activism I have discussed in this book demonstrate that *autonomous* is not necessarily the best term to use. Certainly, these spaces of counteroccupation are characterized by a reorientation of governance and different, more local, people are trying to govern. These counteroccupations could be represented as enclosures of a sort, but they are not wholly separated from their larger milieu in either conceptualization or practice. Instead, as the examples in this book attest, protest counteroccupations are highly connected spaces dependent on all sorts of movements into and out of them. Rather than being autonomous spaces per se, they are spaces where there are rearticulations of how political, economic, geosocial, and human-environment relations occur within the space and beyond it. As I have stressed, looking through the lens of assemblage theory shows that these spaces of countergovernance are about more than what may be traditionally called politics and are quite connected beyond the local in myriad ways. These spaces absorb and reproduce globally circulating ethics of social justice. Their members move in and out of the space. The spaces expand and contract, disappear, and resurface in various forms. In short, they are translocal entities that articulate in particular ways into local and global social fabrics rather than autonomous spaces somehow excised from these fabrics.

4. The Oceans: Making Waves of Change

In concluding this discussion about producing islands of counteroccupation, keep in mind that supplanting governance is, in the end, about people assembling in space and flouting existing systems of law and all of the accompanying agents of repression. As the activist quotes in chapter 4 attest, many people involved in these kinds of counteroccupations have had to overcome dangers and fears to do this kind of work. Also, as the examples in this book show, there are no guarantees of success. Sometimes counteroccupations achieve their goals, and sometimes they do not. They almost always, however, elicit a repressive and violent state response. This does not mean that the state gets its way in the end—it frequently does not. It does mean, however, that it is a high-stakes strategy fraught with more dangers than mere protests, petitions, and voting. The question activists frequently have to ask themselves is whether the potential rewards of counteroccupation are worth the risks associated with the state response.

There are ways, however, to both maximize the chances for the success of counteroccupations and minimize the intensity and efficacy of state repression. This is where it is important to consider the larger assemblages in which both counteroccupations and states are embedded—what I have been metaphorically referring to as the "ocean." One of the advantages of thinking about sovereignty as assemblage—whether exercised by the state or by nonstate actors—is that it forces us to think about the ways that neither states nor counteroccupations are autonomous. Neither states nor any other apparatus of governance can dominate all other social and natural processes and direct them according the whim of some decider. As discussed in reference to the work of Foucault and Noelani Goodyear-Ka'ōpua, there are numerous ways that environmental factors, economic processes, biological demands of living bodies, widespread cultural beliefs and customs, and so on impinge on political decisions and affect the kinds of rules of the game that a governing apparatus can effectively construct. These are, in a sense, the metasovereignties that structure political sovereignties.

These larger milieus—the oceans—not only affect the ability of governing apparatuses to act; they are also themselves capable of being altered. They are not infinitely malleable, of course, but human agency can shift them. For instance, the whole idea of the Anthropocene is built on the premise that what may have been thought of as natural processes are becoming rearranged (intentionally and not) by human action. In terms of social practices, political projects ranging from Marxism to neoliberalism are premised on the idea that economic processes, property relationships, and cultural beliefs about the value of communalism or individualism can all be altered. The larger milieu *is* malleable, and this fact is a vital part of enhancing the potential success of social movement counteroccupations that aim to emplace systems of governance that promote body-centric ethics of inclusion.

One of the primary ways that activists attempt to shape the larger milieu is through influencing public opinion on local, regional, and global levels. Influencing public opinion may sound like a fairly traditional and mundane approach, but it is more powerful than some may give it credit for. It is not just about getting good public relations for a group or reaching out to get direct support for a cause. It is also about challenging and attempting to change cultural values that support oppression. For instance, many of the activist groups in the Pacific have been attempting to make islands of counteroccupation, and they have been trying to demonstrate that the troubles they face are examples of their fundamental human rights being violated. But they are also trying to do something more. They are trying to change what values are acceptable. They are trying to challenge values of white supremacy, of militarism, of paternalism, and of patriarchy that legitimize continued colonialism, militarization, and enforced sacrifice.

We can look at this through the work of Richard Day and see that in addition to the aforementioned old, new, and newest social movement strategies that try to create change either through state capture, petitioning the state for redress of grievances, or producing counteroccupations, respectively, there is also a fourth kind of social movement tactic. Namely, there is the tactic of trying to shift the social milieu in which a state can make decisions. Like other social movement tactics, this one often occurs in tandem with other strategies. For instance, the civil rights movement in the United States or the later movement for LGBTQ+ rights might look somewhat like new social movements in Day's schema in that they petitioned existing states for an expansion of rights, but they also engaged in electoral politics, occupations, and, critically, they also engaged in trying to shape the larger milieu that would condition acceptable state policies.

Put simply, these movements changed cultural values around race and sexuality in the general public (though certainly with conservative resistance and retaliation) in such a way that discriminatory policies became less acceptable to larger and larger segments of the population. This then affected what states could do because there had been a change in what larger publics would support. In a sense, this fourth kind of social movement tactic is one of education, but in an expansive sense of the word. It is not accomplished merely through schools and colleges (though these are some important sites of this ideational struggle) but also through appeals to the public through diverse avenues such as popular music, film, and literature, as well as political and religious debates. To put it in somewhat crass terms, it is about marketing ideas and winning culture wars.

The struggles in the Asia-Pacific region are not just about occupying space and linking local struggles with other struggles. They are also about challenging and changing the globally circulating values that legitimize continued colonialism and militarization in the minds and bodies of locals and distant actors alike. They are not about creating subjects who see themselves as activists so much as changing what larger publics see as acceptable and legitimate forms of political practice. It is much more difficult for a state to flout the values of the majority of their population than to bend to them (at least in the long run, for a state with even nominal forms of democracy).

To put it more theoretically: to create and maintain social and environmental relationships guided by body-centric ethics of inclusion, social movements need to attempt to territorialize these values through islands of counteroccupation, as well as to legitimize these values by making larger publics see their values as desirable, realistic, and attainable ethics of governance. In other words, they need to work to envelop islands of counteroccupation in oceans of supportive waves and currents that nourish—rather than erode—these budding possibilities for governance.

There are, of course, many challenges facing social movements and individuals that are working to make another Pacific and another world possible. There is a need for formal decolonization and for supporting Indigenous rights. There is also a desperate need to construct more peaceful international relations, to produce more just structures of economic equality, and to create systems of governance that level social inequalities and relationships of domination rather than intensifying them. There is also a growing recognition that these concerns can be woven together and that it is possible to not just demand, but to produce arrangements of governance based on a respect for the health and well-being of all people and their enveloping environments. My hope is that the stories I have shared in this book provide a useful perspective on the state of politics in this rapidly changing region. More than that, however, I hope these stories inspire you to imagine more inclusive futures for your own community and motivate you to pursue effective tactics that can make those futures real.

NOTES

INTRODUCTION. VISIONS OF SOVEREIGNTY

1. D. Lakota, December 4, 2014, "American Flags Taken Down by Hawaiian Kingdom Advocates at UH," YouTube, https://www.youtube.com/watch?v=OyUZq6HDAKI.

2. I conducted more than two hundred interviews for this research over the past seventeen years. Based on promises of anonymity during the research process (and Institutional Review Board regulations), the real names of the respondents quoted in this book are not given.

3. In the case of Okinawa, not only was it absorbed by a larger state, Japan, but the political autonomy of Japan itself has been questioned by those that label it a "client state" (McCormack and Norimatsu 2012).

4. However, this is not to say that this is impossible; there are many maps that do just this. There have been maps that describe where the Islamic State held territory versus Syrian or Iraqi forces during its rise and fall, or maps that show which drug cartels control which areas of northern Mexico, or even maps of everyday spaces where people of different genders congregate.

5. As Donald Trump put it, "A country that cannot protect its borders will not last." "Exclusive—Trump: 'A Country That Cannot Protect Its Borders Will Not Last,'" Breitbart.com, July 11, 2014, http://www.breitbart.com/big-government/2014/07/11/must-get-tough-on-border/.

6. J. Niedenthal, "Bikini Atoll Dive Tourism Information," BikiniAtoll.com, 2017, last accessed October 21, 2019, https://www.bikiniatoll.com/divetour.html.

7. *Ontology* means the study of reality or what we think reality is and how it works. *Relational* refers to the idea that objects or other entities come into existence through their relating with other entities.

8. In keeping with indigenous perspectives that words in indigenous languages not be italicized as "foreign" (especially when used in reference to their own places and struggles), I do not italicize Hawaiian, CHamoru or Carolinian terms.

9. Of course, Marxist analyses have long appreciated that the political is not

autonomous at all, and that economic forces may in fact be primary considerations in understanding why state power is deployed in certain ways (i.e., in the service of capital).

CHAPTER 1. SOVEREIGNTY AS ASSEMBLAGE

1. Henoko Blue, Facebook, last accessed October 9, 2019, https://www.facebook.com/henokoblue/.

CHAPTER 2. OCEANS OF MILITARIZATION

1. The whole region colloquially known as Micronesia includes hundreds of islands within multiple official political jurisdictions (the Northern Mariana Islands, Guåhan, Palau, Nauru, Kiribati, the Republic of the Marshall Islands, and the Federated States of Micronesia).

2. See, for instance, Global Fishing Watch, "Fishing Watch Vessel Tracking Map," last accessed October 13, 2019, https://globalfishingwatch.org/map/.

3. Gendered language is intentional and appropriate in this case.

4. Even though it may be problematic according to traditional conceptualizations to call this imperial reaching into the region the exercise of sovereignty, since the power is so clearly being applied outside the formal territories that it is supposed to be ascribed, I argue—following my arguments in chapter 1—that this is actually more the rule to the exercise of state power than the exception. After all, even within the formal boundaries of countries, power is exercised all the time over populations that do not support the policies being enforced (Held 2013; Painter 2010).

5. Singapore does this, for example. The United States did extensive reclamation for its base on Johnston Atoll in the central Pacific. And, of course, the new U.S. Marine Corps base in Okinawa discussed in detail in chapter 1 is to be located on mostly reclaimed coral and sea grass habitat.

6. Certainly, an in-depth Foucauldian archeology of the terms A2/AD and *counterintervention*—from a critical geopolitics perspective that examined the threads of authority and influence that constructed the ideas—is a fascinating and important direction for continued research.

7. In CHamoru the first two letters are capitalized because "ch" is considered one consonant.

8. "Save Ritdian," Facebook, last accessed October 13, 2019, https://www.facebook.com/saveritidian/.

9. Shortly after this, however, the U.S. mainland was put in range when North Korea developed the Hwasong-15 missile.

CHAPTER 3. AGAINST SPHERES OF INFLUENCE

1. Palau also signed a COFA with the United States in 1994, but I will focus here on the RMI and FSM agreements.

2. UNICEF, "Migration Profile: Federated States of Micronesia," n.d., last accessed October 13, 2019, https://esa.un.org/miggmgprofiles/indicators/files/Micronesia.pdf. UNICEF; "Migration Profile: Republic of the Marshall Islands," n.d., last accessed October 13, 2019, https://esa.un.org/miggmgprofiles/indicators/files/MarshallIslands.pdf.

3. An additional $18 million is budgeted annually for the U.S. use of Kwajalein Atoll, but much of that money goes to compensate landowners.

4. See, for instance, the lengthy letter of response by the FSM ambassador to the United States, Akillino Susaia, in the GAO report (2018) decrying the cuts to compact funding.

5. P. Brant, *Chinese Aid in the Pacific Regional Snapshot*, Lowy Institute, 2015, last accessed October 13, 2019, https://chineseaidmap.lowyinstitute.org/.

6. See the full plan at "ETG's Plan in Yap," 2012, last accessed October 13, 2019, https://concernedyapcitizens.wordpress.com/etgs-plan-in-yap-july-2012/.

7. D. Cheng, *Countering Chinese Inroads into Micronesia*, 2016, last accessed October 13, 2019, https://www.heritage.org/asia/report/countering-chinese-inroads-micronesia. See also Australian concerns about a Chinese funded dock in Vanuatu as a security threat to Australia. Agence France-Presse, "Vanuatu Angrily Denies Reports It Plans to Host Chinese Military Base," *Japan Times*, April 10, 2018, last accessed October 13, 2019, https://www.japantimes.co.jp/news/2018/04/10/asia-pacific/australian-media-report-china-proposes-military-base-south-pacific/#.WyFqoFMvwWo.

8. J. Brown, *Germans in Micronesia*, exhibition at the Belau National Museum in Koror, Palau, viewed May 20, 2017.

CHAPTER 4. SHARING THE STRUGGLE

Much of the information for this chapter comes from field research conducted in the fall of 2014 in Gangjeong Village of Jeju, South Korea. Although this chapter is focused on the global scope and transnational connections of these activist networks, it also includes information from interviews I conducted between 2007 and 2017 with activists from other places, such as Guåhan, Hawai'i, Puerto Rico, and Okinawa—some in person and some done as follow-up interviews by phone and Skype. The primary research methods used consisted of semistructured interviews and participant observation. More than one hundred and twenty interviews were conducted over the span of the research. Based on promises for anonymity during the research process, I do not divulge the names of respondents.

1. See *Save Jeju Now*, n.d., last accessed October 13, 2019, http://savejejunow.org.

CHAPTER 5. LEARNING FROM THE CONTEMPORARY PACIFIC

1. See also Davis and Hayes-Conroy (2018) for how these contrasting logics operate in the radioactive areas near the Fukushima Daiichi Nuclear Power Plant in Japan.

REFERENCES

Ackerman, P., and C. Kruegler. 1994. *Strategic Nonviolent Conflict: The Dynamics of People Power in the Twentieth Century*. Santa Barbara: Praeger.

Agamben, G. 2005. *State of Exception*. Chicago: University of Chicago Press.

Agnew, J. 1997. *Political Geography*. Malden, MA: John Wiley & Sons.

———. 2005. "Sovereignty Regimes: Territoriality and State Authority in Contemporary World Politics." *Annals of the Association of American Geographers* 95:437–61.

———. 2009. *Globalization and Sovereignty*. New York: Rowman & Littlefield.

———. 2017. *Globalization and Sovereignty: Beyond the Territorial Trap*. 2nd ed. New York: Rowman & Littlefield.

Aguon, J. 2005. *Just Left of the Setting Sun*. Tokyo: Blue Ocean Press.

———. 2006. *The Fire This Time: Essays on Life under U.S. Occupation*. Tokyo: Ocean Press.

———. 2008. *What We Bury at Night: Disposable Humanity*. Tokyo: Blue Ocean Press.

———. 2017. "When you Live in a Colony, You Are Easy Meat: Guam in the Crosshairs of Warmongering." *In These Times*, August 21, 2017. http://inthesetimes.com/article/20439/Guam-United-States-North-Korea-Donald-Trump-Colonization.

Akaka, M., M. Kahaulelio, T. Kekoʻolani-Raymond, L. Ritte, and N. Goodyear-Kaʻōpua. 2018. *Nā Wāhine Koa: Hawaiian Women for Sovereignty and Demilitarization*. Honoulu: University of Hawaii Press.

Alexander, R. 2016. "Living with the Fence: Militarization and Military Spaces on Guåhan/Guam." *Gender, Place and Culture* 23 (6): 869–82.

Allen, J. 2011. "Topological Twists: Power's Shifting Geographies." *Dialogues in Human Geography* 1:283–98.

———. 2016. *Topologies of Power: Beyond Territory and Networks*. New York: Routledge.

Alvesson, M., and K. Sköldberg. 2017. *Reflexive Methodology: New Vistas for Qualitative Research*. New York: Sage.

Anderson, B. 1991. *Imagined Communities*. New York: Verso.

Anderson, B., and P. Harrison. 2010. *Taking-Place: Non-Representational Theories and Geography*. Aldershot, UK: Ashgate.

Anderson, B., M. Keanes, C. McFarlane, and D. Swanton. 2012. "On Assemblages and Geography." *Dialogues in Human Geography* 2:171–89.

Arrighi, G. 2005. "Hegemony Unravelling II." *New Left Review* 32:23–80.

Baird, I. 2015. "Translocal Assemblages and the Circulation of the Concept of 'Indigenous Peoples' in Laos." *Political Geography* 46:54–64.

Baldacchino, G. 2016. "Diaoyu Dao, Diaoyutai or Senkaku? Creative Solutions to a Festering Dispute in the East China Sea from an 'Island Studies' Perspective." *Asia Pacific Viewpoint* 57:16–26.

Baldacchino, G., and D. Milne. 2009. *The Case for Non-sovereignty*. New York: Routledge.

Bartelson, J. 1995. *A Genealogy of Sovereignty*. Cambridge: Cambridge University Press.

———. 2006. "The Concept of Sovereignty Revisited." *European Journal of International Law* 17 (2): 463–74.

Bélanger, P., and A. Arroyo. 2012. "Logistics Islands: The Global Supply Archipelago and the Topologies of Defense." *Prism: A Journal of the Center for Complex Operations* 3 (4): 55–75.

———. 2016. *Ecologies of Power: Countermapping the Logistical Landscapes and Military Geographies of the US Department of Defense* Cambridge: MIT Press.

Benitez-Rojo, A. 1997. *The Repeating Island: The Caribbean and the Postmodern Perspective*. Durham: Duke University Press.

Bevacqua, M. 2010. "The Exceptional Life and Death of a Chamorro Soldier: Tracing the Militarization of Desire in Guam, USA." In *Militarized currents: Towards a Decolonized Future in Asia and the Pacific*, edited by S. Shigematsu and K. Camacho, 33–62. Minneapolis: University of Minnesota Press.

———. 2017. "Guam through the Eyes of a Child: The N. Korean Missile Conflict." *Guam Guide*, August 14, 2017. http://theguamguide.com/guam-through-the-eyes-of-a-child-the-us-north-korean-missile-conflict-in-perspective/.

Bey, H. 1991. *TAZ: The Temporary Autonomous Zone, Ontological Anarchy, Poetic Terrorism*. New York: Autonomedia.

Bickerstaff, K., and P. Simmons. 2009. "Absencing/Presencing Risk: Rethinking Proximity and the Experience of Living with Major Technological Hazards." *Geoforum* 40:864–72.

Blanchard, J., and C. Flint. 2017. "The Geopolitics of China's Maritime Silk Road Initiative." *Geopolitics* 22 (2): 223–45.

Bohane, B. 2016. "US Stresses 'Unique' Pacific Islands Links, as China's Regional Footprint Grows." *ABC News*, June 2, 2016. http://www.abc.net.au/news/2016-06-01/us-stresses-unique-pacific-islands-links/7466368.

———. 2018. "The United States Is Losing the Pacific." *Asia Pacific Bulleting*, March 26, 2018. https://www.eastwestcenter.org/system/tdf/private/apb414_1.pdf?file=1&type=node&id=36582.

Bonnemaison, J. 1994. *The Tree and the Canoe: History and Ethnogeography of Tanna*. Honolulu: University of Hawaii Press.

———. 2005. *Culture and Space: Conceiving a New Geography*. London: IB Tauris.

Bookchin, M. 1998. *The Third Revolution: Popular Movements in the Revolutionary Era.* London: A&C Black.

Booth, K. 1997. *Critical Security Studies.* Oxford: Blackwell.

Borja, J. 2017. "Guam Receives $1.5M More in Compact-Impact Funding." *Pacific Daily News*, August 2, 2017. https://www.guampdn.com/story/news/2017/08/02/guam-receives-1-5-m-more-compact-impact-funding/531565001/.

Bosco, F. 2007. "Emotions That Build Networks: Geographies of Human Rights Movements in Argentina and Beyond." *Tijdschrift voor economische en sociale geografie* 98:545–63.

Brant, P., P. Jiawei, and D. Cave. 2016. "Chinese Aid in the Pacific." Lowy Institute. Accessed June 17, 2019. https://www.lowyinstitute.org/chinese-aid-map/.

Braun, B., and J. McCarthy. 2005. "Hurricane Katrina and Abandoned Being." *Environment and Planning D: Society and Space* 23 (6): 802–9.

Broudy, D., P. Simpson, and M. Arakaki. 2013. *Under Occupation: Resistance and Struggle in a Militarized Asia-Pacific.* Newcastle-upon-Tyne: Cambridge Scholars Publishing.

Brown, G., and H. Yaffe. 2014. "Practices of Solidarity: Opposing Apartheid in the Centre of London. *Antipode* 46:34–52.

Brown, M., and L. Staeheli L. 2003. "'Are We There Yet?' Feminist Political Geographies." *Gender, Place and Culture* 10:247–55.

Brown, W. 2010. *Walled States, Waning Sovereignty.* Cambridge: MIT Press.

Bruyneel, K. 2007. *The Third Space of Sovereignty: The Postcolonial Politics of US–Indigenous Relations.* Minneapolis: University of Minnesota Press.

Butler, J. 2010. *Frames of War: When Is Life Grievable?* New York: Verso.

Campbell, D., and M. Schoolman. 2008. *The New Pluralism: William Connolly and the Contemporary Global Condition.* Durham: Duke University Press.

Campling, L., and A. Colás. 2018. "Capitalism and the Sea: Sovereignty, Territory and Appropriation in the Global Ocean." *Environment and Planning D: Society and Space* 36 (4): 776–94.

Caroll, C. 2017. "Protecting the South China Sea" *Foreign Policy*, June 9, 2017. https://www.foreignaffairs.com/articles/china/2017-06-09/protecting-south-china-sea.

Chan, J. 2008. *Another Japan Is Possible: New Social Movements and Global Citizenship Education.* Palo Alto: Stanford University Press.

Chandler, D., and J. Pugh. 2018. "Islands of Relationality and Resilience: The Shifting Stakes of the Anthropocene." *Area* 1–8.

Chua, C., M. Danyluk, D. Cowen, and L. Khalili. 2018. "Introduction: Turbulent circulation: Building a critical Engagement with Logistics." *Environment and Planning D: Society and Space* 36 (4): 617–29.

Clement, V. 2019. "Beyond the Sham of Emancipatory Enlightenment: Rethinking the Relationship of Indigenous Epistemologies, Knowledges, and Geography through Decolonizing Paths." *Progress in Human Geography* 43 (2): 276–94.

Clough, N. 2012. "Emotion at the Center of Radical Politics: On the Affective Structures of Rebellion and Control." *Antipode* 44:1667–86.

Clough, N., and R. Blumberg. 2012. "Toward Anarchist and Autonomist Marxist Geographies." *ACME: An International E-Journal for Critical Geographies* 11:335–51.

Collier, S. 2009. "Topologies of Power Foucault's Analysis of Political Government beyond 'Governmentality.'" *Theory, Culture & Society* 26 (6): 78–108.

Collier, S., and A. Lakoff. 2005. "On Regimes of Living." In *Global Assemblages: Technology Politics and Ethics as Anthropological Problems*, edited by A. Ong and S. Collier, 22–39. Oxford: Blackwell.

———. 2009. "On Vital Systems Security." *International Affairs Working Paper 2009-01*. Accessed June 5, 2012. http://test.gpia.info/files/u16/Collier_and_Lakoff_2009-01.pdf.

Compact of Free Association Amendments Act of 2003. 2003. S. J. Res. 16. 108th Congress.

Connolly, W. 2017. *Facing the Planetary: Entangled Humanism and the Politics of Swarming*. Durham: Duke University Press.

Cowen, D. 2014. *The Deadly Life of Logistics: Mapping Violence in Global Trade*. Minneapolis: University of Minnesota Press.

Cresswell, T. 2015. *Place: An Introduction*. Malden, MA: John Wiley & Sons.

Cumbers, A. 2015. "Constructing a Global Commons in, against, and beyond the State." *Space and Polity* 19:62–75.

Cumbers, A., P. Routledge, and C. Nativel. 2008. "The Entangled Geographies of Global Justice Networks." *Progress in Human Geography* 32 (2): 183–201.

Dalby, S. 2014. "Rethinking Geopolitics: Climate Security in the Anthropocene." *Global Policy* 5 (1): 1–9.

Davies, A. 2012. "Assemblage and Social Movements: Tibet Support Groups and the Spatialities of Political Organization." *Transactions of the Institute of British Geographers* 37:273–86.

Davis, J. S. 2005a. "Representing Place: 'Deserted Isles' and the Reproduction of Bikini Atoll." *Annals of the Association of American Geographers* 95:607–25.

———. 2005b. "'Is It Really Safe? That's What We Want to Know': Science, Stories and Dangerous Places." *Professional Geographer* 57:213–21.

———. 2007. "Scales of Eden: Conservation and Pristine Devastation on Bikini Atoll." *Environment and Planning D: Society and Space* 25:213–35.

Davis, S. 2011. "The US Military Base Network and Contemporary Colonialism: Power Projection Resistance and the Quest for Operational Unilateralism." *Political Geography* 30:215–24.

———. 2015. *The Empires' Edge: Militarization, Resistance and Transcending Hegemony in the Pacific*. Athens: University of Georgia Press.

Davis, S., and J. Hayes-Conroy. 2018. "Invisible Radiation Reveals Who We Are as People: Environmental Complexity, Gendered Risk, and Biopolitics after the Fukushima Nuclear Disaster." *Social and Cultural Geography* 19 (6): 720–40.

Day, R. 2005. *Gramsci Is Dead: Anarchist Currents in the Newest Social Movements*. London: Pluto Press.

DeLanda, M. 2006. *A New Philosophy of Society: Assemblage Theory and Social Complexity*. London: A&C Black.

Deleuze, G. 1988. *Foucault.* Minneapolis: University of Minnesota Press.

———. 1992a. "Postscript on the Societies of Control." *October* 59:3–7.

———. 1992b. "What Is a Dispositif?" in *Michel Foucault: Philosopher*, edited by T. Armstrong, 159–68. New York: Harvester Wheatsheaf.

Deleuze, G., and F. Guattari. 1987. *A Thousand Plateaus: Capitalism and Schizophrenia.* Minneapolis: University of Minnesota Press.

DeLoughrey, E. 2007. *Routes and Roots: Navigating Caribbean and Pacific Island Literatures.* Honolulu: University of Hawaii Press.

———. 2017. "Submarine Futures of the Anthropocene." *Comparative Literature* 69 (1): 32–44.

Dewsbury, J. 2011. "The Deleuze-Guattarian Assemblage: Plastic Habits." *Area* 43:148–53.

Diaz, V. 2011. "Voyaging for Anti-Colonial Recovery: Austronesian Seafaring, Archipelagic Rethinking, and the Re-Mapping of Indigeneity." *Pacific Asia Inquiry* 2:21–32.

Dillon, M., and J. Reid. 2009. *The Liberal Way of War: Killing to Make Life Live.* New York: Routledge.

Dittmer, J. 2014. "Geopolitical Assemblages and Complexity." *Progress in Human Geography* 38:385–401.

Dowler, L. 2012. "Gender Militarization and Sovereignty." *Geography Compass* 6:490–99.

Dowler, L., and J. Sharp. 2001. "A Feminist Geopolitics?" *Space and Polity* 5:165–76.

Elden, S. 2009. *Terror and Territory: The Spatial Extent of Sovereignty.* Minneapolis: University of Minnesota Press.

Emel, J., M. Huber, and M. Makene. 2011. "Extracting Sovereignty: Capital, Territory, and Gold Mining in Tanzania." *Political Geography* 30 (2): 70–79.

Enloe, C. 1990. *Bananas Beaches and Bases: Making Feminist Sense of International Politics.* Berkeley: University of California Press.

———. 2000. *Maneuvers: The International Politics of Militarizing Women's Lives.* Berkeley: University of California Press.

———. 2007. *Globalization and Militarism: Feminists Make the Link.* New York: Rowman & Littlefield.

Erickson, A., and J. Wuthnow. 2016. "Barriers, Springboards and Benchmarks: China Conceptualizes the Pacific Island Chains." *China Quarterly* 225:1–22.

Estes, N. 2019. *Our History Is The Future: Standing Rock versus the Dakota Access Pipeline, and the Long Tradition of Indigenous Resistance.* New York: Verso.

Featherstone, D. 2011. "On Assemblage and Articulation." *Area* 43 (2): 139–42.

———. 2012. *Solidarity: Hidden Histories and Geographies of Internationalism.* London: Zed.

Fernandes, B. 2013. "Re-Peasantization, Resistance and Subordination: The Struggle for Land and Agrarian Reform in Brazil." *Agrarian South: Journal of Political Economy* 2 (3): 269–89.

Firth, S. 1987. *Nuclear Playground.* Honolulu: University of Hawaii Press.

Flint, C. 2016. *Introduction to Geopolitics.* New York: Routledge.

Fluri, J. 2012. "Capitalizing on Bare Life: Sovereignty Exception and Gender Politics." *Antipode* 44:31–50.

Fominaya, C. 2010. "Collective Identity in Social Movements: Central Concepts and Debates." *Sociology Compass* 4:393–404.

Foucault, M. 1977. "Nietzsche, Genealogy, History." In *Language, Counter-Memory, Practice: Selected Essays and Interviews*, edited by D. Bouchard, 139–64. Ithaca: Cornell University Press.

———. 1978. *The History of Sexuality*. Vol. 1, *An Introduction*. New York: Vintage.

———. 2007. *Security Territory Population: Lectures at the Collège de France, 1977–1978*. London: Palgrave Macmillan.

Frain, S. 2016. "Resisting Political Colonization and American Militarization in the Marianas Archipelago." *AlterNative: An International Journal of Indigenous Peoples* 12:298–315.

———. 2017. "Women's Resistance in the Marianas Archipelago: A US Colonial Homefront and Militarized Frontline." *Feminist Formations* 29:97–135.

Fregonese, S., and A. Ramadan. 2015. "Hotel Geopolitics: A Research Agenda." *Geopolitics* 20:793–813.

Fravel, M., and C. Twomey. 2015. "Projecting Strategy: The Myth of Chinese Counter-Intervention." *The Washington Quarterly* 37 (4): 171–87.

Freire, P. (1970) 2000. *Pedagogy of the Oppressed*. New York: Continuum Publishing.

GAO (United States Government Accountability Office). 2018. *Actions Needed to Prepare for the Transition of Micronesia and the Marshall Islands to Trust Fund Income: Report to the Chairman, Committee on Energy and Natural Resources, U.S. Senate*. Accessed June 19, 2019. https://www.gao.gov/assets/700/691840.pdf.

García-López, G. 2018. "The Multiple Layers of Environmental Injustice in Contexts of (Un) natural Disasters: The Case of Puerto Rico Post-Hurricane Maria." *Environmental Justice* 11 (3): 1–10.

Gelardi, C., and S. Perez. 2019. "This Isn't Your Island: Why Northern Mariana Islanders Are Facing Down the US Military." *Nation*, June 12, 2019.

Giddens, A. 1984. *The Constitution of Society*. Cambridge: Polity Press.

Gillan, K., and J. Pickerill, J. 2008. "Transnational Anti-War Activism: Solidarity, Diversity and the Internet in Australia, Britain and the United States after 9/11." *Australian Journal of Political Science* 43 (1): 59–78.

Gonzalez, V. 2013. *Securing Paradise: Tourism and Militarism in Hawaii and the Philippines*. Durham: Duke University Press.

Goodyear-Kaʻōpua, N. 2011. "Kuleana Lahui: Collective Responsibility for Hawaiian Nationhood in Activists' Praxis." *Affinities: A Journal of Radical Theory, Culture, and Action* 5 (1): 130–63.

———. 2014. "Introduction." In *A Nation Rising: Hawaiian Movements for Life, Land, and Sovereignty*, edited by N. Goodyear-Kaʻōpua, I. Hussey, and E. Wright, 1–35. Durham: Duke University Press.

Goodyear-Kaʻōpua, N., I. Hussey, and E. Wright. 2014. *A Nation Rising: Hawaiian Movements for Life, Land, and Sovereignty*. Durham: Duke University Press.

Gray, N. 2018. "Charted Waters? Tracking the Production of Conservation Territories on the High Seas." *International Social Science Journal* 68: 257–72.

Grove, K. 2014. "Agency, Affect, and the Immunological Politics of Disaster Resilience." *Environment and Planning D: Society and Space* 32:240–56.

Grydehøj, A., and Z. Ou. 2017. "Deterritorialization of Indigeneity: Indigenous Territory, Development Policy, and the Dan Fishing Community of Hainan (China)." *Political Geography* 61:77–87.

Gwon, G. 2013. "Remembering 4/3 and Resisting the Remilitarisation of Jeju: Building an International Peace Movement." In *Under Occupation: Resistance and Struggle in a Militarized Asia-Pacific,* edited by D. Broudy, P. Simpson, and M. Arakaki, 238–70. Newcastle-upon-Tyne: Cambridge Scholars Publishing.

Hagiwara, M., S. Yamada, W. Tanaka, and D. Ostrowski. 2015. "Litigation and Community Advocacy to Ensure Health Access for Micronesian Migrants in Hawai'i." *Journal of Health Care for the Poor and Underserved* 26 (2): 137–45.

Hammes, T. 2012. "Offshore Control: A Proposed Strategy for an Unlikely Conflict." *Strategic Forum* 278. Washington, DC: National Defense University Press.

Hanlon, D. 1998. *Remaking Micronesia: Discourses over Development in a Pacific Territory, 1944–1982.* Honolulu: University of Hawaii Press.

Hannah, M. 2000. *Governmentality and the Mastery of Territory in Nineteenth-Century America.* Cambridge: Cambridge University Press.

Hardt, M., and A. Negri. 2000. *Empire.* Cambridge: Harvard University Press.

———. 2004. *Multitude: War and Democracy in the Age of Empire.* New York: Penguin.

Harvey, D. 2003. *The New Imperialism.* Oxford: Oxford University Press.

———. 2007. *A Brief History of Neoliberalism.* Oxford: Oxford University Press.

———. 2015. "'Listen Anarchist!' A Personal Response to Simon Springer's 'Why a Radical Geography Must Be Anarchist.'" DavidHarvey.org. Accessed August 23, 2015. http://davidharvey.org/2015/06/listen-anarchist-by-david-harvey/.

Hau'ofa, E. 1994. "Our Sea of Islands." *The Contemporary Pacific* 6 (1): 147–61.

Havice, E. 2018. "Unsettled Sovereignty and the Sea: Mobilities and More-Than-Territorial Configurations of State Power." *Annals of the American Association of Geographers* 108 (5): 1280–97.

Hayes, P., L. Zarsky, and W. Bello. 1986. *American Lake: Nuclear Peril in the Pacific.* New York: Penguin Group USA.

Hayes-Conroy, A. 2018. "Somatic Sovereignty: Body as Territory in Colombia's Legión del Afecto." *Annals of the American Association of Geographers* 108 (5): 1298–312.

Hayes-Conroy, A., and D. Martin. 2010. "Mobilising Bodies: Visceral Identification in the Slow Food Movement." *Transactions of the Institute of British Geographers* 35:269–81.

Hayes-Conroy, A., and A. Montoya. 2017. "Peace Building with the Body: Resonance and Reflexivity in Colombia's Legion del Afecto." *Space and Polity* 21 (2): 144–57.

Hayes-Conroy, J. 2008. "Hope for Community? Anarchism Exclusion and the Non-Human Realm." *Political Geography* 27:29–34.

Hayes-Conroy, J., and A. Hayes-Conroy. 2013. "Veggies and Visceralities: A Political Ecology of Food and Feeling." *Emotion, Space and Society* 6:81–90.

Hayward, P. 2012. "Aquapelagos and Aquapelagic Assemblages." *Shima: The International Journal of Research into Island Cultures* 6 (1): 1–11.

Held, D. 2013. *Political Theory and the Modern State.* Malden, MA: John Wiley & Sons.

Hezel, F. 1978. "Looking Ahead to the End of Trusteeship, Trust Territory of the Pacific Islands." *Journal of Pacific History* 13 (4): 204–10.

———. 2003. *Strangers in Their Own Land: A Century of Colonial Rule in the Caroline and Marshall Islands.* Honolulu: University of Hawaii Press.

Ho, E. 2017. "The Geo-Social and Global Geographies of Power: Urban Aspirations of 'Worlding' African Students in China." *Geopolitics* 22 (1): 15–33.

Hofschneider, A. 2016. "The Fight to Save Pagan Island from US bombs." *Honolulu Civil Beat*, December 2016. http://www.civilbeat.org/2016/12/the-fight-to-save-pagan-island-from-us-bombs/.

Holloway, J. 2002. *Change the World without Taking Power*. London: Pluto Press.

Hörschelmann, K., and E. Reich. 2017. "Entangled (In) Securities: Sketching the Scope of Geosocial Approaches for Understanding Webs of (In) Security." *Geopolitics* 22:73–90.

Hui-Yi, K. 2016. "Re-contemplating the South China Sea Issue: Sailing with the Wind of the 21st-Century Maritime Silk Road." *Chinese Journal of Global Governance* 2 (1): 63–95.

Hyndman, J. 2004. "Mind the Gap: Bridging Feminist and Political Geography through Geopolitics." *Political Geography* 23:307–22.

Immerwahr, D. 2019. *How to Hide an Empire: A History of the Greater United States.* New York: Farrar, Straus and Giroux.

Ince, A. 2012. "In the Shell of the Old: Anarchist Geographies of Territorialisation." *Antipode* 44:1645–66.

Inoue, M. 2007. *Okinawa and the US Military: Identity Making in the Age of Globalization.* New York: Columbia University Press.

Ireland, B. 2010. *The US Military in Hawai'i: Colonialism, Memory, and Resistance.* New York: Palgrave Macmillan.

Isin, E. 2007. "CityState: Critique of Scalar Thought." *Citizenship Studies* 11:211–28.

Jackson, S. 1995. "The Water Is Not Empty: Cross-Cultural Issues in Conceptualising Sea Space." *Australian Geographer* 26 (1): 87–96.

Jaynes, B. 2017. "FSM President Peter Christian Talks about His State Visit to China." *Kaselehlie Press*, April 5, 2017. http://www.kpress.info/index.php?option=com_content&view=article&id=582:fsm-president-peter-christian-talks-about-his-state-visit-to-china&catid=8&Itemid=103.

Jennings, R. 2017. "How China Could Gradually Assume Control of Scarborough Shoal in the South China Sea. *Forbes*, December 29, 2017. https://www.forbes.com/sites/ralphjennings/2017/12/29/chinas-takeover-of-an-islet-disputed-with-the-philippines-3-scenarios/#549383542785.

Jetnil-Kijiner, K. 2017. *Iep jaltok: Poems from a Marshallese Daughter*. Tucson: University of Arizona Press.

Johnson, G. 2019. "Trump Meets FAS Family." *Marshall Islands Journal*, May 23, 2019. https://marshallislandsjournal.com/trump-meets-fas-family/.

Jones, J., K. Woodward, and S. Marston. 2007. "Situating Flatness." *Transactions of the Institute of British Geographers* 32:264–76.

Jones, L., and D. Sage. 2010. "New Directions in Critical Geopolitics: An Introduction." *Geojournal* 75:315–25.

Jones, R. 2016. *Violent Borders: Refugees and the Right to Move*. New York: Verso.

———, ed. 2019. *Open Borders: In Defense of Free Movement*. Athens: University of Georgia Press.

Jose, C., K. Wall, and J. Hinzel. 2015. "This Dome in the Pacific Houses Tons of Radioactive Waste—And It's Leaking." *Guardian*, July 3, 2015. https://www.theguardian.com/world/2015/jul/03/runit-dome-pacific-radioactive-waste.

Kajihiro, K. 2013. "Moananuiākea or 'American Lake'? Contested Histories of the US Pacific." In *Under Occupation: Resistance and Struggle in a Militarized Asia-Pacific*, edited by D. Broudy, P. Simpson, and M. Arakaki, 126–60. Newcastle-upon-Tyne: Cambridge Scholars Publishing.

Kennedy, P. 1987. *The Rise and Fall of the Great Powers: Economic Change and Military Conflict from 1500 to 2000*. New York: Random House.

Keown, M. 2017. "Children of Israel: US Military Imperialism and Marshallese Migration in the Poetry of Kathy Jetnil-Kijiner." *Interventions* 19 (7): 930–47.

Khal, C., and H. Brands. 2017. "Trump's Grand Strategic Train Wreck." *Foreign Policy*, January 31, 2017. http://foreignpolicy.com/2017/01/31/trumps-grand-strategic-train-wreck/.

Kim, C. 2018. "Bases that Leave: Consequences of US Base Closures and Realignments in South Korea." *Journal of Contemporary Asia* 48 (2): 339–57.

Kirk, G. 2008. "Gender and U.S. Bases in Asia-Pacific." *Foreign Policy in Focus*, March 14, 2008.

Kirsch, S., and C. Flint. 2011. *Reconstructing Conflict: Integrating War and Post-War Geographies*. Burlington, VT: Ashgate.

Klein, N. 2007. *The Shock Doctrine: The Rise of Disaster Capitalism*. New York: Macmillan.

Koopman, S. 2011. "Alter-Geopolitics: Other Securities Are Happening." *Geoforum* 42:274–84.

———. 2015. "Social Movements." In *The Wiley Blackwell Companion to Political Geography*, edited by J. Agnew, 339–51. Oxford: Blackwell.

Krasner, S. 1999. *Sovereignty: Organized Hypocrisy*. Princeton: Princeton University Press.

Krepinevich, A. 2015. "How to Deter China: The Case for Archipelagic Defense." *Foreign Affairs* 94:1–6.

Krepinevich, A., B. Watts, and R. Work. 2003. *Meeting the Anti-Access and Area Denial Challenge*. Washington, DC: Center for Strategic and Budgetary Assessments.

Latour, B. 1993. *We Have Never Been Modern*. Cambridge: Harvard University Press.

Larsson, O. 2013. "Sovereign Power beyond the State: A Critical Reappraisal of Governance by Networks." *Critical Policy Studies* 7 (2): 99–114.

Lefebvre, H. 1991. *The Production of Space*. Cambridge: Blackwell.

Legg, S. 2009. "Of Scales Networks and Assemblages: The League of Nations Apparatus and the Scalar Sovereignty of the Government of India." *Transactions of the Institute of British Geographers* 34:234–53.

———. 2011. "Assemblage/Apparatus: Using Deleuze and Foucault." *Area* 43:128–33.

Lemke, T. 2001. "The Birth of Bio-Politics: Michel Foucault's Lecture at the Collège de France on Neo-Liberal Governmentality." *Economy and Society* 30:190–207.

Leon Guerrero, V. 2017. "An Open Letter from Guam to America." *Boston Review*, August 11, 2017. http://bostonreview.net/war-security/victoria-lola-m-leon-guerrero-open-letter-guam-america.

Leverett, F., and W. Bingbing. 2017. "The New Silk Road and China's Evolving Grand Strategy. *China Journal* 77 (1): 110–32.

Lilomaiava-Doktor, S. 2009. "Beyond 'Migration': Samoan Population Movement (Malaga) and the Geography of Social Space (Vā)." *Contemporary Pacific* 21 (1): 1–32.

Lisle, D., and A. Pepper. 2005. "The New Face of Global Hollywood: *Black Hawk Down* and the Politics of Meta-Sovereignty." *Cultural Politics* 1 (2): 165–92.

Louis, R. 2017. *Kanaka Hawai'i Cartography: Hula, Navigation, and Oratory*. Corvallis: Oregon State University Press.

Loyd, J. 2012. "Geographies of Peace and Antiviolence." *Geography Compass* 6:477–89.

Loyd, J., E. Mitchell-Eaton, and A. Mountz. 2016. "The Militarization of Islands and Migration: Tracing Human Mobility through US Bases in the Caribbean and the Pacific." *Political Geography* 53:65–75.

Lummis, D. 2019. "'It Ain't Over 'till It's Over': Reflections on the Okinawan Anti-Base Resistance." *Asia-Pacific Journal*, January 1, 2019. https://apjjf.org/2019/01/Lummis.html.

Lutz, C. 2006. "Empire Is in the Details." *American Ethnologist* 33 (4): 593–611.

———. 2009. *The Bases of Empire: The Global Struggle against US Military Posts*. New York: New York University Press.

MacArthur, D. 1965. *A Soldier Speaks: Public Papers and Speeches of General of the Army, Douglas MacArthur*. Santa Barbara: Praeger.

Mahan, A. 1890. *The Influence of Sea Power upon History, 1660–1783*. Boston: Little, Brown and Company.

Man, S., A. Paik, and M. Pappademos. 2019. "Violent Entanglements: Militarism and Capitalism." *Radical History Review* 133:1–10.

Massey, D. 1994. *Space, Place and Gender*. Minneapolis: University of Minnesota Press.

Matelski, T. 2016. "America's Micronesia Problem." *Diplomat*, February 19, 2016. https://thediplomat.com/2016/02/americas-micronesia-problem/.

Mattis, J. 2018. "Read: James Mattis' Resignation Letter." CNN, December 21, 2018. https://www.cnn.com/2018/12/20/politics/james-mattis-resignation-letter-doc/index.html.

McCaffrey, K. 2002. *Military Power and Popular Protest: The US Navy in Vieques Puerto Rico*. New Brunswick, NJ: Rutgers University Press.

McCormack, F. 2011. "Rāhui: A Blunting of Teeth." *Journal of the Polynesian Society* 102 (1): 43–56.

———. 2017. *Private Oceans: The Enclosure and Marketisation of the Seas.* London: Pluto Press.

McCormack, G., and S. Norimatsu. 2012. *Resistant Islands: Okinawa Confronts Japan and the United States.* New York: Rowman & Littlefield Publishers.

McFarlane, C. 2009. "Translocal Assemblages: Space Power and Social Movements." *Geoforum* 40:561–67.

McNamara, K., and C. Gibson. 2009. "'We Do Not Want to Leave Our Land': Pacific Ambassadors at the United Nations Resist the Category of Climate Refugees." *Geoforum* 40 (3): 475–83.

Megoran, N., F. McConnell, and P. Williams. 2016. "Geography and Peace." In *The Palgrave Handbook of Disciplinary and Regional Approaches to Peace*, edited by O. Richmond, S. Pogodda, and J. Ramović, 123–38. London: Palgrave Macmillan.

Meick, E., M. Ker, and H. Chan. 2018. "China's Engagement in the Pacific Islands: Implications for the United States." *U.S.-China Economic and Security Review Commission Staff Research Report*, June 14, 2018. https://www.uscc.gov/sites/default/files/Research/China-Pacific%20Islands%20Staff%20Report.pdf.

Melucci, A. 1995. "The Process of Collective Identity." In *Social Movements and Culture*, edited by H. Johnston and B. Klandermans, 41–63. Minneapolis: University of Minnesota Press.

Mezzadra, S., and B. Neilson. 2012. "Between Inclusion and Exclusion: On the Topology of Global Space and Borders." *Theory, Culture & Society* 29:58–75.

Mitchell, K., and K. Kallio. 2017. "Spaces of the Geosocial: Exploring Transnational Topologies." *Geopolitics* 22:1–14.

Mountz, A. 2013. "Political Geography I: Reconfiguring Geographies of Sovereignty." *Progress in Human Geography* 37:829–41.

Mulalap, C. 2017. "Federated States of Micronesia." *Contemporary Pacific* 29 (1): 94–104.

Müller, M. 2015. "Assemblages and Actor-Networks: Rethinking Socio-Material Power Politics and Space." *Geography Compass* 9:27–41.

Nadarajah, Y., and A. Grydehøj. 2016. "Thematic Section: Island Decolonization Island Studies as a Decolonial Project (Guest Editorial Introduction)." *Island Studies Journal* 11 (2): 437–46.

Na'puti, T. 2019. "Archipelagic Rhetoric: Remapping the Marianas and Challenging Militarization from a Stirring Place." *Communication and Critical/Cultural Studies* 16:4–25.

Na'puti, T., and M. Bevacqua. 2015. "Militarization and Resistance from Guåhan: Protecting and Defending Pågat." *American Quarterly* 67:837–58.

Na'puti, T., and S. Frain. 2017. "Decolonize Oceania! Free Guåhan! Communicating Resistance at the 2016 Festival of Pacific Arts." *Amerasia Journal* 43 (3): 3–34.

Nathan, A., and R. Ross. 1997. *The Great Wall and the Empty Fortress: China's Search for Security.* New York: W. W. Norton.

Natividad, L., and G. Kirk. 2010. "Fortress Guam: Resistance to US Military Mega-Buildup." *Asia-Pacific Journal* 19:1–10.

Naylor, L. 2017. "Reframing Autonomy in Political Geography: A Feminist Geopolitics of Autonomous Resistance." *Political Geography* 58:24–35.

Nicholls, W. 2009. "Place Networks Space: Theorising the Geographies of Social Movements." *Transactions of the Institute of British Geographers* 34:78–93.

Nolan, P. 2013. "Imperial Archipelagos: China, Western Colonialism and the Law of the Sea." *New Left Review* 80:77–95.

Norimatsu, S. 2011. "Hatoyama's Confession: The Myth of Deterrence and the Failure to Move a Marine Base Outside Okinawa." *Asia-Pacific Journal* 9 (February 28): 1–19.

Nye, J. 2004. *Soft Power: The Means to Success in World Politics.* New York: Public Affairs.

Ó Tuathail, G. 2000. "The Postmodern Geopolitical Condition: States, Statecraft, and Security at the Millennium." *Annals of the Association of American Geographers* 90:166–78.

Ó Tuathail, G., and S. Dalby. 1998. *Rethinking Geopolitics: Towards a Critical Geopolitics.* New York: Routledge.

Olds, K., and N. Thrift. 2007. "Cultures on the Brink: Reengineering the Soul of Capitalism on a Global Scale." In *Global Assemblages: Technology Politics and Ethics as Anthropological Problems*, edited by A. Ong and S. Collier, 270–90. Oxford: Blackwell.

Oliveira, K. 2014. *Ancestral Places: Understanding Kanaka Geographies.* Corvallis: Oregon State University Press.

Oslender, U. 2016. *The Geographies of Social Movements: Afro-Colombian Mobilization and the Aquatic Space.* Durham: Duke University Press.

Osorio, J. 2014. "Hawaiian Souls: The Movement to Stop the U.S. Military Bombing of Kahoʻolawe." In *A Nation Rising: Hawaiian Movements for Life, Land, and Sovereignty*, edited by N. Goodyear-Kaʻōpua, I. Hussey, and E. Wright, 137–60. Durham: Duke University Press.

Paik, K. 2015. "Islanders Unite to Resist a New Pacific War." *Common Dreams*, November 4, 2015. http://www.commondreams.org/views/2015/11/04/islanders-unite-resist-new-pacific-war.

Pain, R., and S. Smith. 2008. *Fear: Critical Geopolitics and Everyday Life.* Burlington, VT: Ashgate.

Painter, J. 2006. "Prosaic Geographies of Stateness." *Political Geography* 25:752–74.

———. 2010. "Rethinking Territory." *Antipode* 42:1090–118.

Panda, A. 2018. "South China Sea: US Destroyer Conducts Freedom of Navigation Operations near Scarborough Shoal." *Diplomat*, January 21, 2018. https://thediplomat.com/2018/01/south-china-sea-us-destroyer-conducts-freedom-of-navigation-operations-near-scarborough-shoal/.

Pasternak, S. 2017. *Grounded Authority: The Algonquins of Barriere Lake against the State.* Minneapolis: University of Minnesota Press.

Pasternak, S., and T. Dafnos. 2018. "How Does a Settler State Secure the Circuitry of Capital?" *Environment and Planning D: Society and Space* 36 (4): 739–57.

Patrick, S. 2017. *The Sovereignty Wars: Reconciling America with the World.* Washington, DC: Brookings Institute Press.

Pearl, H. 2017. "Pacific Island leaders Express Dismay at US Leaving Paris Climate Accord." *SBS News*, February 6, 2017. https://www.sbs.com.au/news/pacific-island-leaders-express-dismay-at-us-leaving-paris-climate-accord.

Peattie, M. 1992. *Nan'yo: The Rise and Fall of the Japanese in Micronesia, 1885–1945.* Honolulu: University of Hawaii Press.

Perez, C. 2014. *From Unincorporated Territory.* Richmond, VA: Omnidawn Publishing.

Peters, K., P. Steinberg, and E. Stratford. 2018. *Territory beyond Terra.* New York: Rowman & Littlefield.

Poyer, L., S. Falgout, and L. Carucci. 2001. *The Typhoon of War: Micronesian Experiences of the Pacific War.* Honolulu: University of Hawaii Press.

Pugh, J. 2013. "Island Movements: Thinking with the Archipelago." *Island Studies Journal* 8 (1): 9–24.

———. 2016. "The Relational Turn in Island Geographies: Bringing Together Island, Sea and Ship Relations and the Case of the Landship." *Social & Cultural Geography* 17 (8): 1040–59.

———. 2018. "Relationality and Island Studies in the Anthropocene." *Island Studies Journal* 13 (1): 1–18.

Raymundo, S. 2017. "Guam Residents Rally for Peace amid North Korean Missile Crisis." *Pacific Daily News*, August 14, 2017. http://www.guampdn.com/story/news/2017/08/14/guam-residents-rally-peace-amid-north-korean-missile-crisis/563928001/.

Robbins, P. 2011. *Political Ecology: A Critical Introduction.* Malden, MA: John Wiley & Sons.

Roberts, B., and M. Stephens. 2017. *Archipelagic American Studies.* Durham: Duke University Press.

Rodriguez, M., L. Losinio, and B. Carreon. 2017. China Is Making Inroads in Micronesia. *Pacific Island Times*, February 6, 2017. https://www.pacificislandtimes.com/single-post/2017/02/06/China-is-making-inroads-in-Micronesia.

Rogers, R. 1994. *Destiny's Landfall: A History of Guam.* Honolulu: University of Hawai'i Press.

Rose-Redwood, R. 2006. "Governmentality Geography and the Geo-coded World." *Progress in Human Geography* 30:469–86.

Routledge, P. 1996. "Critical Geopolitics and Terrains of Resistance." *Political Geography* 15:509–31.

———. 2015. "Territorialising Movement: The Politics of Land Occupation in Bangladesh." *Transactions of the Institute of British Geographers* 40:445–63.

Santana, D. 2002. "Resisting Toxic Militarism: Vieques versus the US Navy." *Social Justice* 29:1043–578.

Scott, J. 1998. *Seeing Like a State: How Certain Schemes to Improve the Human Condition Have Failed.* New Haven: Yale University Press.

———. 2009. *The Art of Not Being Governed: An Anarchist History of Upland Southeast Asia.* New Haven: Yale University Press.

Sharp, G. 1973. *The Politics of Nonviolent Action*. Boston: Porter Sargent.

Shigematsu, S., and K. Camacho. 2010. *Militarized Currents: Toward a Decolonized Future in Asia and the Pacific*: Minneapolis: University of Minnesota Press.

Shuster, D. 1998. "Political Leadership in Palau: The Roman Tmetuchl Period." In *Leadership in the Pacific islands: Tradition and the Future*, edited by D. Shuster, P. Larmour, and K. Von Strokirch, 27–57. Canberra: National Centre for Development Studies.

Simons, M. 2016. "Marshall Islands Can't Sue the World's Nuclear Powers, U.N. Court Rules." *New York Times*, October 5, 2016. Retrieved from https://www.nytimes.com/2016/10/06/world/asia/marshall-islands-un-court-nuclear-disarmament.html.

Simpson, A. 2014. *Mohawk Interruptus: Political Life across the Borders of Settler States*. Durham: Duke University Press.

Sixth Commission of the EZLN (Ejército Zapatista de Liberación Nacional). 2016. *Critical Thought in the Face of the Capitalist Hydra: I*. Brisbane: Paperboat Press.

Smith, J. 2018. *To Master the Boundless Sea: The U.S. Navy, the Marine Environment, and the Cartography of Empire*. Chapel Hill: University of North Carolina Press.

Soja, E. 1996. *Thirdspace: Journeys to Los Angeles and Other Real-and-Imagined Places*. Malden, MA: Blackwell.

Sparke, M. 2007. "Geopolitical Fears, Geoeconomic Hopes, and the Responsibilities of Geography." *Annals of the Association of American Geographers* 97:338–49.

———. 2013. "From Global Dispossession to Local Repossession: Towards a Worldly Cultural Geography of Occupy Activism." In *The Wiley-Blackwell Companion to Cultural Geography*, edited by N. Johnson, R. Schein, and J. Winders, 387–408. Oxford: Blackwell.

Springer, S. 2014. "Why a Radical Geography Must Be Anarchist." *Dialogues in Human Geography* 4:249–70.

Star, S. 2010. "This Is Not a Boundary Object: Reflections on the Origin of a Concept." *Science, Technology, & Human Values* 35 (5): 601–17.

Stavridis, J. 2017. *Sea Power: The History and Geopolitics of the World's Oceans*. New York: Penguin.

Steinberg, P. 2001. *The Social Construction of the Ocean*. Cambridge: Cambridge University Press.

———. 2018. "Editorial: The Ocean as Frontier." *International Social Science Journal* 68:237–40.

Steinberg, P., and K. Peters. 2015. "Wet Ontologies, Fluid Spaces: Giving Depth to Volume through Oceanic Thinking." *Environment and Planning D: Society and Space* 33:247–64.

Stratford, E., G. Baldacchino, E. McMahon, C. Farbotko, and A. Harwood. 2011. "Envisioning the Archipelago." *Island Studies Journal* 6 (2): 113–30.

Tan, J. 2018. "China Outbound Tourism Hits Record High in 2017. *Caixin*, March 5, 2018. https://www.caixinglobal.com/2018-03-05/china-outbound-tourism-hits-record-high-in-2017-101217260.html.

Teaiwa, T. 2000. "Bikinis and Other S/Pacific N/Oceans." In *Voyaging through the Con-*

temporary Pacific, edited by D. Hanlon and G. White, 91–112. New York: Rowman & Littlefield.,

Thang, N. 2012. "Fisheries Co-operation in the South China Sea and the (Ir)relevance of the Sovereignty Question." *Asian Journal of International Law* 2:59–88.

Tobin, M. 2019. "U.S.-China Battle for Dominance Extends across Pacific, above and below the Sea." *South China Morning Post*, January 19, 2019. https://www.scmp.com/week-asia/geopolitics/article/2182752/U.S.-china-battle-dominance-extends-across-pacific-above-and.

Trask, H. 1999. *From a Native Daughter: Colonialism and Sovereignty in Hawai'i*. Honolulu: University of Hawaii Press.

Trump, D. 2017. "Inaugural Address." January 20, 2017. Washington DC.

———. "Remarks by President Trump to the 74th Session of the United Nations General Assembly." September 25, 2019. New York.

Underwood, R. 2019. "The End of Micronesia." *Pacific Island Times*, May 29, 2019. *https://www.pacificislandtimes.com/single-post/2019/05/29/The-end-of-Micronesia.*

Vine, D. 2009. *Island of Shame: The Secret History of the U.S. Military Base on Diego Garcia*. Princeton: Princeton University Press.

———. 2019. "No Bases? Assessing the Impact of Social Movements Challenging US Foreign Military Bases." *Current Anthropology* 60:S158–S172.

Wainwright, J., and S. Kim. 2008. "Battles in Seattle Redux: Transnational Resistance to a Neoliberal Trade Agreement." *Antipode* 40 (4): 513–34.

Wallerstein, I. 2004. *World-Systems Analysis: An Introduction*. Durham: Duke University Press.

Warf, B. 1997. "The Geopolitics/Geoeconomics of Military Base Closures in the USA." *Political Geography* 16:541–63.

West, P. 2006. *Conservation Is Our Government Now: The Politics of Ecology in Papua New Guinea*. Durham: Duke University Press.

Whatmore, S. 2002. *Hybrid Geographies: Natures Cultures Spaces*. Thousand Oaks: Sage.

White, M. 2016. *The End of Protest: A New Playbook for Revolution*. Toronto: Knopf Canada.

Wilson, R. 2000. *Reimagining the American Pacific: From South Pacific to Bamboo Ridge and Beyond*. Durham: Duke University Press.

Wirth, C. 2016. "Securing the Seas, Securing the State: Hope, Danger and the Politics of Order in the Asia-Pacific." *Political Geography* 53:76–85.

Woodward, R. 2004. *Military Geographies*. Malden, MA: Blackwell.

Yamada, S. 2011. "Discrimination in Hawai'i and the Health of Micronesians and Marshallese." *Hawaii Journal of Public Health* 3 (1): 55–57.

Yang, J. 2011. *The Pacific Islands in China's Grand Strategy: Small States, Big Games*. New York: Springer.

Yeo, A. 2010. "US Military Base Realignment in South Korea." *Peace Review* 22 (2): 113–20.

———. 2013. "A Base for (In)Security? The Jeju Naval Base and Competing Visions of Peace on the Korean Peninsula." In *Under Occupation: Resistance and Struggle in a*

Militarized Asia-Pacific, edited by D. Broudy, P. Simpson, and M. Arakaki, 224–37. Newcastle-upon-Tyne: Cambridge Scholars Publishing.

Yoshihara, T. 2014. *Going Anti-Access at Sea: How Japan Can Turn the Tables on China* (Maritime Strategy Series). Washington, DC: Center for a New American Security.

Yu-Lin, K. 2017. "Trump's Asia Trip: 10 Best Quotes." *Straits Times,* November 14, 2017. Retrieved from https://www.straitstimes.com/world/united-states/ten-of-trumps-best-quotes-on-his-trip-to-asia.

Zalik, A. 2018. "Mining the Seabed, Enclosing the Area: Proprietary Knowledge and the Geopolitics of the Extractive Frontier beyond National Jurisdiction." *International Social Science Journal* 1–10.

Zibechi, R. 2010. *Dispersing Power: Social Movements as Anti-State Forces.* Oakland: AK Press.

INDEX

GEOGRAPHIES OF JUSTICE AND SOCIAL TRANSFORMATION

1. *Social Justice and the City*, rev. ed.
   BY DAVID HARVEY
2. *Begging as a Path to Progress: Indigenous Women and Children and the Struggle for Ecuador's Urban Spaces*
   BY KATE SWANSON
3. *Making the San Fernando Valley: Rural Landscapes, Urban Development, and White Privilege*
   BY LAURA R. BARRACLOUGH
4. *Company Towns in the Americas: Landscape, Power, and Working-Class Communities*
   EDITED BY OLIVER J. DINIUS AND ANGELA VERGARA
5. *Tremé: Race and Place in a New Orleans Neighborhood*
   BY MICHAEL E. CRUTCHER JR.
6. *Bloomberg's New York: Class and Governance in the Luxury City*
   BY JULIAN BRASH
7. *Roppongi Crossing: The Demise of a Tokyo Nightclub District and the Reshaping of a Global City*
   BY ROMAN ADRIAN CYBRIWSKY
8. *Fitzgerald: Geography of a Revolution*
   BY WILLIAM BUNGE
9. *Accumulating Insecurity: Violence and Dispossession in the Making of Everyday Life*
   EDITED BY SHELLEY FELDMAN, CHARLES GEISLER, AND GAYATRI A. MENON
10. *They Saved the Crops: Labor, Landscape, and the Struggle over Industrial Farming in Bracero-Era California*
    BY DON MITCHELL
11. *Faith Based: Religious Neoliberalism and the Politics of Welfare in the United States*
    BY JASON HACKWORTH
12. *Fields and Streams: Stream Restoration, Neoliberalism, and the Future of Environmental Science*
    BY REBECCA LAVE
13. *Black, White, and Green: Farmers Markets, Race, and the Green Economy*
    BY ALISON HOPE ALKON
14. *Beyond Walls and Cages: Prisons, Borders, and Global Crisis*
    EDITED BY JENNA M. LOYD, MATT MITCHELSON, AND ANDREW BURRIDGE
15. *Silent Violence: Food, Famine, and Peasantry in Northern Nigeria*
    BY MICHAEL J. WATTS
16. *Development, Security, and Aid: Geopolitics and Geoeconomics at the U.S. Agency for International Development*
    BY JAMEY ESSEX
17. *Properties of Violence: Law and Land-Grant Struggle in Northern New Mexico*
    BY DAVID CORREIA
18. *Geographical Diversions: Tibetan Trade, Global Transactions*
    BY TINA HARRIS
19. *The Politics of the Encounter: Urban Theory and Protest under Planetary Urbanization*
    BY ANDY MERRIFIELD
20. *Rethinking the South African Crisis: Nationalism, Populism, Hegemony*
    BY GILLIAN HART
21. *The Empires' Edge: Militarization, Resistance, and Transcending Hegemony in the Pacific*
    BY SASHA DAVIS
22. *Pain, Pride, and Politics: Social Movement Activism and the Sri Lankan Tamil Diaspora in Canada*
    BY AMARNATH AMARASINGAM
23. *Selling the Serengeti: The Cultural Politics of Safari Tourism*
    BY BENJAMIN GARDNER
24. *Territories of Poverty: Rethinking North and South*
    EDITED BY ANANYA ROY AND EMMA SHAW CRANE
25. *Precarious Worlds: Contested Geographies of Social Reproduction*
    EDITED BY KATIE MEEHAN AND KENDRA STRAUSS
26. *Spaces of Danger: Culture and Power in the Everyday*
    EDITED BY HEATHER MERRILL AND LISA M. HOFFMAN

27. *Shadows of a Sunbelt City: The Environment, Racism, and the Knowledge Economy in Austin*
BY ELIOT M. TRETTER

28. *Beyond the Kale: Urban Agriculture and Social Justice Activism in New York City*
BY KRISTIN REYNOLDS AND NEVIN COHEN

29. *Calculating Property Relations: Chicago's Wartime Industrial Mobilization, 1940–1950*
BY ROBERT LEWIS

30. *In the Public's Interest: Evictions, Citizenship, and Inequality in Contemporary Delhi*
BY GAUTAM BHAN

31. *The Carpetbaggers of Kabul and Other American-Afghan Entanglements: Intimate Development, Geopolitics, and the Currency of Gender and Grief*
BY JENNIFER L. FLURI AND RACHEL LEHR

32. *Masculinities and Markets: Raced and Gendered Urban Politics in Milwaukee*
BY BRENDA PARKER

33. *We Want Land to Live: Making Political Space for Food Sovereignty*
BY AMY TRAUGER

34. *The Long War: CENTCOM, Grand Strategy, and Global Security*
BY JOHN MORRISSEY

35. *Development Drowned and Reborn: The Blues and Bourbon Restorations in Post-Katrina New Orleans*
BY CLYDE WOODS
EDITED BY JORDAN T. CAMP AND LAURA PULIDO

36. *The Priority of Injustice: Locating Democracy in Critical Theory*
BY CLIVE BARNETT

37. *Spaces of Capital / Spaces of Resistance: Mexico and the Global Political Economy*
BY CHRIS HESKETH

38. *Revolting New York: How 400 Years of Riot, Rebellion, Uprising, and Revolution Shaped a City*
GENERAL EDITORS: NEIL SMITH AND DON MITCHELL
EDITORS: ERIN SIODMAK, JENJOY ROYBAL, MARNIE BRADY, AND BRENDAN O'MALLEY

39. *Relational Poverty Politics: Forms, Struggles, and Possibilities*
EDITED BY VICTORIA LAWSON AND SARAH ELWOOD

40. *Rights in Transit: Public Transportation and the Right to the City in California's East Bay*
BY KAFUI ABLODE ATTOH

41. *Open Borders: In Defense of Free Movement*
EDITED BY REECE JONES

42. *Subaltern Geographies*
EDITED BY TARIQ JAZEEL AND STEPHEN LEGG

43. *Detain and Deport: The Chaotic U.S. Immigration Enforcement Regime*
BY NANCY HIEMSTRA

44. *Global City Futures: Desire and Development in Singapore*
BY NATALIE OSWIN

45. *Public Los Angeles: A Private City's Activist Futures*
BY DON PARSON
EDITED BY ROGER KEIL AND JUDY BRANFMAN

46. *America's Johannesburg: Industrialization and Racial Transformation in Birmingham*
BY BOBBY M. WILSON

47. *Mean Streets: Homelessness, Public Space, and the Limits of Capital*
BY DON MITCHELL

48. *Islands and Oceans: Reimagining Sovereignty and Social Change*
BY SASHA DAVIS

49. *Social Reproductions and the City: Welfare Reform, Child Care, and Resistance in Neoliberal New York*
BY SIMON BLACK

50. *Freedom Is a Place: The Struggle for Sovereignty in Palestine*
BY RON J. SMITH

www.ingramcontent.com/pod-product-compliance
Lightning Source LLC
Chambersburg PA
CBHW010139270326
41926CB00022B/4504